INTERKULTURELLE BEGEGNUNGEN 18

Studien zum Literatur- und Kulturtransfer

Hrsg. von Rita Unfer Lukoschik
und Michael Dallapiazza

Zu Qualitätssicherung und Peer Review der vorliegenden Publikation

Die Qualität der in dieser Reihe erscheinenden Arbeiten wird vor der Publikation durch beide Herausgeber der Reihe geprüft.

Notes on the quality assurance and peer review of this publication

Prior to publication, the quality of the work published in this series is reviewed by both editors of the series.

Roberta Mullini

Healing Words

The Printed Handbills of Early Modern London Quacks

PETER LANG
EDITION

Bibliographic Information published by the Deutsche Nationalbibliothek
The Deutsche Nationalbibliothek lists this publication in the Deutsche Nationalbibliografie; detailed bibliographic data is available in the internet at http://dnb.d-nb.de.

Library of Congress Cataloging-in-Publication Data
Mullini, Roberta, author.
Healing words : the printed handbills of Early Modern London quacks / Roberta Mullini.
pages cm. – (Interkulturelle Begegnungen. Studien zum Literatur- und Kulturtransfer; Band 18)
Includes bibliographical references and index.
ISBN 978-3-631-66477-3 (Print) – ISBN 978-3-653-05699-0 (E-Book)
1. Advertising–Great Britain–Language–History. 2. Advertising fliers–Great Britain–History. 3. Medicine–Language–History. 4. Literature and medicine–Great Britain–History. 5. Physicians–Great Britain–History. 6. Social medicine–Great Britain–History. 7. Medical ethics–History. 8. London (England)–History. I. Title.
P301.5.A38M85 2015
808.06'6659–dc23 2015011607

This book has been published with the financial backing of the Department of International Studies. HISTORY, CULTURES, AND LANGUAGES of the University of Urbino Carlo Bo.

Cover illustration: A Mountebank (coloured engraving, after Marcellus Laroon, 1688. Wellcome Library, London).

ISSN 2195-1160
ISBN 978-3-631-66477-3 (Print)
E-ISBN 978-3-653-05699-0 (E-Book)
DOI 10.3726/978-3-653-05699-0

Peter Lang Edition is an Imprint of Peter Lang GmbH.

Peter Lang – Frankfurt am Main · Bern · Bruxelles · New York · Oxford · Warszawa · Wien

This publication has been peer reviewed.

www.peterlang.com

Medicine is a Science, which hath beene (as wee haue sayd) more professed, than labored, & yet more labored, than aduanced; the labor hauing been, in my iudgement, rather in circle, than in progression. For, I finde much Iteration, but small Addition.

(Francis Bacon, *The Advancement of Learning*)

The Argument

That there can be no Safety in relying upon any Remedy, left up-and-down the Town to be sold at Tradesmen's Shops, and publish'd by Bills dispersed for that Purpose, or Advertisements in the News-papers; the same being usually made up by ignorant People, who themselves know not their real Use; or by profess'd Quacks, who for base Lucre only, expose the same to Sale.

(*The Modern Quacks Detected*)

Contents

List of Plates

List of Tables

List of Abbreviations

551a32	*A Collection of 231 advertisements*, etc. *The greater part English and chiefly relating to quack medicines, the rest German descriptions of commemorative coins and medals [1675–1715].*
C112f9	*A Collection of 185 advertisements, chiefly relating to quack medicines. The greater part English, the rest French, German and Italian [1660–1716].*
ECCO	Eighteenth Century Collections Online (accessed via The Wellcome Library Remote Access to e-Resources)
EEBO	Early English Books Online (accessed via The Wellcome Library Remote Access to e-Resources).
ESTC	*English Short Title Catalogue* (British Library, <http://estc.bl.uk/F/?func=file&file_name=login-bl-estc>)
EMEMT	Early Modern English Medical Texts – CD ROM, in Irma Taavitsainen and Päivi Pahta, eds, *Early Modern English Medical Texts*, Amsterdam: John Benjamins, 2010. [CD ROM included.]
Harley 5931	*A Collection of Titlepages, fragments of printed books and other material assembled by John Bagford. [1528–1715]*
MEMT	Irma Taavitsainen, Päivi Pahta, and Martti Mäkinen, eds, *Middle English Medical Texts*, a CD-ROM, Amsterdam: John Benjamins, 2005.
ODNB	*Oxford Dictionary of National Biography*
OED	*Oxford English Dictionary*

A Note on Quotations and References

Whenever possible first editions have been quoted. Original spelling and punctuation have always been preserved (only in a few cases have erroneous forms been signalled by [sic]). Quotations from the texts included in the EMEMT CD reproduce the graphical conventions used in it.

In order not to overload the notes, all titles will be shortened in the notes themselves. Full titles are referenced in Appendix C, and in the Bibliography at the end of the volume.

Preface

Interest in the development of science in early modern times has been growing in recent decades, particularly in the field of socio-medical studies, perhaps because of our contemporary focus on the body, which has caused scholars to investigate whatever – in the past – can be connected to it. Consequently medicine has become an area of privileged and ever-growing concern, especially when linked to, and seen through, its possible connections either with other sciences or, more specifically, with literature and culture at large. Pre-scientific medicine – or "physick" as it was named in England at least till the end of the seventeenth century – has become a ground where interdisciplinarity is still yielding generously. Investigated in its multifaceted historical aspects, in the relationships with play- and novel-writing, in the psychological effects it produced on people, the progress of medicine has revealed – and is still revealing – how it moulded society and how society was mirrored in scientific thought, including the understanding of gender, cultural and post-colonial tenets. Medicine, after all, deals with human life and death and therefore nothing is more human than the interest it has always aroused.

Medicine, like all other disciplines, has subjects and objects. It is enacted by someone for the benefit of someone else; it is based on theoretical principles, but badly needs experimentation; it uses old and new substances to cure man's ailments; it tries to prolong man's life. The fascination of medical studies and of their history, therefore, will always intrigue mankind.

In the following pages, though, the issues dealt with will be very limited when compared with a science that has existed – in its various cultural forms – for thousands of years: my research focuses on the printed ephemera of the irregular medical practitioners who worked in London (according to some critics contrary to them they actually "flooded" the town) between the sixteenth and the seventeenth centuries. Some of these ephemera (both handbills and pamphlets) are spread in various libraries, but the majority of them is held by the British Library in three collections which assemble them in somewhat random sets. Here the focus will be on two of them only: the first – *A Collection of 231 advertisements*, etc. *The greater part English and chiefly relating to quack medicines, the rest German descriptions of commemorative coins and medals [1675–1715]* is shelfmarked 551a32; the second – *A Collection of 185 advertisements, chiefly relating to quack medicines. The greater part English, the rest French, German and Italian [1660–1716]* – is shelfmarked C112f9. The third set – *A Collection of Titlepages, fragments of printed books and other material assembled by John Bagford. [1528–1715]* – will be seldom taken into account, since it mainly collects sundry items, i.e. not medical adverts published by irregular practitioners. Furthermore this third set includes many handbills already present in the other two collections (its shelfmark is Harley 5931).[1]

All three collections have been used and quoted by scholars studying medical social history, such as Roy Porter, Margaret Pelling, Andrew Wear, Kevin Siena and others, both as foils to regular physicians' practice and as witnesses of the multifaceted variety of health care in early modern London.[2] Never, though, were they taken into consideration as constituting a larger set of texts through which to analyse on the one hand what irregular practitioners wrote about themselves, about their conceptions of illness, their ideas of health care; on the other how they worded their medical practice, that is, their rhetorical strategies aiming at capturing the reader's attention in what appears to be one of the first forms of printed advertising. In other words, the interest of irregular practitioners' texts lies in what they contain (with much information about London as well) and how they are written. From them the real language of quacks (as irregular practitioners will be often called in the present research, independently from the negative aura the term has acquired in time, starting exactly in early modern times) is made visible, in spite of the 'romance' grown around them especially in the eighteenth century in such works as *The Harangues or Speeches of Several Famous Mountebanks in Town and Country*, an anthology which evidently sold

---

1 The three collections will always be quoted by their shelfmarks: 551a32, C112f9, and Harley 5931, respectively, followed – between square brackets – by the number of individual handbills, as pencilled on each of them.

2 Roy Porter, *Health for Sale: Quackery in England 1650–1850* (1989). This volume was reprinted later with the title *Quacks: Fakers and Charlatans in Medicine* (2000). Below, the "Illustrated paperback edition" of this latter will be quoted (2003); Margaret Pelling, *The Common Lot* (1998), and *Medical Conflicts in Early Modern London* (2003); Andrew Wear, "The Popularization of Medicine in Early Modern England" (1992), *Health and Healing in Early Modern England* (1998), and *Knowledge and Practice in English Medicine* (2000); Kevin Siena, "'The 'Foul Disease' and Privacy" (2001), and *Venereal Diseases* (2004).
An early twentieth-century study of 'London Quacks' is C. J. S. Thompson, *Quacks of Old London* (1928), but this very rich work, albeit seminal, does not provide any information as to its sources, apart from a short phrase in the "Foreword" touching quacks' bills "which have now been brought together from various collections" (p. vii); however, no further bibliographical detail is given.

well, since it was published in various formats at different times in the same century, though one cannot absolutely be certain of its reliability and truth.[3]

The language of quacks (or charlatans, mountebanks, or empirics)[4] is the specific topic of an article by Roy Porter, but in that work the author considered medical ephemera mainly as a source of historical information, while describing the "language of quackery" with the usual labels deriving from the allegations against irregular practitioners' "prattle" and "babble", and their magniloquent and hyperbolic speech.[5] In other words, quacks' printed documents were not seen on their whole as building up a text type researchable as such. In the present work, on the contrary, the two collections 551a32 and C112f9 will be studied in their entirety, but excluding non-relevant documents, in order to find out what kind of information can be retrieved from them, from many points of view. The focus will be on them as a store of linguistic details about quacks' rhetorical (and performative) attitudes in approaching their targets and selling their remedies, of data about their lexicon especially related to the popular naming of illnesses, of information about their use of print and orality in early modern London medical life.

The texts of the two collections have accordingly been typed, so as to make them into an electronically searchable corpus made of a single specific text type, and analysed by means of a concordancer.[6] This has allowed the investigation

---

3 D. G., *The Harangues or speeches of several famous Mountebanks in Town and Country* (1700[?]), BL General Reference Collection 1038.g.46). The collection actually contains eleven "harangues or speeches", but the majority of them appears to be literary inventions, and not transcriptions of real quacks' orality (see Chapter 4 below). The last 'speech' printed is nothing but Volpone's tirade in Ben Jonson's homonymous play (II.2). This anthology is also mentioned in Hugh Ormsby Lennon, *Hey Presto! Swift and the Quacks* (2011, pp. 57–58). Lennon also introduces many quotations from the handbills of the two BL Collections (see especially pp. 50–70). The author uses them to show the connection between Swift's satirical writing of *A Tale of a Tub* (1704) and the "popular culture of mountebankery" (p. 18), made of street medicine vendors and "stage-itinerants".

4 For the problem of defining the boundaries of each of these terms see below.

5 Roy Porter, "The Language of Quackery in England" (1987), pp. 73–103.

6 A concordancer is a software which allows the electronic search of a corpus, by creating concordances. According to corpus linguistics a concordance is "a list of lines of text containing a node word, nowadays generated by computer as the principal output of a search of a corpus showing the word in its contexts and thus representing a sum of its usage" (Wolfgang Teubert and Anna Čermáková, *Corpus Linguistics. A Short Introduction* (2007), p. 141).

of individual keywords on which to construe some interpretative hypotheses. From the corpus, in order to make it reliable and consistent, I have eliminated multiple copies of a single handbill, and other items written in German and in Italian. In the end, the corpus consists of 304 leaflets (plus 12 pamphlets, separately searchable).

Of course other primary sources were added to the handbills, including visual evidence, together with the relevant secondary studies. Among primary sources there will also be included broadsides, pamphlets and publications printed during the time span from the sixteenth to the early eighteenth century, when of interest to the principal topic, i.e. how irregular practitioners used English, both orally and in the written form. Therefore some witnesses of the ongoing war between regulars and irregulars are encompassed, as satirical evidence of the troublesome presence of empirics and of their discourse. Their speech – oral and written – had a double task: it served first to appeal to customers, and then to cure them (or so irregulars said it would). Its healing power passed through the innovative technique of selling medicines by approaching the undifferentiated and anonymous sick orally from a stage or in writing via handbills.

The project aims at furthering the research in the history of medical language, and at possibly filling a gap in our knowledge of early modern irregular practitioners as a culturally relevant social phenomenon.

My approach is interdisciplinary, involving mainly linguistic and cultural (but also gender) studies. Literature (especially drama) will surface now and then, because not only did quacks belong to the cultural panorama of the time span under study, but they were also showmen, playing their own roles on their own public stages.

The Chapters

Chapter 1, The Historical Context

Charlatanism was not a conspicuous phenomenon in London only, on the contrary it was widespread in Europe and, specifically, it had originated in Italy, as many early modern texts attest and as our contemporary hypotheses still witness. The fact that Thomas Coryate described Venetian mountebanks with utmost care testifies to his admiration, on the one hand, and contemporarily to his blame of their selling techniques on the other.[7] Chapter 1 presents Italian and English

---

7 Thomas Coryate, *Coryats Crudities* (1611).

sources juxtaposed in order to highlight similarities and differences in the two countries as concerns the mixed activities of charlatans, made of health care, selling medicines, and spectacle. It also focuses on the particular situation of London medicine market.

The aim of this chapter is to offer a cultural and historical backdrop against which to interpret the spread of handbills printing in the following parts of the book. It does not absolutely pretend to be a 'history of quackery' (which such specialists as those mentioned in note 2 above have already written), and, because I am neither a historian *tout court* nor a medical historian, it must needs rely mainly on what dedicated researchers have studied. Mine will be the slant and some additional information, especially drawn from disciplinary fields other than medicine and history.

Chapter 2, A Corpus-based Approach to the Language of Quacks

Chapter 2 deals specifically with the corpus of handbills and with the multifarious information it can make available. By comparing the London handbills with their Italian counterparts studied by David Gentilcore,[8] it first aims at defining a model structure of the former, then – by discussing some high-ranking key words connected to London trades – it pinpoints the web of medicine dealers in the city, among whom booksellers and coffeehouse owners appear to be the most involved in selling irregular practitioners' remedies.

The Chapter also examines the information concerning how irregular practitioners conveyed the address of their practices, the 'format' of the cures they offered (pills, elixirs, spirits, lozenges…), and at which prices.

Chapter 3, Common Complaints in Corpora from the Medical Domain

Chapter 3 is devoted to presenting and discussing the results deriving from the search of the names of illnesses – as key words – in the corpus, so as to show which diseases quacks said they were able to cure, with particular attention to some of them (such as the scurvy, the pox, and the green sickness). Key words connected to health problems are listed in a first table, while a second shows the ranking of specific disease names. The scurvy, the pox and the green sickness are dealt with in separate paragraphs, and special emphasis is given to melancholy because of its cultural relevance. To assess the corpus data referring to

8 *Medical Charlatanism in Early Modern Italy* (2006).

melancholy, data deriving from other corpora in the medical domain are also considered.[9]

Chapter 4, How Quacks Addressed their Audience

With Chapter 4 the data resulting from the handbills, while still remaining the main working basis, are enriched with diverse sources. It aims at addressing the discursive procedures and techniques introduced by quacks in their handbills and at handling the spoken/written word relationship as it is testified by contemporary literature. Roy Porter often remarks that "quackspeak" was a patter built on hyperboles, flattery, and boasts, but he never deals with it as present in documents constituting a text type *per se*.[10]

If it is relatively easy to handle quacks' bills as a specific text type, it is certainly harder to analyse their orality, since – of course – no real recording survives. In order to try and recover some rhetorical traits of quacks' orality, some of their "harangues and speeches" (among those collected in D. G.'s *Harangues*) will be of interest, albeit mainly literary products. Indeed they may help in my analysis as terms of comparison, because the anonymous 'editor' of the collection tried to make them sound as realistic as possible. Therefore Chapter 4 will be devoted to studying the traces of quacks' genuine speech in writing as mediated testimonies of oral performances.

Chapter 5, Quacks and the Media

Chapter 5 presents the multimodal analysis of some handbills that include images, decorations, and/or particular fonts. Even if quacks' handbills belong to 'cheap print', nevertheless they sometimes show a particular care of typography; therefore typographical details such as asterisks, pointing fingers, and special fonts are studied, besides three cases displaying very impressive illustrations.

Together with this, the Chapter hosts a discussion of anti-quack satire as it results in an often reprinted – with different images – broadside whose wording is copied from D. G.'s collection of *Harangues* mentioned above ("Pharmacopola Circumforaneus or, the Horse Doctor's Harangue to the Credulous Mob"). The analysis of coeval literature has also brought to the discovery of a previously unknown possible source of the latter text.

---

9 Especially those studied in Taavitsainen and Pahta, eds, *Early Modern English Medical Texts* (2010), and – by the same editors – *Medical Writing in Early Modern English* (2011).

10 Porter, "The Language of Quacks", p. 76.

Chapter 6, Three Case Studies: Men, Women, and a Courtier

The final Chapter, 6, encompasses three case-studies, always grounded on the corpus. The first covers the production of two quacks belonging to the same family (the Winters, of Italian origin), and wants to investigate the continuity of medical (popular) vocabulary in the printed matter of father and son along half a century (from 1647 to c. 1700). A sub-set of the Winters' handbills is thus searched for key words which are listed in tables in order to assess father's and son's usage of specific medical terminology.

The following study concentrates on handbills and pamphlets advertising beauty products, and therefore envisaging women as their primary target in the marketplace; tables here as well help visualise the relevance of the lexical items used to market toiletries. It also stresses the role of women in health care, therefore showing them as both subjects and objects of medical advertising.

The third case-study is devoted to the pamphlet published by John Wilmot, second Earl of Rochester, who – under the cover of Dr Alexander Bendo – spent some time of his unruly life on a mountebank's stage. As a parallel text this sub-Chapter is also underpinned by a nearly contemporary document sent in 1687 by Thomas Alcock, a servant of the Earl of Rocherster's, to the earl's daughter.[11]

Acknowledgments

Writing a book may initially be a solitary enterprise, but it soon grows into a collective activity. In my case the beginning, too, was somewhat due to a joint effort, since my interest in early modern medical practitioners began when some years ago I was asked by Italian colleagues to take part in a national research project focussing on "spectacles from the margins in early modern England" and, out of various possibilities (such as public executions, puppets, automatons, ballad singers…), I picked charlatans. My knowledge of the subject was nearly null at that time, and my choice depended on what I knew of Italian medicine vendors and on what I had read on them especially in sixteenth-century texts. In the end, the project – notwithstanding the very positive refereeing – was not financed, but in the meantime I had started my personal research on my topic and had been fascinated by what I was finding. Then I also benefited from a sabbatical from my department ("Dipartimento di Studi Internazionali. Storia, Lingue, Culture" of the University of Urbino Carlo Bo), of which I was (and still am)

11 Thomas Alcock, and John Wilmot, *The Famous Pathologist, or the Noble Mountebank* (1961).

greatly appreciative. To my department I am also thankful for the research funds which have made this publication possible.

Along my way towards this volume I profited from friends' and colleagues' advice and support, especially when partial results were presented at conferences. I am particularly grateful to the members of the Italian Association for Shakespearean and Early Modern Studies (IASEMS), who discussed two contributions of mine during the association's annual conferences, and to the friends of the "Associazione di Storia della Lingua Inglese" (the History of the English Language Association, SLIN) who accepted me among them even if I was not a proclaimed linguist.

Furthermore I want to express my gratitude to Rita Unfer Lukoschik and Michael Dallapiazza for hosting my book in the series they edit, and to Ute Winkelkötter of Peter Lang Publishers for her kind answers to my many doubts. And – since some of the outcomes of my research, which here I present in revised and augmented versions, were published in the past – to the following publishers and journals for their permission to reuse those contributions:

- *Biblos* (Revista da Faculdade de Letras, Universidade de Coimbra), which hosted my "Was Waltho van Claturbank's Speech ever spoken? The Fashion of London Quacks' Speeches between the Seventeenth and the Eighteenth Centuries" (2009).
- *Textus* (the journal of the Italian Association of English Studies, AIA) which issued my "'With such flourishes as these': The Visual Politics of Charlatans' Handbills in Early Modern London" (2009).
- The Cambridge Scholars Publishing who published "'Gull'd by the enchanting Tongues of *Quack* and *Zany*': The Rhetoric of Nostrum Marketing in Speech and Print in Early Modern London" in N. Brownlees, G. Del Lungo, J. Denton, eds, *The Language of Public and Private Communication in a Historical Perspective* (2010).
- The Italian publishers Polimetrica who accepted my article "'Family Sayings': Two Generations of Italian Quack Doctors in 17th-Century London" in their volume T. Canziani, K. Grego, and G. Iamartino, eds, *Perspectives in Medical English* (2014).

I also want to thank the British Library and the University of Michigan Library for allowing me to reproduce some of the documents they hold, but a special thank goes to the London Wellcome Library for their invaluable gift in opening up vast fields of research to their readers through the remote access to e-resources, and also for permitting the free download of many images in their collections.

My debts of gratitude are many, especially towards those people who propped me up during the whole process: my friends and colleagues Jan Marten Ivo Klaver and Romana Zacchi who patiently read and commented on the final product, Simon Jarvis who tried to eliminate my obstinate tendency to Italianise the English language, Peter Basham of the Royal College of Physicians of London for giving me information held at the College Heritage Centre, Margaret Pelling who generously gave me access to information previously unknown to me. The soul of the whole operation, though, has been Paola Pugliatti, without whose warm encouragement I do not think I would ever have tried to sit down and give volume form to my ideas. But since I am a rather stubborn person, what will be found as defects in this volume is due only to my resistance to these friends' kind advice.[12]

Finally I want to express my deep thanks to my son Alessandro Zanarini, who has helped me arrange Figure 4 and drawn the map in Appendix B, besides solving all technical problems and taming the computer (or, rather, showing to a human how to behave with 'him') when the fight between the machine and me was particularly violent. My gratitude also goes to Giulio, who pardoned my ups and downs and has always understood why.

12 When Joel S. Berson made the results of his research about dating Waltho van Claturbank's broadside available to me, the proofs of this volume had already been processed and I could not intervene in my text. Nevertheless I thank him, because the information he passed will certainly be useful for a future research.

1 The Historical Context

It is strange notwithstanding in these dayes to behold, with what senselesse madnesse, men are become worshippers of medicines.

(John Cotta, *A True Discovery of the Empiricke*)

Selling Medicines in Early Modern Times

In the first Act, Scene 5, of Gaetano Donizetti's opera *L'elisir d'amore* (*The Elixir of Love*, 1832)) Dulcamara, a self-proclaimed doctor, enters on stage standing on a gilded carriage and holding bottles and sheets of papers in his hands. Behind him comes a servant playing a trumpet. When all the village people gather around him, he starts singing the famous 'cavatina' "Udite, udite, o rustici" [Give ear, now, ye rustic ones],[1] in order to sell them his panacea, good to destroy mice and bedbugs, but also to rejuvenate old men's sexual prowess, to cure love sickness, to eliminate wrinkles from elderly ladies' faces, to cure such diseases as the king's evil, palsy, apoplexy, asthma, hysteria, diabetes, rickets and liver. This medicine he has sold successfully everywhere in the world, simply because this "specific" of his is a "mirabile liquore" [wondrous liquor], and a "balsamico elisire" [balsamic elixir]. The price would be high, as it is in all other places, but "here", in this village, it falls to just a few "lire", about one thirtieth of the supposed price requested elsewhere. The plot of the opera sees Dulcamara's elixir becoming really successful in producing love effects (of course completely independent of the chemical and pharmaceutical – if any – ingredients of the medicine), just because events develop towards a happy ending. And at the end (II.9) Nemorino and Adina (the two lovers) bless both the doctor and the medicine, while Belcore, whose love Adina in the end rejects, curses Dulcamara in this way: "Ciarlatano maledetto, | che tu possa ribaltar!" [Away, you cursed mountebank! | Marplot of my hopes, may you be upset!].

During his first appearance on stage (I.5) Dulcamara also boasts of his proprietary remedy by producing the "certificati autentici | bollati" [authentic and stamped certificates] which testify to its efficacy. If this procedure very probably mirrors the behaviour of real early nineteenth-century medicine vendors, it nevertheless comes from the past. William Langland, when condemning a different

1 Quotations from Felice Romani's libretto of Donizetti's opera and their translations are taken from *Grand Opera Librettos* (1885), pp. 10, 27. All other translations in this volume are mine unless differently specified.

sort of seller – the medieval pardoner selling pardons and relics – in his *Piers Plowman*, laments that

> Þere preched a Pardonere as he a prest were,
> Brouȝte forth a bulle with bishopes seles,
> And seide þat hym-self myȝte assoilen hem alle
> Of falshed of fastyng of vowes ybroken.[2]

The bulls stamped with episcopal seals are, to a pardoner, what the stamped certificates are to Dulcamara: both social types – a pardoner and a charlatan – claim to sell something the goodness of which is guaranteed by an external authority, all this made visible through the exhibition of written documents. Manuscript or printed, both sellers' papers sound either counterfeit or fallacious. Chaucer's Pardoner, as well, in the "Prologue to the Pardoner's Tale", even before starting to extol the value of his pardons, immediately declares:

> First I pronounce whennes that I come,
> And thanne my bulles shewe I, alle and some;
> Oure lige lordes seel on my patente,
> That shewe I first, my body to warente,
> That no man be so boold, ne preest ne clerk,
> Me to destourbe of Cristes hooly werk.
> And after that thanne telle I forth my tales,
> Bulles of popes and of cardynales,
> Of patriarkes and bishopes I shewe,
> And in Latyn I speke a wordes fewe,
> To saffron with my predicacioun,
> And for to stire hem to devocioun.[3]

He too, then, has written documents which testify to his (holy and sanctified) qualifications. And when the Catholic John Heywood, in the early sixteenth century, wrote his two interludes with pardoners among the main characters (*The Pardoner and the Frere* and *The Foure PP*), he resorted to Chaucer's text to blame them in the light of the deeply felt need for a reformation of the Church.[4]

This necessarily short overview of literary sources cannot but end with Volpone's speech in the homonymous play by Ben Jonson. Here, "into an obscure

---

2 William Langland, *Piers the Plowman*, B-text, "Prologus", ll. 68–71.

3 Geoffrey Chaucer, "Prologue to the Pardoner's Tale", ll. 335–346; *The Canterbury Tales*, in *The Riverside Chaucer*.

4 The two plays are to be found in *The Plays of John Heywood* (1991). On Heywood's pardoners see my *La scena della memoria* (1988), *Mad merry Heywood* (1997), and "The First Medical Practitioners in English Drama" (2011).

nook of the Piazza" in Venice (II.ii.39), Volpone, disguised as the mountebank Scoto of Mantua, exhibits his "blessed unguento" (l. 91) and an "ampulla" (l. 165) containing his "Oglio del Scoto" (l. 129) together with his "printed receipt" (l. 105) which, as the stage direction suggests, is now pointed at by the orator.[5]

This operatic and literary introduction, without confusing literature and reality but considering how literature draws on reality especially when dealing with social types, does not aim at diverging from the main topic of this research, but only at showing how selling techniques for centuries have relied both on the seller's rhetoric and on something conferring authoritativeness to the seller as such and to their products.[6] The street and the market square were – and still are – the location of this sort of vendors, either peddlers travelling from village to village, or mountebanks and empirics selling their wares from a raised platform in a town square or at fairs. Even if now, in our contemporary society, marketing can rely on highly technological devices, perhaps its basic procedures are not so different from the medieval and early modern ones, since each selling action tends to follow a stereotyped routine consisting of various stages: 1) attract attention; 2) arouse interest; 3) stimulate desire; 4) create conviction; 5) get action.[7]

The English Situation

The main part of what follows will deal with those people who in public spaces such as streets and squares, sold medicaments to the general public, availing themselves of printed advertising, even if they were neither physicians nor apothecaries, or – although they might have acquired such professional titles – they were not admitted to the corresponding official companies and guilds. Time and place will be limited to early modern London, where permission to perform cures was granted by the College of Physicians, according to its rigid statutes. This sort of practitioner was generally and disparagingly called by various names, differing slightly according to period. While such terms as 'practitioner' and 'empiric', as attested by the *OED*, were 'neutral' terms connected to

---

5 Quotes draw on Ben Jonson, *Volpone*, in *Three Comedies* (1966). The original stage direction reads "*Pointing to his bill and his glasse*". I have checked the quote with the play text published in Ben Jonson, *Workes of Benjamin Jonson* (1616), II.2.469. For an analysis of this scene see Tanya Pollard, "'No Faith in Physic': Masquerades of Medicine Onstage and Off" (2004).

6 The purely oral and rhetorical skills of a street vendor can be appreciated in Rutebeuf's *Dit de l'Herberie*, a French text of the thirteenth century.

7 Vestergaard and Schrøder, *The Language of Advertising* (1994), p. 49.

the practice of medicine, variously modified according to their accompanying adjectives and therefore acquiring negative meaning only when preceded for instance by 'unlearned' and 'doltish' as early as the sixteenth century,[8] 'mountebank', 'charlatan' and 'quack' entailed the concept of deceit and fraud. These latter words are variously distributed in time: 'mountebank', with the meaning of "An itinerant charlatan who sold supposed medicines and remedies, freq. using various entertainments to attract a crowd of potential customers" while being on a raised platform is attested as early as 1566. 'Charlatan', meaning "A mountebank or Cheap Jack who descants volubly to a crowd in the street; *esp.* an itinerant vendor of medicines who thus puffs his 'science' and drugs" appears in 1607 (in the Italian plural form "ciarlitani" in the scene from Jonson's *Volpone* quoted above). 'Quack' in the sense of "A person who dishonestly claims to have medical or surgical skill, or who advertises false or fake remedies; a medical impostor" appears only later, in 1638.[9] All three terms, anyway, are not attested earlier, and the dates show that 'quack' was the latest to be used.[10]

From the *OED* definitions the three nouns appear as belittling and discrediting, implying artifice, dishonesty, and falsity. In other terms, sixteenth-century mountebanks became first charlatans and then, in the seventeenth century, quacks, but in spite of the different labels, they were all considered as medical impostors, selling and puffing their remedies, often deceiving patients with good-for-nothing preparations.[11] Their names could also be used as synonyms,

---

8 The first modifier is used in the 1527 English translation of Hieronymus Brunschwig's *Liber de arte distillandi* (1527), and the second by William Bullein in his *Bulwarke of Defence* (1562). (*OED*, 2.a.).

9 *OED*, definition 1.a. for 'mountebank', 'charlatan', and 'quack'.

10 Roy Porter ("Before the Fringe" (1988), p. 3) prefers to use the term as a convenient one, according to one of Dr Johnson's three definitions, i.e. a quack is "one who proclaims his own medical abilities in publick places". In this article, though, Porter omits the first part of the definition itself, which reads "A vain boastful pretender to physick", which contains the usual accusation of counterfeiting (Samuel Johnson, "Quack (noun)", in *A Dictionary of the English Language*, 1755). The whole definition, on the contrary, is reproduced in Porter, *Quacks*, p. 19, together with the two others, which sound of similar negative meaning. Actually Porter comments: "In short, the appellation 'quack' marked out a man as Mr False Pretences" (p. 20). Nevertheless, Porter uses *quack* (without inverted commas) as a working term. Personally, I will follow suit.

11 Names were evidently interchangeable if, as late as 1654, to the title of his *Zωotomia* Richard Whitlock added the phrase "With an usefull detection of Mountebanks of both sexes". For the connections of the various terms, see Gentilcore, *Medical Charlatanism*, esp. pp. 53–58.

or in a series: the anonymous self-proclaiming "Italian doctor" "lately come to London" proudly boasts of being neither "any stage-quack or mountebank" (C112f9[150]), whereas Daniel Defoe, in his *Journal of the Plague Year*, laments the people's "running after Quacks and Mountebanks" during the 1665 visitation of the pestilence.[12]

That the two terms are used with the same meaning is clear from the title of the broadsheet *The Infallible Mountebank, or Quack Doctor*, datable to the very end of the seventeenth century or the beginning of the following one.[13] Richard Steele, in his turn, wrote of "[o]rdinary quacks and charlatans",[14] thus varying the composition of the 'duo' on the one hand, but on the other showing the interchangeability of the three terms at least around the 1710s.

Generally the bias against all irregular practitioners, whatever their name, has always tended to censure and disgrace them, but in the last decades of the twentieth century, and more recently, medical historians have underlined that the state of official medicine up to the end of the seventeenth century (and even later) was still linked to Galen, Hippocrates and their humoral theories, and had actually not progressed towards scientific medicine.[15] Therefore what a licensed physician might prescribe was very probably not so different from what a mountebank/charlatan/quack offered. Neither can the constraints imposed by the College of Physicians be overlooked when considering the satire and the accusations addressed against medical 'pretenders': for example, an applicant to enter the College had to show his skill in reading and understanding Latin (i.e. his academic education) and, quite often, that his medical degree had been obtained in England. This meant that many doctors who had graduated abroad were not admitted,[16] so that modern historians tend now to use the more neutral

---

12 Daniel Defoe, *A Journal of the Plague Year* (1722), p. 36.

13 For a discussion of this broadsheet, see Chapter 4 below.

14 Richard Steele, *The Tatler*, n. 240, 21 October 1710 (1831), p. 391.

15 In this volume, which does not pretend to be either a history of quackery or of early modern medicine, many basic concepts are given for granted. Among these, on the one hand there are those connected to Galen's humoral theory (according to which illness was imputed to the imbalance of the four bodily humours: phlegm, blood, yellow bile, and black bile). On the other there are the issues related to Paracelsus' defiant reaction to Galenism, in a mixture of esoterism and alchemical principles: the human body suffered from external causes which had to be fought with chemicals and minerals.

16 Once again I refer to Whitlock's work: when translating into English a passage from Dr Primerose's *De erroribus vulgi* on this topic (translated into English in 1651 with the title *Popular Errours*), the author – "because the fault is not confined to Italy" – writes: "many Medicasters, pretenders to Physick, buy the degree of Doctor abroad,

term 'irregular practitioners' for all medical figures who crowded and practised in London, especially in the seventeenth century, without having a licence. With the exception, of course, of those who clearly were 'counterfeit physicians'.[17]

The phenomenon of quackery, i.e. of those who were not doctors at all but only pretenders, was Europe-wide, and also connected to popular medicine. In England, in 1512, King Henry VIII's Parliament had promulgated a law which observed that

> the science and cunning of Physick and Surgery (to the perfect knowledge whereof be requisite both great learning and ripe experience) is daily within this Realm exercised by a great multitude of ignorant persons, of whom the greater part have no manner of insight in the same, nor in any other kind of learning. Some also can no letters on the Book, so far forth that common Artificers, as Smiths, Weavers, and Women boldly and customably take upon them great Cures, and things of great difficulty; in the which they partly use Sorcery and Witchcraft, partly apply such Medicines unto the disease, as be very noyous, and nothing meet.[18]

In this way, non-licensed people were prohibited from practising medicine and surgery within the city of London and "within seven miles of the same", and punished with fines in money up to £5. The license had to be obtained from religious authorities (the bishop of London or the Dean of St. Paul's in London; in the provinces licences were given by the bishop of the local diocese) who availed themselves of university physicians. Some years after that (in 1518, the tenth year of Henry's reign), the College of Physicians was created via a royal letter patent, giving Thomas Linacre and other royal physicians – all of them university graduates – the privilege to constitute a corporation in charge of testing would-be physicians. As a consequence only after obtaining the College's approbation

---

and come home and sel it for the Lives and Monyes of their own Countrymen." (*Zωotomia*, p. 107). In this way Whitlock shows all his spite for those countrymen of his who got their degrees outside England, by buying it (of this he accuses them), no matter if the foreign university was a renowned one such as Leiden, Montpellier, or Padua. By the way, this sounds strange, since Primerose himself got his MD degree at the university of Montpellier (see Pelling, *Medical Conflicts*, p. 173).

17 See ibid., particularly Chapter 5 for the various irregulars prosecuted by the College of Physicians and for the professional diversity of the former. The online resource connected with the volume is Margaret Pelling and Frances White, *Physicians and Irregular Medical Practitioners in London 1550–1640: Database*, 2004. See also Margaret Pelling and Charles Webster, "Medical Practitioners" (1979).

18 Christopher Merret, *A Collection of Acts of Parliament* (1660), pp. 1–2.

was a physician allowed to practice in London.[19] Henry's intervention was in response to a long-standing request from both universities that non-graduates be prohibited from practising the medical profession.[20] But in spite of these restrictions some time afterwards, in 1542, the king issued a bill which was to become known as "The Quacks' Charter", allowing men and women with no official qualifications to practice external cures, again recognizing the medical role of those men and women who had herbal knowledge. This law, probably due to the small number of university doctors in the country and – as the document declares – because of the *Chirurgeons*' "minding only their own lucres", gave permission to practise to everyone "as well men as women, whom God hath endued with the knowledge of the nature, kind and operation of certain herbs, roots and waters, and the using and ministering of them, to such as been pained with customable diseases". These people were allowed to work "within any part of the Realm of England, or within any other of the Kings Dominions", provided that their healing remedies were limited to "outward sore[s]" for the "relief and health of the Kings poor Subjects".[21] In other words, the College's power emerged hedged and limited and the role of empirics and cunning women was recognized and tolerated by law. At the same time, Henry's 1542 bill acknowledged the validity of popular medicine and accepted the role of women as healers both in village and town cultures, whereas university physicians at the time were obviously only male. The "Quacks' Charter", then, resulted in the free circulation of healers all over the kingdom, they no longer being indictable of breaking any law when complying with Henry VIII's decree. Only in London, therefore, was the power of the College of Physicians applicable and, elsewhere, healers might be prosecuted only when operating outside the limits imposed by their 'charter'.

In the 1540s the number of folk healers also rose due to the Dissolution of the Monasteries, which 'released' many friars, monks and nuns throughout the country. Most of them – according to a century-long tradition – were well-trained in growing, collecting and using herbs both as simples and compounds, not only for their communities' necessities but also to relieve the poor who crowded in for help.[22] Many non-university physicians, then, were available around England, and administered remedies to the sick, especially performing external cures

19 See ibid., pp. 9–10. For the series of royal physicians of Tudor and Stuart sovereigns, see Elizabeth Lane Furdell, *The Royal Doctors, 1485–1714: Medical Personnel at the Tudor and Stuart Courts* (2001).

20 See Carole Rawcliffe, *Medicine & Society in Later Medieval England* (1997), p. 120.

21 Merret, pp. 27–29.

22 See Eric Maple, *Magic Medicine and Quackery* (1968), pp. 66–67.

(thus leaving the cure of internal diseases to university educated physicians), so much so that Thomas Gale attacked the "rude Emperikes" and those "who, under the name of Chirurgians be nothing els but open murtherers", they being favoured because "without penaltie and correction of lawes frelye [they] take on them the practise of Chirurgerie".[23]

Two factors must also be taken into consideration, i.e. that outside London the College could not intervene, and that religious and urban authorities were entitled to issue medical licenses. At a time – both in the sixteenth and seventeenth century – when "early modern people were obsessed with health, its fragility, and with the means for preserving it",[24] health care was provided by a vast range of practitioners, from university graduates to surgeons and apothecaries, from barber-surgeons to local practitioners (not only women in general and midwives, but also other part-time laypeople). This was because, notwithstanding the often poor therapeutic results, there was "a high level of lay expertise and involvement in medicine in the early modern period" and a great "professional diversity" was available.[25]

Sixteenth-Century Charlatans in Italy and England

As stated above, uneducated healers were present all over Europe,[26] but the phenomenon became particularly acute in the early modern period, when mobility increased due to situations in individual countries (for example the ban on Jews in Spain, religious troubles after the Reformation elsewhere on the Continent, when people were compelled to leave their own country and look for a living in another, or had to turn to new ways of earning a living; other social problems such as poverty spread in the English countryside because of the enclosures, which pushed many people to vagrancy and beggary).[27] What was new, or at least perceived as such, was the way medicine vendors practised in order

23 Thomas Gale, *Certaine VVorkes of Chirurgerie* (1563), fols ii^{v} and Cii^{r}, respectively. This is an exemplary case where the neutrality of the noun 'empiric' is modified by a negative adjective.

24 Pelling, *The Common Lot*, p. 5.

25 Margaret Pelling, "Medicine and the Environment in Shakespeare's England", p. 31.

26 About the situation in Italy see Piero Camporesi, ed., *Il libro dei vagabondi* (1973); Giorgio Cosmacini, *Ciarlataneria e medicina* (1998); Piero Gambaccini, *I mercanti della salute* (2000); David Gentilcore, *Healers and Healing in Early Modern Italy* (1998), and *Medical Charlatanism*.

27 See Paola Pugliatti, *Beggary and Theatre in Early Modern England* (2003), esp. "Part One" for England, and Gentilcore, *Medical Charlatanism*, pp. 91–117 for Italy.

to sell their wares. If rhetorical skills had always been a resource to sellers, on the one hand the invention of print offered a more sophisticated tool, allowing a wider dissemination of information to non-present potential patients, on the other travelling actors' companies shared their stages with charlatans or were, as sometime happened, actors and charlatans at the same time. The documented routes of Commedia dell'Arte performers in the late sixteenth century and the entire seventeenth century, together with the treatises published about (mainly against) their activities, bear witness to the vastness of the territories they covered.[28] Actually, in Italy, the activities of remedy vendors and actors overlapped almost completely, especially because contemporary charlatans were at the same time masters in the art of entertainment.[29]

Nearly all early modern Italian writers stress the connection between quackery and theatrical performance, given charlatans' ability to collect large audiences through tricks, jokes, jugglery, music and animal taming. As Tomaso Garzoni highlighted (later quoted by both Mercuri and Ottonelli), Italian squares were brimful of charlatans who first entertained their audience, and only later started selling their remedies. At the end of his discourse devoted to "Ceretani" [charlatans] Garzoni listed the main types of performers:

> [c]hi fa uedere mostri stupendi, e horribili all'aspetto; chi mangia stoppa, e getta fuori una fiamma […] chi si laua il uolto col piombo liquefatto; chi finge di tagliar il naso a uno con un cortello artificioso; chi si caua di bocca diece braccia di cordella; chi fa trovare una carta all'improuiso in man d'un altro. (Garzoni, p. 764)

> [There are those who show marvellous monsters, and horrible in their appearance; those who eat oakum, and breathe out flames […] those who wash their faces with liquefied lead; those who pretend to cut somebody's nose with a stage knife; those who pull twenty feet of rope out of their mouths; those who make a card suddenly appear in another's hand]

---

28 See M. A. Katritzky, *Healing, Performance and Ceremony* (2012) for performers' activities in France through the writings of German-speaking physicians. As for attacks on Italian healers, see Scipione Mercurii [Mercurio], *De gli Errori popolari d'Italia* (1603), and the five tomes of Giovanni Domenico Ottonelli, *Della christiana moderatione del teatro* (1646–52). Mercurio's books were written in the wake of Laurent Joubert, *Erreurs populaires* (1578), to which Primerose also belongs. As for French culture, see also Thomas Sonnet de Courval, *Satyre contre les Charlatans* (1610). As early as 1585 Tomaso Garzoni blamed charlatans in his discourse "De' Formatori di spettacoli in genere, & de' Ceretani, o Ciurmatori massime" (in *La piazza universale*, pp. 757–64); the whole passage came to be known later as "Discourse CIV".

29 See below for these aspects in Italian culture.

All this was often enhanced by the presence of at least one woman on the stage ("la putta") whose function, he wrote, was to arouse "un strano desiderio al popolo della sua lasciuia grata" (Garzoni, p. 761) [a strange desire in the people with her lascivious grace].[30]

Giovanni Domenico Ottonelli also listed the stratagems used by charlatans in order to gather the largest possible number of people around their banks:

> E per hauer concorso vsano varj allettamenti, tra' quali alcuni si possono chiamar giuochi marauigliosi per allettare. Tali sono il caminar, ò ballare sù la corda; il far le forze d'Hercole: l'vsare salti mortali: il volare da vn luogo ad vn altro con vna fune: il giuocar d'arme in varij modi: il caminar con le mani à piedi alzati: il far ballar, e saltare vna bestia, ouero una donna vestita da huomo; l'ingannar gli occhi altrui con varie destrezze di mano: il solleuare vn peso grandissimo con i soli capelli: il ferirsi qualche parte del corpo, e presto risanarsi. Et altre cose di simil fatta, ouero superstitiose, che si possono numerare, e delle quali si sono seruiti anche gli antichi Ciarlatani, o Comedianti.[31]

> [And in order to gather an audience they use various allurements, some of which may be called wonderful tricks designed to entice. Such are rope walking or dancing; Hercules' games [human pyramids]; somersaults; flying from one place to another hanging on a rope; various weapon games; walking on one's hands with feet in the air; getting animals to dance and jump; or a woman dressed in man's attire; beguiling people through sleight of hand; raising a huge weight with only one's hair; inflicting wounds to one's body and soon recovering. And other things of a similar sort, i.e. superstitious, which can be listed, and of which the old Charlatans or Comedians also made use.]

The last words of the quotation show the author's tendency to put charlatans and Commedia actors on the same level ("Ciarlatani, o Comedianti"), so much so that later in his treatise he offered a further revealing description:

> Voglio dire, che i Ciarlatani molte volte trasferiscono dalla nobiltà della Scena, e del Theatro alla viltà del banco la Comedia; & iui la fanno comparire ad arrecar diletto infino all'vltima, e vilissima ciurma della plebe cenciosa, e stracciata: quasi che vna Cittadina onorata debba riceuere affronto da simili bassezze. Horsù così và il Mondo: i Ciarlatani diuentano Comedianti: e si seruono della Comedia, come di mezzo efficace, per allettare al banco; d'onde fanno lo spaccio delle loro mercantie, e bussolotti. E quando sono osceni meritano tutti que' vituperi, che si sono accennati altroue contro i dishonesti Professori dell'Arte Comica [...] Mà vediamo la pratica de' Comici Ciarlatani. Comparisce alle volte

30 I quote David Gentilcore's translation (*Medical Charlatanism*, p. 327). For a general appreciation of Garzoni's and Ottonelli's views about actresses and women on mountebank stages, see M. A. Katritzky, *Women, Medicine and Theatre* (2007), pp. 215–19.

31 Giovanni Domenico Ottonelli, *Della christiana moderatione del theatro libro, detto L'ammonitioni a' recitanti* (1652), [fourth volume of the series, by a different printer], p. 439.

in vna Città una Compagnia di questi Galant'huomini: conducono seco Donne bene all'ordine, e della lor professione; perche senza Donne stimano di dar in nulla, & essere giudicati Comedianti degni di poco plauso: spargono voce di voler seruire al publico, vendendo eccellenti segreti, e facendo belle Comedie; e tutte, per dar spasso e piacere, e senza pagamento: eleggono luogo nella publica piazza: oue composto vn palco, vi salgono à fare prima il Ciarlatano, e poi il Comediante. Ogni giorno à hora comoda comparisce in quella scena bancaria vn Zanni, ò altro di simil fatta, e comincia ò sonando, ò cantando ad allettare il Popolo al circolo, & all'audienza: poco dopo si fà vedere un'altro, e poi un'altro, & anche spesso vna Donna, e quiui tutti insieme con zannate, ò con altro fanno un miscuglio di popolari allettamenti: quando ecco viene il principale, che è lo Spacciatore del secreto, e l'Archiciarlatano: e con buona maniera s'introduce alla lode grande, & incomparabile del suo marauiglioso medicamento; di cui fattosi buono spaccio, e radunati i soldi, si termina quella vendita principale; dopo cui vn altro Ciarlatano comincia la sua, se prima non l'hà fatta; e poi anche la Signora spaccia i suoi moscardini, ò qualche altra gentilezza: alla fine si auuisa al popolo così.

Horsù La Comedia si cominci, la Comedia; e serrate le scatole, e leuati i bauli; il banco si cangia in scena, ogni Ciarlatano in Comediante, e si da principio a vn dramatico recitamento, che all'vso comico trattiene per lo spatio di circa due hore il Popolo con festa, con riso, e con solazzo. (Ottonelli, *L'ammonitioni a' recitanti*, pp. 454–56)

[I mean that Charlatans often transfer Comedy from the nobility of stage and theatre to the ignominy of a bank; and there they display it for the delight of all and sundry, down to the poorest and meanest scum of the ragged, tattered populace, as if an honoured townswoman must needs be affronted by this baseness. But this is the way of the world: Charlatans turn Comedians and use Comedy as an effective tool to allure people to their stage, from which they carry on a brisk sale of their stock-in-trade. And when they are obscene they deserve all those accusations mentioned elsewhere against the dishonest Professors of the Comic Art [...] But let us look more closely at the practice of Comedians-Charlatans. Sometimes a company of these Gentlemen arrives in a town: they take well-proportioned women with them, of the same profession as theirs, because they deem themselves worthless when without women, and to be judged Comedians of little merit. They spread the news they are there to serve the public, and sell excellent secrets and perform beautiful Comedies, everything to please and entertain, gratis. They choose a place in the public square where, after raising a stage, they mount it to play the Charlatan first and then the Comedian. Every day, at a convenient hour, on that raised stage a Zanni appears, or another similar personage, who by playing an instrument or by singing, starts pleasing and luring the onlookers to form an audience around him. After a while, another is called, and another, and often even a woman, and hereon all together with jests [*zannate*], or with various pranks they offer a mixture of popular allurements. Then, hey presto! the star comes on, the dealer of the secret and the Archcharlatan. With urbanity, he sets about extolling the virtues of his wondrous and incomparable medicament; then it is sold widely, money is collected, and the main sale is over. After that another Charlatan begins his, if he has not already, and the Lady also sells her dainties and other delicacies. At the end, the following announcement is made to the people.

> Let the Comedy begin, the Comedy! And once boxes are closed and trunks taken away, the bank is transformed into a stage, each Charlatan into a Comedian, and a dramatic performance gets started which, according to the comic custom, entertains the people for about two hours, with merriment, laughter, and delight.][32]

The interconnectedness of performing and selling medicines as described in this long but revealing passage will remain a feature of medicine vendors, and so will the condemnation of non-professional healers. But procedures developed differently in different countries. If we accept Garzoni's and Ottonelli's descriptions of Italian charlatans' actions – and nothing stands against that – Coryate's surprise at seeing mountebanks' shows in Venice in 1608 testifies to profound diversity between the strategies of English and Italian empirics.

In his *Heptameron of Civill Discourses* George Whetstone, when presenting "the thirde Nightes Pastime" at the fictional Italian court of Queen Aurelia, introduced a "Mountebanke" with his "Zanni", who played with "Adders" and "Snakes" only for the recreation of "Segnior Philoxenus", "and not with the intent of common Mountebanckers, to deceive the people with some unprofitable Merchandise". In the marginal gloss, the author commented that "mountebanks of Italie, are in a maner, as Englysh Pedlers", thus showing that the term was still rather new to his readers and pointing to the entertainment provided by these performers, while denying – as laudable – any attempt at selling on their part.[33]

The Jesuit John Rastell had also written of mountebanks in his work printed in Antwerp in 1566, and in a similar vein, i.e. without accusing the mountebanks "that goe abroad with diuerse thinges for mens Bodies" of anything but their will to earn money, a reason why they are judged far less dangerous than the "Mountebankes for the Soule" "that sel [...] everlasting life".[34] Before shooting his darts against Calvinism and Luther's Reformation, Rastell described the detailed manners of mountebanks on five of his small pages, concluding that

> A Montebank then, may crake, and lie, and outface his Aduersarie, and make somewhat of nothing, and mingle sporte with sadnesse, and play what part he will in the sight of the people, and hundreds will gase upon him, but none will reproue him.[35]

Thomas Coryate, as touched on above, visited Venice in 1608 and in his *Crudities* published in 1611 inserted a long passage devoted to Venetian mountebanks, firstly because they were the most famous ones in Italy, secondly because

---

32 Another translation of part of this passage is in David Gentilcore, "'Charlatans, mountebanks and other similar people'" (1995), p. 309.

33 George Whetstone, *An Heptameron of Civill Discourses* (1582), fol. Liii^{v}.

34 John Rastell, *The third booke* (1566), fols Aiii^{r}, Av^{v}.

35 Ibid., fol. Av^{r-v}. Rastell's whole passage about mountebanks will be discussed later.

they "oftentime ministered infinite pleasure vnto me", and also because he was convinced of the 'otherness' of these characters to English culture:

> neither doe I much doubt but that this treatise of them will be acceptable to some readers, as being a meere nouelty neuer before heard of (I thinke) by thousands of our English Gallants. (Coryate, p. 272)

The extended details Coryate relates include a mountebank's whole procedures, from his arriving in the Piazza and mounting the stage, the selling proper being preceded by instrumental music, songs, tricks and jests, till the moment when the

> principall Mountebanke [...] opens his truncke, and sets abroach his wares; after the musicke hath ceased, he maketh an oration to the audience of halfe an houre long, or almost an houre. Wherein he doth most hyperbolically extoll the vertue of his drugs and confections. (Coryate, p. 273)

Some women also belong to the company ("for there are divers women also amongst Mountebanks, [who] are attyred with habits according to that person that they sustaine"). The novelty of this kind of spectacle was evidently great if Coryate describes it with such a wealth of details, notwithstanding the comparison of mountebanks to peddlers offered by Whetstone. Particularly striking is the oratorical skill of these sellers, for which the author uses such phrases as "admirable volubility and plausible grace", "singular variety of elegant jests and witty conceits" (p. 273). A mountebank's rhetoric, Coryate witnessed, is

> intermingle[d] with such sauory iests (but spiced now and then with singular scurrility) that they minister passing mirth and laughter to the whole company, which perhaps may consist of a thousand people that flocke together about one of their stages. (p. 274)

Nearly all the ingredients of charlatans' marketing policy are here attested, even if there is no mention of printed matter (apart from ballads and songs) being distributed among the audience. Nevertheless, what Coryate saw in Venice aroused his curiosity and interest in such a manner, that he considered it worth relating in detail to the English, evidently because he noticed the differences between English and Italian medicine vendors. For those who also provoked his laughter and merriment, though, Coryate reserves a final negative judgment when he states that what a mountebank sells consists only in "trifles", thus shielding his own conscience from the temptation of praising something and somebody far from acceptable to his insular culture: "The principall things that they sell are oyles, soveraigne waters, amorous songs printed, Apothecary drugs, and a Common-weale of other trifles" (p. 274).[36]

---

36 On Coryate's description of Venetian mountebanks see Paola Pugliatti, "The Hidden Face of Elizabethan-Jacobean Theatre" (2010).

Forty years earlier Rastell had also described mountebanks' behaviour, as mentioned, but without setting their activities in any particular place. One can surmise, though, that the author's stay in the Spanish Netherlands after his flight from England had favoured his knowledge of and acquaintance with the phenomenon. According to this early mention of mountebanks (the earliest use of the word, according to the *OED*), these people "are a free kind of wanderers, pedlars, Surgeans, Physitians, Historiographers, poetes, or what so ever name besides you will geue unto them, men altogeather for the penie, which is the cause that they professe so many thinges". What puts all these sorts of people together is their greed, whatever their previous profession; certainly to find historiographers in the company appears rather strange, but possibly Rastell meant storytellers or news vendors. Their eloquence is praised, which is used to "commend" their goods, "But they doe it with such a Grace, with such a Constancie, with such Copie of words, with such mouing of Affections, that it is wonderful" (Rastell, fols Aiii^{r}, Aiii^{v}). Rastell does not seem to be interested in any particular town or country where he might have met mountebanks, but in their appearance and behaviour, so that in his work the basic structure of many speeches and harangues by later quacks can be found, including the appeal to the spectators' feelings.[37] A mountebank is "[a]rayed in his silkes and veluettes, And all to be rayed with braslettes & bowed peeces of golde, And chained about the neck with a great thing (of copper and gylt, as many iudge, but) of pure and fine gold" (Rastell, fol. Aiii^{v}): the irony about the fake jewels worn by these men is clear from the wary use the author makes of parentheses, even if a deeper distrust of mountebanks as vagrants dissimulating poverty can be perceived.[38] As for the speech proper, a lengthy (but fascinating) quotation is here better than any summary:

> He will tell his Audience: That he is come unto them for good wils sake, moued in him by the Fame and worthines of them and theyr Citie or Toune; He will tell them, that he can not tarie long, & that, before he depart, he would faine bestow upon them some token of his good affection: Then will he bring furth that water or pouder, or conceipt, which he would utter, and say, That it was brought from beyonde Calecut, or the Red Sea: and then wil he point with his finger towardes Calecut, and make a like disgression, to declare how far that is of, from their Countrie [...]: after this, he wil show the vertue and strength of his Pouder: And further declare, how much thereof hath been bought in greate Cities, and noble Personages which he will name: and further yet, he wil make

37 See D. G., *Harangues*, and Chapter 4 below.

38 I thank Paola Pugliatti for this observation. On the performance of beggary in early modern England and the social and political prejudices against vagrancy see Pugliatti, *Beggary*.

> them think, that it is al that he hath leaft, that which he offereth to be bought of them: He wil also disgrace other Mountebankes that goe abroad the Countrie, and say, That their wares are but counterfeit, but that his are fine, and pure, and fresh. For why he seeketh not after gaines, as the couetous and beggarly knaues doe, but as it becommeth a good Gentleman, he trauaileth farre and wide upon his own Charges to get such geare, as may bring Commodities to whole Countries. In Conclusion, when he hath spoken as much as he can, then he prouoketh the hearers againe and againe to bye. And if it be a water that he commended, he putteth in Glasses, made for the purpose, half a skore or a skore of droppes thereof: If it be a pouder, he putteth as much as he can hold betwen his Thombe and Forefinger, in seueral papers, and beginneth to make merchandise. And that which as it should seeme by his tale, should be wel worth a Croune a droppe, he wil sel, with good gaines, for a myte or two, of which twelue do make but a penie. (Rastell, fol. Aiiii^{r-v})

The various phases of a salesman's oration are well outlined here, and are very similar to those considered to be effective for today's advertising. To them, typical market-square strategies are added, e.g. the diminution of the price of a certain ware in favour of those customers who are present, together with something which sounds quite modern, i.e. 'comparative advertising', as it were, when the mountebank boasts of his goods as better than those of any competitor, up to the overt denigration of rivals.[39] No woman is present on the stages of Rastell's mountebanks, whereas Coryate noticed them, especially because they were "attyred with habits according to that person that they sustaine", that is, they acted in the performance at a time when women were absent from English theatrical stages (Coryate, p. 273). Ottonelli, as quoted above, mentions that, after the selling of the main mountebank, the others start selling their own wares, and among them "anche la Signora spaccia i suoi moscardini, o qualche altra gentilezza" (Ottonelli, p. 456) [the Lady also sells her dainties and other delicacies], meaning perhaps that these remedies are "of her own making".[40] Women, therefore, were common figures on Italian mountebank stages,[41] but the same does not

39 Ben Jonson 'copied' these same phases when writing Volpone's oration in II.2 of the homonymous play, a procedure which very probably contributed to this speech being reproduced in the various editions of D. G., *Harangues* (see Chapter 4 below).

40 Bella Mirabella, "'Quacking Delilahs'" (2005), p. 97.

41 Thompson, pp. 29–30. For mountebanks in France at the end of the sixteenth century as attested in Thomas Platter's diary, see Katritzky, *Healing*, esp. pp. 143–59. Both Katritzky's volumes (*Women* and *Healing*) contain many illustrations showing women on mountebank stages. For the Italian domain the most relevant study on charlatans remains Gentilcore, *Medical Charlatanism*, (esp. pp. 171–74, for women charlatans in Italy).

seem to be the case in England, even if Thompson, without quoting his source, mentions the case of Tomazine (Thomasina) Scarlet, who was fined and imprisoned with the accusation of having "hundreds under her cure to whom she gave medicines" although "she confessed she knew nothing of Physick, neither could read or write".[42] From Thompson's words, though, it is impossible to understand whether Thomasina was simply a healer, or actually mounted a stage for her cures. As happened later in the seventeenth century, English medical practitioners, especially in London, lived and worked in town at a specific address where they had their 'surgery', without disdaining, though, to mount a street platform or travel around the country.

As already noticed, Rastell's presentation of mountebanks is broad and delocalised, so far as to constitute a model for future harangues, while Coryate's text links his 'reportage' from Venice to the town's sellers. Both writers recognised – either explicitly or with subtle irony – how deceitful mountebanks were; however they both overtly admired not only charlatans' selling techniques and oratory skills, but also their positive effect (the action) on the bystanders. Rastell, who wondered why the local authorities did not prohibit such shows, acquitted them because of the social 'relief' they brought "by Singing, or plaieng upon Instrumentes", so that "for theyr fitte of mirth onely, they are worthy of somewhat" (Rastell, fol. Av^{r}).

Medicine in Seventeenth-Century London

The science of medicine, from the therapeutic point of view, did not make any significant progress in the seventeenth century, although Francis Bacon's empiricism favoured some development in many fields, including medicine. William Harvey's studies on the circulation of the blood were certainly fundamental for

42 Thomasina Scarlet was repeatedly condemned by the College of Physicians between 1588 and 1610, but the Annals of the College do not mention any activity of hers as a mountebank. Summoned to court on 4 August 1598, she "was accused by Caldwell, an official of the Bridewell, and by Mrs Heyborne, whose husband she had treated for ulcerated knee with an ointment made of mercury. She confessed to having given antimony in white wine. He became paralysed. She also admitted treating a man in Thyckin's house in Redcross Street, and to having frequently given stibium, even to children." Because of this, she was "imprisoned and fined £10", as the Annals report (Pelling and White 2004, s.v.; see also Margaret Pelling, "Thouroughly Resented?" (1997), p. 75). From the fact that she is still mentioned in the anonymous *The Modern Quacks Detected* (1752), p. 24, her case evidently became notorious: she is listed "with other Women" among the "Delinquents formerly called to Account" by the College.

advancement in physiology, but were not followed by decisive discoveries concerning medicaments, and people continued to be cured with the old remedies. Medicine, in other words, was still based on Galen and Hippocrates, while chemistry was still far from offering reliable substances. Even the chemical intuitions of Paracelsus from the previous century did not help to improve the cures for the many diseases and epidemics from which people and whole countries suffered. Neither did Vesalius' anatomical works bring about immediate significant progress. Patients, therefore, could only rely either on 'learned' but expensive medicines, or on cheaper, but empiric, folk remedies, and they could profit from iatrochemistry and alchemical results (such as the use of some minerals, including dangerous ones). Furthermore, medicines prescribed by physicians and prepared by apothecaries were mainly based on herbal knowledge, i.e. exactly the same that was followed by traditional healers.[43] The main differences between a

---

43 Apothecaries, who were united in a guild only in 1617 under the title of "Society of Apothecaries", sustained many controversies with physicians, accused as they were of preparing medicaments different from physicians' prescriptions, and of attempting to supersede doctors in curing patients. Thomas Coxe disparagingly calls them "Quacking Apothecaries" in his *A Discourse* (1669), pp. 198, 207, 316. Actually this work's title also claims that *Many Abuses of the Apothecaries in the Preparing their Medicines are detected, and Their Unfitness for Practice Discovered.* See also *The Accomplisht Physician*, whose anonymous author – but the book is attributed to Christopher Merret – called apothecaries "Hermaphrodite Apothecary-Doctor[s]", for their attempts at 'dethroning' physicians (Merret [?] (1670), p. 93). As early as 1566 John Securis had also spoken contemptuously of those "ignorant potecaries" who wanted "to play the phisitions" (*A Detection and Querimonie*, fol. Diiii^{r}). In 1618 the *Pharmacopoeia Londinensis* was published under the auspices of the College of Physicians; besides being a collection of official remedies it was designed to regulate apothecaries' activities and limit their freedom in creating their own medicines outside the physicians' prescriptions. In 1649 Nicholas Culpeper, in line with his agenda about bringing medicine to the people, published a translation into English of the *Pharmacopoeia*, with the title *A Physical Directory or A Translation of the London Dispensatory*. It was a revolutionary enterprise, for it allowed all literate people to read and prepare their own remedies: "What made Nicholas's book revolutionary and courageous, if not fool-hardy, was that, as the title-page promised, it included 'many hundred additions which the reader may find in every page marked with this letter A'" (Benjamin Woolley, *Heal Thyself* (2004), p. 289). Culpeper's translation provided an invaluable collection of recipes and their dosages, to be joined to the numerous family collections of healthcare to which almost all resorted for self help. At the same time it also furnished irregular practitioners with accessible medical knowledge as a basis for their own more or less 'secret' medicines.

physician's medicine and a charlatan's (apart from the price) were that the former consisted of known ingredients and was not sold in public places such as streets and squares, and the latter – not always of uncertain composition, but often grounded on traditional home recipes – was sold on the basis of what might now be termed long and hard 'advertising campaigns'.[44] To popular remedies – either sold by mountebanks or ministered by old women – magic, if not witchcraft proper, was also associated:

> [...] the inadequacy of orthodox medical services left a large proportion of the population of Tudor and Stuart England dependent upon traditional folk medicine. This was essentially a mixture of common-sensical remedies, based on the accumulated experiences of nursing and midwifery, combined with inherited lore about the healing properties of plants and minerals. But it also included certain types of ritual healing, in which prayers, charms or spells accompanied the medicine.[45]

It is not difficult to understand, therefore, that official and non-official medicine were not so different from each other, and that proprietary remedies were often preferred by both the well-off and the poor, thus determining the popular success of charlatans or, as they more often came to be named in the seventeenth century, 'quacks'.

Not all quacks were ignorant pretenders: some, as already stated, had graduated in medicine abroad, and some were simply 'empirics' (or barber-surgeons, who were not obliged to attend university courses), that is, people who practised medicine, even successfully, but without an official licence from the College (for London) or from ecclesiastical and urban authorities in other towns and in the provinces, as previously hinted at. Francis Bacon himself, when highlighting the deficiencies of the medical profession, had written that what was desirable for physicians and empirics was that learning and practice went hand in hand in both categories: "they be the best Phisitians, which being learned incline to the traditions of experience; or being Emperiques, incline to the methods of learning".[46] However, Bacon distinguished clearly between physicians and impostors (including "Witches, and old women"), "which minister the same medicines to all patients", and "which commonly haue a fewe pleasing receits, whereupon

44 As Andrew Wear observes, "[t]here are examples in seventeenth-century England of doctors as well as patients using folk remedies" ("The Popularization of Medicine", p. 22). On the role of home medicine and of manuscript recipe collections see Elaine Leong and Sara Pennell, "Recipe Collections" (2007).

45 Keith Thomas, *Religion and the Decline of Magic* (1991), p. 210.

46 Francis Bacon, *THE Tvvoo Bookes of FRANCIS BACON. Of the proficience and aduancement of Learning* (1605), II, fol. 41^{r}.

they are confident and aduenturous, but know neither the causes of diseases, nor the complexions of Patients, nor perill of accidents, nor the true methode of Cures". Evidently he did not accept their usurpation of the medical title and profession, and attributed most of these people's success to the "weaknesse and credulitie of men [...], as they will often preferre a Montabanke or Witch, before a learned Phisitian".[47] Nevertheless, irregular practitioners, especially in the mid- and late seventeenth century, were not illiterate (even though the College of Physicians insisted in calling them so): literacy had grown "among the craftsmen and tradesmen of early modern London" and was still growing, and since many people practising medicine came from the varied world of guilds and trade companies, "in spite of the College's terminology it was more a matter of rival literacies, rather than illiteracy itself. It was, for example, perfectly possible to know Latin and not to have been at university at all".[48]

Neither were all irregular practitioners cheats and swindlers. Margaret Pelling has made a thorough study of the situation of non-Collegiate practitioners up to 1640, finding that many of them – besides those with a foreign degree – belonged to the apothecaries' guild or to the barber-surgeons'. In other words they were able professionals, even if the College accused them of malpractice, especially because they often practised inward medicine (also against the "Quacks' Charter" according to which unlicentiates were allowed outward cures only).[49] Considering that medical practitioners might be defined as those persons (men and women) "whose occupation is basically concerned with the care of the sick",[50] it is evident how broad the category turns out to be, including on the one hand capable and experienced health carers, and on the other charlatans and tricksters, in a continuum showing a variegated professional diversity.

47 Ibid., fols 40^{r}, 77^{r}; I, fol. 8^{r}, and II, 39^{v}, respectively.

48 Margaret Pelling, "Knowledge Common and Acquired" (1995), pp. 269, 262.

49 See ibid., pp. 267–70. See also Pelling, *Medical Conflicts*, pp. 138–41, and Figures 5.2. and 5.3. in the same volume (pp. 156–57) for the various occupations of the irregulars registered (and fined) by the College. The already mentioned "Annals" of the College of Physicians of London (on which Pelling's research is based), constitute the internal history of the College itself and record the proceedings against irregulars. They have never been published, but those parts written in Latin have been translated, and the whole is now microfilmed (they are held at the Royal College of Physicians in London).

50 Pelling and Webster (1979), p. 166.

Printing to Sell

Throughout the seventeenth century what mostly disturbed the College physicians was the aggressive methods launched by irregulars to sell their remedies and practice, i.e. advertising by print. That was nothing totally new, if one considers that William Caxton himself – as all studies on the history of English advertising inform us – produced a print ad for a book of his (*The Pyes of Salisbury*) in 1477, and that a medical ad by a Master Gervaes goes back to the mid-sixteenth century.[51] But it was the quantity of both irregular practitioners and of their publications (and of course the latter's content) that irritated the College. A 'good' doctor was not supposed to address patients through vernacular print, especially when one considers that the printed items were thin sheets of cheap paper usually crammed with thick letters, very often badly written, and printed in "small workshops, or corner presses".[52] These leaflets were either distributed to the people surrounding a stage or walking along the streets, or left for reading in coffeehouses, or pasted on walls and poles. Advertisements in the periodical press must also be added to handbills (from the second half of the seventeenth century), together with medical information printed in almanacs.[53] It goes without saying that irregular practitioners were not the only ones to resort to these means of communication (in fact, sometimes College physicians used them as well), and that, as a result, the market for medicine became too crowded for the

---

51 See Chapter 5 below. Caxton's advertisement is reproduced in T. R. Nevett, *Advertising in Britain* (1982), facing p. 18.

52 Elizabeth Lane Furdell, *Publishing and Medicine in Early Modern London* (2002), p. 143. The seminal studies about print and the medical domain, analising the quantitative and qualitative impact of vernacular medical printed books in early modern England, remain Paul Slack, "Mirrors of Health and Treasures of Poor Men" (1979), and Harold J. Cook, *The Decline of the Old Medical Regime in Stuart London* (1986), esp. Chapter 1, "The Medical Marketplace of London"; see also a fairly recent article by Mary E. Fissell, "The Marketplace of Print" (2007).

53 See R. B. Walker, "Advertising in London Newpapers, 1650–1750" (1973), esp. pp. 126–29, and Diane Wales, "Equally Safe for Both Sexes" (2005); for almanacs, see Louise Hill Curth, "The Medical Content of English Almancs" (2005), and "Medical Advertising in the Popular Press" (2006). About newspaper advertising see Maurizio Gotti, "The English of Eighteenth Century Advertising" (1994), and "Advertising Discourse in 18th-Century English Newspapers" (2005). Almanacs published by women are the subject of A. S. Weber, "Women's Early Modern Medical Almanacs" (2003). As already stated, I will deal only with advertising via handbills; therefore readers interested in other early modern media such as newspapers and almanacs will profitably resort to the specialized bibliography quoted here.

College to accept, hence all the latter's belittling strategies and the satirical campaigns against quacks.[54]

From some handbills it appears that not all quacks were enthusiastic about publicising their profession in print; in fact some of them were (or wanted to appear) reluctant to use ads. On the one hand there is the "German Gentlewoman" Anne Laverenst who declares that

> Being but very lately arriv'd in this Kingdom, and so consequently a Stranger, I could not propose a better method to make my self known, than by this Printed Paper, without which; I might for some Years have remained unknown to you; and so consequently incapable of imploying that Talant which Heaven hath bestowed on me, for all your benefits and good. (551a32[31])[55]

thus showing that she acknowledged advertising as a powerful means of communication, especially for a foreign woman starting her practice in a new country. On the other hand "The great TRAVELLER Major J. C. one of his Majesties Chymists", who sells his "in a manner miraculous [teething] Necklaces", also claims to have recourse to print, but only in order to make himself known to the poor, in this way letting readers understand how charitable he is: "He had not appeared in Print, but for the good of such as have not much money to lay out upon Physick." (C112f9[87]).

A different reason for apologising for the resort to print is given by the "Gentleman" living "At the Sign of the Moon and Star in Leopard's Court in Baldwins-Garden near Holborn", who similarly offers the knowledge he has acquired after his "learned Education in the University of Louvain" to help the sick, but fearing counterfeits has had to make use of print: "And were it not to prevent you from being imposed on by ignorant Pretenders he would never have appeared in Print." (551a32[37]).

Another practitioner, selling pills against "the Scurvey, Pox, and Dropsie" (remedies whose origin he attributes to Robert Boyle: "Of which Pills the ever honoured Esquire BOYLE was the Author"), proclaims his love for mankind, which he wants to preserve from the torment of mistaken cures, by asserting that

> the Publisher [of the present medicine] did for a long time decline all thoughts of printing, but being at last prevail'd upon by the unanswerable perswasions of worthy

54 For a critical discussion of the use (and abuse) of "'[m]arket' mechanisms and terminology" in the historical medical domain, see Mark S. R. Jenner and Patrick Wallis, "The Medical Marketplace" (2007).

55 As already stated, references to single handbills will always be quoted in the text.

> men, he is to tell the world, that if they will avoid the horrid tortures of ill Cures […] (551a32[118])

In this way, he kills two birds with one stone, since (through his words) he communicates both his humanitarianism and his will to oppose fakes.

To print, however, all practitioners did resort, including some College physicians. Evidence of this phenomenon are the various bills distributed by John Pechey in which, either when revealing his name or simply declaring himself a "Physician", he claims to be "a Graduate in the University of Oxford and a Member of the College of Physicians in London" (551a32[9]).[56] The College as such also used bills, if not exactly to advertise nostrums, at least to inform people of their own activities:

> Advertisement
> The Physitians of the Colledge, that us'd to consult twice a week, for the benefit of the Sick, at the Consultation house, at the carv'd Angel and Crown in Kings street, near Guild Hall, meet now four times a week; and therefore give publick notice, that on Mondays, Wednesdays, Thursdays and Fridays, from two in the afternoon till six, they may be advis'd with by the known poor, and meaner families for nothing; and that their expectations and demands from the middle rank, shall be moderate: but as for the rich, and noble, liberality is inseparable from their quality and breeding. (551a32[226])

There survives a bill, though, that shows that no less a figure than Dr Charles Goodall – a Collegiate and the author of a history of the College of Physicians through the relevant documents[57] – resorted to printed advertisements in order

---

56 Pechey's bills in the two British Library Collections clearly demonstrate that the same practitioner would print various handbills producing only minor changes to a basic text: some of his bills vary just in minor lexical choices (for example in 551a32[163] the physician is said to 'dwell' instead of 'living' in London, whereas in 551a32[211] he wrote of being "a graduate in one of our own Universities" without stating which one). That all these handbills refer to the same person is guaranteed by the address printed on each of them, it being always the same, i.e. "At the Angel and Crown in Basing-Lane, being the Second Turning in Bread-Street from Cheapside". In order to assure the public of his credentials, he also printed a grant he received "from the Colledge of Physicians in the year 1684", which had "examin'd and approv'd of, and elected [him] into our Colledge" (551a32[168]). On Pechey's biography and his struggle with the College, see Thompson, pp. 132–35.

57 See Charles Goodall, *The Royal College of Physicians of London* (1684). This work also includes information about the punishment of offenders and proceedings "against Empiricks" before the Restoration. The College was called "The Kings Colledge of Physitians in the Cittie of London" by Charles II in a charter issued on 26 March of his fifteenth regnal year (i.e. 1663), printed ibid., pp. 62–118 (the quote is on p. 69).

to publicise "a Superfine Sort of Jesuits Bark ready powder'd and paper'd into Doses" which was sold "at the Coach and Horses in Physicians Colledg in Warwick-Lane" (C112f9[28]), and to attack apothecaries' abuses.[58]

Quacks' Handbills and Popular Medicine

One is legitimately entitled to wonder how different the remedies offered by irregular practitioners were from Collegiate physicians' and whether the former relied on folk and popular medicine. According to the major scholars of early modern health care, it would be rather difficult to detect a deep divide between the two, since both still had Galen's humoral pathology as their basis together with the widespread knowledge of herbs and plants. Medical pluralism in early modern times (especially in the sixteenth and seventeenth centuries) did not mean that there were such differences as to justify assertions about orthodox and heterodox medicines. According to Roy Porter, who deals with this problem in detail, "[p]re-modern quackery did not seek to create alternative understandings of health and disease: it battened on to those already existing".[59] What was different were the forms of dealing with patients: on the one hand the physician's practically daily visit and bed care of patients, plus his detailed prescriptions to the apothecary for the preparation of a medicine, and on the other the probable non-contact between quacks and their clients, who bought ready-made and secret remedies (i.e. the ingredients of which remained unknown) either at a mountebank's stage or even by post, after reading an advertisement. Family health care, not only in the countryside, continued to be in women's hands, and village healers were still the daughters and nieces of late medieval wise-women, by now often rid of any accusation of magic and witchcraft. The 'popular errors', so disparaged by learned physicians all over Europe (and by John Securis in England) in their volumes with this title, were rather the demonstration of the university physician's anger at seeing the growing commercialization of medicine and the massive entry of irregulars into the medical field, than an analysis of really different medical practices. These volumes had "a mission": in David Gentilcore's words, it was "to rid [the] world of medical 'errors'", attributed mainly to charlatans and women.[60]

58 See Thompson, pp. 233–34.

59 Porter, *Quacks*, p. 205.

60 David Gentilcore, "Was there a 'Popular Medicine' in Early Modern Europe?" (2004), p. 152. I am applying Gentilcore's phrase to all writers of "popular errors literature", but originally the author uses it only for Scipione Mercuri.

Doreen G. Nagy, in her turn, underlines that "popular practitioners used the same treatments as the professionals to treat a broad spectrum of ailments and achieved similar results", and that "popular practice was at the centre of health care, not its fringe".[61] And this obtains especially because in those centuries "[t]here were not two distinct medical cultures"[62] – or because people, even if they recognized the differences between the "learned physician trained in the universities and the empiric or mountebank", were not troubled by them: "in practice those distinctions were often ignored".[63] This also underlines the fact that popular remedies were made more or less of the same ingredients (mainly herbal ones) used by Collegiate physicians, and that – once again – a distinction must necessarily be drawn in the wide range of remedies between the often dangerous or useless hotchpotch administered by cheats and the traditional infusion prepared by a cunning woman.

Certainly handbills and their writers did not often show a university education; the leaflets were written for the public at large with no social distinction (and actually attracted patients from all ranks of life), who were only asked to be personally able to read (or to have someone to do that for them), and to let themselves be persuaded to try the nostrum sold by an ever growing medical marketplace:[64]

> Dear Friends, let your Disease be what God will
> Pray to him for a Cure, Try CASE's Skill;
> Who may be such an healing Instrument,
> As will Cure you to your own Heart's Content.
> His Medicines are Cheap, and truly Good,
> Being full as safe as your daily Food.[65]

And people did try, not least because, as Case's lines highlight, quacks' remedies were (relatively) cheap, allegedly "as safe as your daily Food", and, mainly, they also guaranteed the patient's "Heart's Content", i.e. they 'spoke' to people's feelings and perceptions about sickness: "[w]hether or not quack medicines did much good, they showed sensitivity to customer demand".[66]

---

61 Doreen G. Nagy, *Popular Medicine* (1988), pp. 3, 79.

62 Slack, p. 173.

63 Wear, "The Popularization of Medicine", p. 17.

64 The term 'marketplace' is not used in its strictly ideological modern meaning, since in early modern times "if any transactions occurred, they were social rather than economic" (Wear, *Knowledge*, p. 29).

65 From a bill by John Case (551a32[131]).

66 Porter, *Quacks*, 205.

One of the main issues I dealt with at the beginning of my research was whether the empirics' handbills can be considered as part of popular culture, given that they are printed and therefore not available to the illiterate. While working on them, though, I have become more and more convinced that they do belong to it, and for various and different reasons. First, they do not represent official medical positions, even if what they offer cannot be defined 'alternative medicine'. Furthermore, the cost of empirics' and wise women's cures was lower than the very expensive remedies regular physicians prescribed and had the apothecaries prepare, therefore these cures were available to larger social classes.[67] Second, in an age in which printing had become more and more widespread and literacy levels had risen hugely, children at least – if not their fathers – might be considered capable of reading (the writing skill, of course, is something which can well be separated from reading, as research in the field has shown). As a consequence, handbills were targeted at a public endowed with at least basic reading skills.[68] Thirdly, the language used by medical practitioners, in spite of its being interspersed with far-fetched, resounding words, some of them in Latin, is very basic; their lexicon is limited, so as not to create problems in understanding but at the same time betraying the writer's lexical deficiency; the often inaccurate grammatical structures let the reader 'overhear' the casualness of speech. Neither is the syntax complex, and they often use pre-formed clusters which pass from one bill to another, thus revealing their repetitive character and clear residues of orality. Besides, one mustn't forget that the so called blackletter ballads of the time (and of the preceding decades, too, of course) were also intended mainly for the illiterate,[69] since they were composed to be sung rather than read. Moreover, to spread the knowledge of a ballad even in the absence of singers, it was sufficient

67 But cf. Porter, "Before the Fringe", p. 17, where the author contests this view of irregular practitioners' medicine. Porter's position is quite understandable since his research mainly deals with eighteenth-century medicine and with "top quacks of the Georgian age" who "grew rich and famous".

68 The problem of literacy (and, consequently, of the potential readership of written texts) has been debated and studied by various scholars. Adam Fox writes that in the sixteenth and seventeenth centuries literacy, especially in London, "was dispersed quite widely in society" (*Oral and Literate Culture* (2000), p. 14). See also Jonathan Barry, "Literacy and Literature in Popular Culture" (1995), esp. pp. 78–85; David Cressy, *Literacy and the Social Order* (1980), and *Society and Culture in Early Modern England* (2003).

69 Ballads, nevertheless, fascinated the literate as well, as is testified by Samuel Pepys' collection of 1800 ballads, in five volumes (now held at the Pepys Library at Magdalene College, Cambridge).

that one literate person read it aloud to an audience of listeners. With medical handbills something very similar might have happened, especially considering that some of them were distributed at the foot of empirics' stages (and therefore were reminders of what had already been listened to during an individual empiric's performance), and that many handbills were posted in London coffeehouses, where the literate could read them aloud.[70]

70 In the copious late seventeenth-century anti-quack literature, though, the accusations against irregular practitioners also include doubts about quacks' real reading and writing skills. The anonymous author of *The Quacks Academy* (1678), p. 8, advises would-be practitioners in this way: "Take two large Sheets of paper, on the one write down (or get the Book-lear'd Scribe that writes your Bills to do it for you) the Names of all ordinary *Distempers*; on the other all celebrated *Medicines*" (underscoring mine). In the same way, and with similar words, the author of *The Character of a Quack-Doctor* (Anon., 1676), p. 3, stigmatises any quack that "ingages some Friend that's *Book-Learn'd* to correct the false English" (on this text see more in Chapter 5 below).

2 A Corpus-based Approach to the Language of Quacks

A handbill had the power to prolong the charlatan's public performance, bringing his words into homes, shops, and other places, independent of the charlatan's own physical presence.

(David Gentilcore, *Medical Charlatanism in Early Modern Italy*)

The Two British Library Collections

As the titles given by the British Library to the two collections show, they include 185 and 231 advertisements (C112f9 and 551a32, respectively). In effect, though, not all documents are ads, even if they contain something related to advertising. Pages are not numbered, but each individual item has a faintly pencilled number on it at the top left corner (added probably by a librarian in the past), which in the present work is placed between square brackets and added to the BL shelf mark in order to identify each single document. Some handbills are printed on both pages, some only on the recto. In both series there are six booklets of instructions (of "directions") about certain medicaments. Neither collection follows any particular order: the various items are simply juxtaposed one after the other randomly, each leaflet glued on a white page (so as to allow the reading of the verso side), and bound in a volume.

Among the handbills collected in C112f9 there are ten Italian recipes of remedies from the "Spezieria de Padri di S. Spirito di Fiorenza" [the apothecary of the Fathers of the Holy Ghost in Florence], from [106] to [115];[1] a document dated 1664 with information about "The Cargo's of Seven East-India Ships" ([118]); another dated 1685 containing certificates of people who had used the "Patentees Engine for making Salt Water Fresh" ([157]); an undated list of the "Governors of the Hospitals of Bridewell and Bethlem, London" ([163]); a curious handbill publicizing an Italian dentist, printed in French on one side and in German on the other ([164]); a plea to the "Officers and Gentlemen of the Army" to give money for and take care of disabled soldiers, of their children and of pensioners of the "Royal Hospital at Chelsea" ([165]), which mentions an episode which happened in 1709; a document of the Company of Merchants of Great Britain

1 This is the only case in this collection of similar leaflets being ordered in a sort of invisible 'section', but why here and not before or afterwards cannot be explained.

dated 1714 ([170]); a sheet with the drawings and measurements of (Catholic) priests' and deacons' tonsures ([175]). Other interesting documents – but necessarily, together with the above mentioned ones, excluded from my research – are a 1663 Milanese passport testifying that a certain person was not hit by the plague ([180]); a leaflet advertising the presence in London of a bearded woman ([181]); a 1714 list of the "Prices of Stocks" ([176]); a couple of ads for baths and spas; a sample of typographical characters; a page with drawings of plants and flowers, evidently ready to be printed in a herbal, or copied from one. The present long lists reveal to the researcher that this collection is not made up of medical ads only, but of various and sundry articles, even though most items are medical ones.

This is also true for 551a32. In it the following prints can be found, which do not correspond to a medical advertisement at all: eleven leaflets in German printed to celebrate particular military successes of Continental sovereigns, but a couple also in homage to Queen Anne ([98]-[108]);[2] an ad of a key seller ([203]); copies of a list of the cargo of "the Rochester arrived from Fort St. George the 21th of October, 1689" ([209]); more than one copy of an advertisement proclaiming the virtues of "a new, light, hollow Girdle" to prevent "from Drowning in any kind of Water [...] by Francis Cruys", i.e. a swimming girdle ([205r]).[3]

All the various items which do not deal with medicine have not been transcribed, neither have those handbills which are clearly identical copies of another document. On the other hand, I have typed some documents which are only similar to others, in so far as they are demonstrably a new release of a previous item (punctuation and capitalization may be changed, or some textual detail reads differently). These diversified copies, anyway, show a continuity in a practitioner's career, and/or its changes (information may be added or subtracted, addresses changed...). The total number of relevant handbills (therefore excluding the 12 booklets) amounts to 304 out of 416, of which 141 from C112f9 and 163 from 551a32, i.e. 73.07 per cent of them all.

As stated above, there are also twelve pamphlets in the two collections, all of them consisting of four or eight pages, usually numbered: C112f9[35], C112f9[41],

2 This 'section' of the present collection is analogous to what was highlighted in the previous note. The only apparent reason for both is the non-English language in which the leaflets are written.

3 The leaflet has no date, but Francis Cruys published his *Art nova natandi, or, New swimming girdles* in 1698. Therefore a possible date for the handbill is around that year.

C112f9[162], C112f9[168], C112f9[169], C112f9[169bis];[4] 551a32[45], 551a32 [128], 551a32[177], 551a32[190], 551a32[202], 551a32[222]. All of them can be labelled "books of directions" about taking the various medicines (and/or beauty products) they advertise, or – according to the MEMT and EMEMT researchers – "Remedies and Materia medica".[5] Therefore they are a slightly different text type from handbills, as regards size, format and structure. The majority of these booklets are undatable, but the one advertising "Fletcher's Powder" (551a32[202]) has a date for 1679 at the end; at the bottom of the damaged front-page of C112f9[168] there remain two faded digits for 17…, whereas on the last page (n. 4) the writer, Paul Chamberlen M.D., shows a date for "Sept. 13, …16"; in C112f9[169] the year 1716 is overtly stated, as it is in C112f9[169bis].

One feature emerging from the above is that not all documents clearly state their dates of printing – actually very few of them do; in particular most irregular practitioners' handbills are devoid of time references, so that dating them is extremely difficult. This explains the BL title of both collections: the documents come from various decades of the seventeenth century and the early eighteenth century, but do not exceed the latest date shown (1715–16). As for the printing place, even if this is very rarely stated, it can be surmised that all handbills were printed in London, given the names of churches, streets and other topographical detail embedded in the bills.

The Structure and the Format

"Unlike ads in periodicals, handbills remained untaxed", writes Elizabeth Lane Furdell,[6] thus becoming a very cheap way to the medicine marketplace. Certainly their printing cannot have been expensive, their paper being flimsy, the characters

---

4 The numbering C112f9[169bis] has been added by myself, since the item following C112f9[169] has no pencilled digits, numbers restarting from 170 after the document at issue.

5 MEMT is the acronym for *Middle English Medical Texts*, a CD-ROM published separately (Irma Taavitsainen and others, eds, *Middle English Medical Texts*, (2005) as a 'companion' to Irma Taavitsainen and Päivi Pahta, eds, *Medical and Scientific Writing in Late Medieval English* (2004). The EMEMT (*Early Modern English Medical Texts*) CD-ROM accompanies the volume Irma Taavitsainen and Päivi Pahta, eds, *Early Modern English Medical Texts* (2010). Each CD ROM collects a vast variety of medical texts from its respective period, thus offering electronically searchable corpora of medical works. Both corpora have been used in some of the following chapters as benchmarks to check the originality and/or the standardization of the language of quacks.

6 Elizabeth Furdell, *Publishing and Medicine* (2002), p. 142.

crammed in order to use all the possible space, with little refinement unless some special features were introduced, such as woodcuts, decorated frames, pointing hands. I postpone the analysis of these typographical details to a later chapter, whereas here the focus will be on bills as rhetorically styled artefacts, i.e. their argumentative structure.

David Gentilcore, in his exhaustive study of Italian charlatanism, outlines the typical format of Italian handbills as follows:

> [t]he typical Italian Charlatans' handbill [...] begins with: (i) a more or less lengthy title introducing the charlatan and his remedy/remedies. It then passes onto: (ii) the diseases and complaints treated by the remedy. This takes up most of the main body of the text. This is then followed by: (iii) a brief mention of dosages, before passing on to: (iv) the charlatan's credentials, usually in the form of licences and privileges awarded, sometimes by mentioning illustrious cures. It sometimes concludes with: (v) the price of the remedy and where to find the charlatan or buy his remedy and take advantage of any other services offered.[7]

Did London handbills resemble this structure and the order of its parts? It would be difficult and even dangerous to generalise, but perhaps a certain format can also be envisaged for the English products. Two 'model' handbills can be taken into consideration, one embellished with a picture and one just made up of words. Let's start by analysing two illustrated handbills, one from each collection, attributable to the first category (illustrated bills).

C112f9 is richer in images than 551a32, the handbills of the latter being mainly – when at all – decorated with (royal) coats of arms. Nevertheless two similar examples from the two collections can be compared (see Figures 1 and 2):

7 Gentilcore, *Medical Charlatanism*, p. 351. Later on the same page Gentilcore explains that "[s]ection one" is the textual place which "gave charlatans the chance to identify themselves to the public, giving name, stage-name, place of origin, and any titles in bold print."

Figure 1: Handbill C112f9[77], recto. By courtesy of the British Library Board

With Liberty of the Colledge of Phiſitians of the Royal Head City of *LONDON* in *ENGLAND*.

BE it made known by this, to all high and lower Perſons, that here lately is Arrived, an Experienc'd, moſt Famous, *German*, *Turkiſh*, and *Imperial* Phyſitian, whoſe like has not been in this Kingdom, who hath Learned ſuch a curious and ſtrange Art, which no other Doctor doth underſtand, and can Cure all ſorts of Patients which are left off by other Doctors. He can ſhow his Teſtimonies from 3 Emperors and 9 Kings, as alſo from 7 Dukes and Electoral Princes, as the *Romiſh*, *Turkiſh*, and *Japaniſh* Emperors; he can ſhow his Teſtimonies in 36 Languages, which no other Doctor can ſhow: He hath Cured the Brother of the *Turkiſh* Emperor, which was Blind 13 years, and hath obtained his Natural Sight again. This *German* Phyſitian has Travelled through 3 parts of the World.

1. He lets underſtand, that he is ſo Famous, that the like of him is not to be found, an Occuliſt, Stone, and Rupture-Cutter, *Medicina Chymicus Practicus*, if any ſuch Patients do meet, which are troubled with blindneſs of the Eyes, though they were Born Blind from the very Womb, he knows to Cure thoſe Patients, with the help of God, for their Life time, as there are Cataracts, Obſtructions, Suffuſions, all ſorts of Blindneſs, Darkneſs of the Eyes, that Men muſt Write and Read by Spectacles, thoſe he Cures by the help of God, that they may Write and Read without them. He alſo Cureth Redneſs, Horneſs, or running of the Eyes, or any other Diſtemper of the Eyes which are not mentioned here, by the help of God he cures in a very ſhort time.

2. He helps alſo all Burſten or broken Bellies, either in Men, Women or Children, whether the Rupture be in the Groin or Navel, and if the Rupture be as bigg as a Mans Head, then truſt to God, and his Art, you ſhall have your Cures, that you may go about in a ſhort time without a Truſs, if they have been Burſten for 20 or 30 years together. He maketh alſo Artificially all ſorts of Truſſes, which no other Doctor doth underſtand, the Patients may go in the ſame, Ride, Dance, and Spring, and do what they will without any danger, which healeth Artificially under the ſame. Of theſe Ruptures are found ſeven ſorts, as *Hernia Inteſtinalis*, *Ventoſa*, *Aquoſa*, *Carnoſa*, *Humoralis*, *Zirbatis*, *Hernie*; all theſe this Famous Doctor can help in a ſhort time, either by Cutting, or without Cutting, according as he finds the Patients.

Figure 2: Handbill 551a32[112], recto. By courtesy of the British Library Board

In Bruges-Street *in* Covent-Garden, *over-againſt the* Kings-Play-Houſe *or* Roſe-Tavern, *where you will ſee the* Kings-Arms *Hang over the* Balconey, *Dwelleth*, Cornelius à Tilbourn, *the Famous* German *Phyſitian and* Operator, *Sworn Chyrurgeon to the late King* Charles *the* II. *And now Priviledg'd by Our Gracious Soveraign King* William, *who*

BY His great Diligence and Study, hath lately found out ſome admirable Remedies, which was never yet made Publick in any of his former Bills: Theſe are therefore to Advertiſe all Perſons concern'd, that have either Weak or Dimm Sight, occaſion'd by Age or otherwiſe, and are oblig'd to wear *Spectacles*, He undertakes to bring them to ſee well without them in a Weeks time, altho' they have uſed them 20 Years before: He Infallibly Cures all ſorts of Sore Eyes whatſoever, otherwiſe demands no Money for his Pains. He takes off all Pearls. Pins, Webbs, Cataracts, both White and Black, and Skins of all kinds, growing upon, or ſettled in the Eye, and gives immediate Sight to thoſe that are termed Stone-Blind, where

It is interesting to analyse these handbills by adopting Gentilcore's (simplified) list of features, in order to see whether the English samples present a similar structure, i.e.:

1) a title
2) the diseases
3) a brief mention of dosages
4) the charlatan's credentials
5) the price of the remedy and where to buy it (address)

At the top of C112f9[77] the wording "With Liberty of the Colledge of Phisitians of the Royal Head City of LONDON in ENGLAND" immediately shows – as if it were a title, or a headline to catch the reader's attention with a particularly effective piece of information (1) – the true (or false?) local credentials of the practitioner (4), to which the sentence printed inside the image also adds an explanation for the image itself: "This High-German Doctor, cured the Emperor of the Turk's Brother, who was Blind 13 Years". The characters in the picture, placed in an elegantly paved interior and dressed in exotic attire, include a standing turbaned and crowned figure on the right (the Turkish emperor, one can guess), another standing turbaned person centre-left shown while helping the doctor who – with something in his right hand, which looks like a surgical instrument – is attending to the head of a man (the Turkish emperor's brother who "was Blind 13 Years"). The following text (which is prolonged in the verso of the leaflet) contains 1380 words, well crammed on one page and a half. As can be read in the Appendix A to this volume, which reproduces the texts of the handbills discussed here, after unfolding the communication function of the leaflet ("Be it made known by this": let's call it phase 6, communication), and fully proclaiming all possible credentials received from the world's royalty and aristocracy (4), the text starts listing, in ten numbered paragraphs, the various ailments for which the "High-German Doctor" guarantees his cures (2 + 3; the ten paragraphs are followed by six shorter others which specify further details of the doctor's practice). Finally, in blackletter, there follow the doctor's address and instructions on how to reach his dwelling (5). The sequence for this bill is thus 1), 4), 6), 4), 2 + 3), 5).

Handbill 551a32[112] has no pseudo-title. The woodcut again represents a patient sitting in an interior, being seen by another man (we can deduce "the famous German Physitian and Operator" Cornelius à Tilbourn, whose name is printed in the paragraph underneath the picture), who is actually touching one of the patient's eyes.[8] On the threshold of a side door on the left stands another younger personage looking at the scene. The wording opens with (5), i.e. the doctor's address as a header, followed, in the same paragraph, by (4), the credentials. The following text, consisting of 538 words written in smaller type, is divided into unnumbered paragraphs. The communication function (6) is embedded in the second: "These are therefore to Advertise all Persons concern'd", while all the rest is devoted to listing the marvellous remedies Cornelius à Tilbourn offers to cure all possible distempers (2+3). The phases, therefore, are: 1=0), 5), 4), 6), 2+3).

Let's now consider C112f9[117] and 551a32[139], two handbills with no images. If the choice of the previous bills was based on the presence in both leaflets of a picture occupying half a page, this time it is made on the basis of the use of various font types and, especially, of the practitioner's address at the top, in the title position.[9]

C112f9[117] consists only of 234 words on a single page. In the title position (1) there is the advertising physitian's address, "At the Golden-Ball in Princes-street, near Stocks Market, you may have", so that (1) and (5) are joined. The second paragraph, immediately following and grammatically coherent with what precedes, clearly states the sickness and its cure (in reversed order, actually: "A Certain, Safe and Private Cure for any Venereal Pox or Clap"), i.e. phase (2). The same portion of text also contains accusations against the "Upstart Pretenders" who, from the writer's point of view, hinder the really good and valiant practitioners: we might distinguish this part as a phase in itself, of a very mobile character, since, while present in many handbills, it does not seem to have a definite position in the bill text (it might be called (7), accusation against rivals and self-defence). No hint is made of the doses of the remedy proposed, so phase (3) is totally missing. There is a "Note" at the end, giving further explanation about the doctor's address, thus completing (5). The names of the diseases (pox, clap, running of the reins) and the name of the cure ("Perfect Cure") are in black-letter, together with an addition "Advice of Proper Medicines in any Distemper" just before the note, as if the author wanted to embellish his bill and, contemporarily, make the names of what he considered more relevant stand out. The sequence of functions is the following: 1+5), 2), 7), 3=0), 5).

---

8 Cornelius à Tilbourn (or Tilburg, or Tilbourg) is one of the few irregular practitioners who overtly declared their name. See Thompson, pp. 86–90, Leslie G. Matthews, "Licensed Mountebanks in Britain", (1964), esp. pp.36–39, and Porter, *Quacks*.

9 In the following and previous examples large use is made of italics. This phenomenon will not be discussed here, but see Chapter 5 below.

"IN Frogmorton-Street" in large blackletter fonts occupies the title position in 551a32[139], (1). The text is longer than C112f9[117] (595 words), printed recto and verso, therefore a more articulated structure with more details can be expected. The first paragraph in fact contains additional information about not only the doctor's address (5), but also the curable diseases (2), the cost of the remedy (5), the practitioner's credentials (4), the existence of rivals (7), and prolonged explanations of the symptoms and causes of syphilis. Two separate paragraphs on the verso are preceded by pointing hands: the first signals that patients unwilling to go to visit the doctor personally "may have Medicines sent them for a perfect Cure" (a phase that can be tagged as (8), services for distant patients); the second hand points to issues which can be jointly labelled under (2), the diseases. Two very short sentences close the text: information about the practitioner's 'office hours' (identifiable as phase 9), and the invitation to "Keep this Bill, and bring it with you", whose presence, although not so frequent, is testified in some other bills (it may be included within the communication function, 6). The overall structure is therefore 1+5), 2), 5), 4), 7), 8), 9), 6).

When comparing the four structures, we have:

C112f9[77]:	1), 4), 6), 4), 2 + 3), 5)
551a32[112]:	1=0), 5), 4), 6), 2+3)
C112f9[117]:	1+5), 2), 7), 3=0), 5)
551a32[139]:	1+5), 2), 5, 4), 7), 8), 9), 6)

Certainly a systematics cannot be derived from the collation of only four cases out of 304, but some constant features can be outlined, and some conclusions drawn. First it is worth noting that the partitions sketched by Gentilcore referring to Italian charlatans' handbills may or may not be totally comparable with their English 'brethren'. Second, that some functions are mixed, one included in another, and – in particular – that other functions must also be identified and taken into account, especially considering that seventeenth-century London irregular practitioners worked in the town in which they lived, that is, they were not always itinerant medicine vendors. Therefore rivalry was a frequent issue in their handbills, and so was the necessity to make themselves known to an ever growing population, to lead potential customers to their homes, and to inform them of the time when the doctor was "to be spoken with". To this the availability of special services (such as the delivery of medicines to the patient's house either by a third person or by post) must be added. Among these the offer of private lodgings has also to be considered.

Not only from the previous limited analysis, but also from a broader look at all handbills, it appears that one recurrent feature of London handbills is the practitioner's address at the beginning of the leaflet. This gives immediate notice not only of the location of the 'practice', but also of possible moves. For example 551a32[24] starts with "The Gentlewoman who lived in Red-Lyon-Court, is now removed to Racket-Court near Fleet-bridge", and 551a32[220] begins by signalling that "J. Russel, Occulist, Professor of Physick and Surgery, etc" is now "Removed from Smithfield to Leather-Lane in Holborn, by the Hole in the Wall, the corner House against Baldwin's Garden, near Hatton-Garden".[10] A further example is offered by C112f9[8], a bill which announces that "That Famous Friendly Pill, Electuary, and Balsam of Balsams of Dr George Jones of Hatton Garden, is now sold by Eliz. Russel, that was Dr Jones's Widow, who is removed from Hatton-Garden, to the two Blew Posts against Grayes-Inn in Holbourn.": here the function of spreading information concerning the practitioner's abode is joined to the immediate notice about the proprietary medicine being advertised. Then, as now, a product was sold by also quoting a known brand, i.e. by building up a historical aura around it.

To inform probable patients of a practitioner's whereabouts was evidently of extreme relevance in such a growing city as London in the second half of the seventeenth century, before and after the Great Fire.

A characteristic of many London handbills is, as already stressed, the presence of attacks on rivals. The defence against 'pretenders' and 'counterfeiters' goes from the simple sentence "Beware of Counterfeits, for they Swarm" concluding C112f9[16], to more complex and articulated paragraphs. A few examples will suffice:

> Pray observe the Coat of Arms here above, and on the Bottles, viz. A Cross ingrailed Ermin, for the Crest a Moor Cock; if the Bottles be not always sealed with the same, and you have not a Printed Paper of Directions, stamp'd with the same with each Bottle, it is a Counterfeit, and imitated only. (C112f9[17])[11]

> To prevent Abuses and Dangers which may ensue from such Counterfeits, I have (by their MAJESTIES Order) published the said Pills frequently in the *Gazette*, and am also advised to give Notice in this manner: That Dr Anderson's, or the Scots Pills, are only truly and faithfully made by Mrs Isabella Inglish (with the Care and Inspection of her Husband Mr Ja. Inglish, Philo-Chymist) who alone is authorized by their MAJESTIES to prepare and publish the same. (C112f9[31])

> [M]y said Spirits becoming deservedly Famous throughout the three Nations, several Whistling Upstarts have since presumed to Counterfeit them, and deceive the unwary,

---

10 The same John Russel starts another bill of his with "J. Russel. Professor of Physick, and Oculist. At the Two Blew Posts against Grays-Inn in Holbourn" (C112f9[1]), thus confirming that to state one's address was of the utmost importance.

11 This handbill publicises the "ELIXIR MAGNUM Stomachicum".

whose Fraud and Boldness I have in former Papers detected, and hope (if we may hope for any Modesty in such Graceless Animals) they will be Ashamed for the future to Abuse the World; or at least that People so fairly forewarn'd, will grow wiser then to be Abused by them.

However finding their Counterfeiting designs frustrated. There is of late a certain Elixir-monger, or Chymical Piece-Broker, who amongst the rest of his Small Wares and Slip Slops that he wants Money for, pretends to sell the Elixir of Horse-Radishe; which he would perswade People, Exceeds the Spirit of Scurvey-Grass, etc. But the Reader must Note, that he has only this Mercenary Hucksters word for it, and that the Persons Name that prepares it is Concealed, as being probably ashamed to own either his work or the Impudence of that Assertion, as well he may, since 'tis known that that Churlish Plant has been long repudiated by the most Judicious and Wary Physitians, as too violent in its operation, Nor will this Blustering Incognito with a few hard words and noise of Essential, Seminal, Balsamick Crafts of Vegetables of Unity in the Concrete, and the like Conjuring bumbastian Cant, from the musty leaves of Paracelsus, be able to Charm the Discreet so far as to make them sacrifice their Health or Lives to his Avarice and Ignorance.

But---Quid opus est Verbis? --- Spectemur Agendo. (C112f9[54], advertising the "The True SPIRITS of SCURVEY GRASS Both PLAIN and GOLDEN")

The third quotation, in particular, shows that not only were irregular practitioners attacked by the Collegiate physicians, but some of them were also the target of 'friendly fire', so to speak, given the lively and often violent competition in the London medical marketplace. Worth noting also is the mention of Paracelsus and chemical medicine, here scorned and sneered at as if the sixteenth-century physician were a juggler, and chemistry only deadly smoke in the patients' eyes, thus revealing that irregular practitioners' medicine did not belong to a 'fringe' movement based on different and unorthodox principles, but that, on the contrary, it remained well inside traditional boundaries.[12] Some Latin words, a coat of arms (not always present on the bill describing it), some acquaintances in the royal sphere: all these were weapons in the hands of those who wanted to try and clear the ground of rivals who, in this way, were belittled and disparaged by another irregular practitioner with exactly the same hard and incriminating words used by the university graduates against the whole category of quacks.[13]

---

12 See Porter, "Before the Fringe".

13 As explained in Chapter 1, the status of 'irregular practitioner' is applied to all those who practised medicine in London without being licensed by the College. This neutral phrase (with similar others, such as unlicentiates, empirics and quacks) is used here – and throughout the present research – for convenience, i.e. with no pretence of defining professional differences; neither does it entail any moral judgment. Given the main purpose of the present research (the study of the written products of medical practitioners), all handbills and all their writers are considered together notwithstanding the

To sum up what emerges from this paragraph apropos of the format of London practitioners' handbills, the following list of functional features can be suggested, by integrating those outlined by Gentilcore with the new ones:

1) a title
2) diseases
3) dosages
4) credentials
5) price and address
6) communication
7) accusation of rivals
8) services
9) practice hours

The previous list obtains if a methodological *caveat* is kept in mind, that is, a) the ranking of functions is not stable (apart from positions 1 and 9 that, when present, play the roles of *incipit* and *explicit* of these texts); b) some functions may not be present in individual bills; c) some may merge with others; d) the relevance of a single function may prevail over others; e) a function may surface more than once in the same bill.

The Handbills as a Corpus

The corpus resulting from my transcription numbers 10,397 word types and 200,583 tokens (including, naturally, the graphic variants), a workable enough set which might be called a 'special' corpus, since it unites entries from one text-type only dealing with the same topic. My corpus also includes bills that are similar to, but differ in some details from others, so that they cannot be simply considered copies of something else, but very probably represent different phases of a practitioner's career, when pre-existing documents were only updated, so to speak, in order to reduce printing costs. For example, of Dr Jones's widow communicating her change of address there survive two handbills (the already quoted C112f9[8] and C112f9[105]): the two have whole paragraphs which are identical, but also others with noticeable differences. Another example, taken from the pamphlets, shows that "Dr Salmon's Pills, Drops & Balsam" were advertised through two like versions of a booklet, but in one the use of capital letters is extensive, while it is

already highlighted differences, especially because the College objected absolutely to this form of self-presentation and endorsement from whoever it came.

much more sporadic in the other; the lists of retailers ending both pamphlets are totally different (551a32[128] and 551a32[222]).

When keyboarding the handbills, I copied them as they were, even if I was tempted to correct old and/or wrong spellings with modern ones. But I decided not to, since the corpus as it is now could also be used for historical research on popular print processes (no proof reading – or at the most a very rough and superficial one – is supposed to have taken place for these products). Besides, the various graphic forms in which the same lexical item appears demonstrate that as late as the end of the seventeenth century English was still on its way towards spelling stability. Therefore the non-standardization of typographical variants allows a historical linguistic research (which will not be undertaken here, though), even if it (partially) affects the results deriving from the processing of the corpus with the chosen concordancer. That is, separated word types are counted for, say, 'days' and 'dayes'.[14]

The highest ranking word types are the usual function words, i.e. articles (THE occupies the first position with 12,119 occurrences), conjunctions (AND ranks second with 7939 occurrences), prepositions (OF occurs 6971 times, thus occupying the third position). The first personal pronoun in the word list is HE, and this bears witness to the fact that in most cases handbills introduce this or that male practitioner by using the third person, even if they very often turn to the first person pronoun I (the two pronouns rank at position n. 17 and 20, with 1473 and 1318 cases, respectively, whereas the feminine form SHE is down in the list: n. 88, with 295 occurrences). The prevalence of masculine pronouns is also relevant in showing that the majority of irregular practitioners whose handbills are extant were men. It is no wonder that the first lexical word type is CURE (n. 25 and 974 occurrences), given this particular text type, handbills being medical advertisements to sell medicines. Besides that, searching for the stem CUR*,[15] one finds that it is repeated 2728 times in the corpus. Counting the word tokens for MEDICINE*, it emerges that they occur 538 times, thus pinpointing – at a simple quantitative analysis – the nature of the corpus as a special one dealing with medical issues (with this number of cases, MEDICINE/S would rank in fiftieth position, as the second lexical word soon after CURE).

14 I availed myself of the freely downloadable concordancer AntConc, in its various releases, designed by Laurence Anthony. The site has been accessed on several occasions since 2009.

15 Here and elsewhere an asterisk (used as a wildcard) signals that a word has been searched both in the singular and in the plural form, if a noun, and in all the possible forms derived from a stem, if a verb or an adjective. In the text small capitals are used for lexical items as keywords.

Information from the Handbills

A lot of information can be drawn from the handbills, even if what is historically most relevant (i.e. the names of the writers/practitioners, of the printers, and the dates of printing) is very often missing. In spite of that, though, much can be retrieved about other details such as street names, the location of taverns and inns, a lot of citizens' surnames and professions,[16] how people were to be found when house numbers did not exist yet, besides, of course, the names of the most dreaded illnesses and the sometimes extraordinary names of the products sold by irregular practitioners. When considering the information included in a handbill, what strikes one most is the abundance both of detailed testimonials and of lists of addresses where that specific practitioner's products could be bought. From them, London (and certain parts of the town, in particular) appears as an intricate web of retailers in whose shops and work places all kinds of remedies were sold, some retailers even selling medicines of different provenance. The abundance of addresses to be found in the bills offers a real picture of busy London life, in coffeehouses, shops and taverns. On a map of the town one might almost imagine the traffic of people heading to a certain grocer's to buy some particular pills, crossing others who went to a nearby bookseller's to buy another remedy, a bottle of elixir or a box of lozenges.

Booksellers and Coffeehouses

From the corpus I have built, the most frequent retailers of irregular practitioners' nostrums turn out to be the category of booksellers with 148 occurrences (see Fig. 3), followed by coffeehouse owners referred to 120 times.[17]

16 Londoners, but sometimes also people from other towns, are mentioned mainly in their capacities as either retailers of medicines, or witnesses of the success of a particular cure.

17 The number of occurrences of COFFEE, 128, must be recalculated as 120, since in eight cases the word is used as the name of the substance: in the total, though, coffee-man and coffee-merchant have been included, since they exactly identify a retailer.

Figure 3: A selection of concordances for BOOKSELLER*

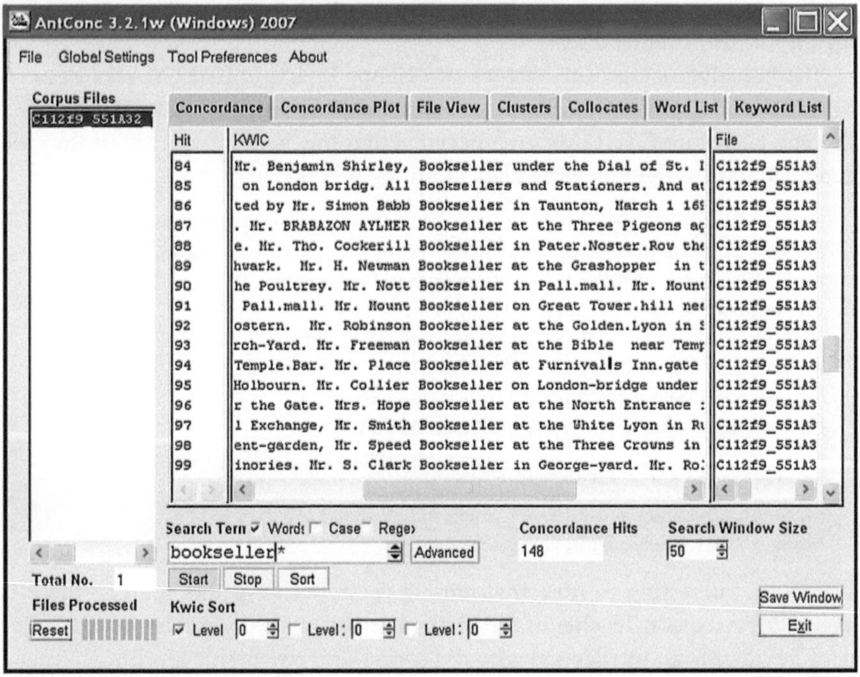

In the list of retailers, grocers, stationers and cheesemongers follow, with 43, 39 and 35 occurrences respectively, and sixth come milliners and chandlers (30 and 29 occurrences respectively). Other salespersons can also be found but the high numbers of booksellers and coffeehouses signal the concentration of medicine retailing in the hands of the abovementioned categories. Evidently, quacks counted on retailers with a large clientele, booksellers included, since these – whose shops were the place where people also bought newspapers in the second half of the century – were the fittest tradesmen to distribute medicines both in town and out of it, because they could avail themselves of the postal news-service routes.[18]

18 Quite an interesting annotation is added at the end of handbill C112f9[37]:

> By the new ingenious Way of the Penny-Post, any Person may send for it [the medicine on sale], from any part of the City or Suburbs, writing plain Directions where to send it to them: if for half a dozen Glasses, they will be brought as safe, as if fetch'd by themselves, and as cheap as one. But who sends this way, must put a Penny in the Letter (besides Six Pence for each Glass) to pay for the

As regards coffeehouses, the possibility, already mentioned, that educated customers read handbills aloud to the illiterate made these meeting places an ideal forum for medical publicity.[19]

The bill advertising "The Virtues and Happy Effects of BATEMAN's Famous SPIRITS of SCURVY-GRASS, both Plain and Golden, and particular CURES thereby performed" (C112f9[16]) declares that the "famous spirits" of the title can be bought at the following places (among others), all of them booksellers:

> Mr BRABAZON AYLMER Bookseller at the Three Pigeons against the Royal Exchange.
> Mr Tho. Cockerill Bookseller in Pater.Noster.Row the Corner of Warwick Lane. […]
> Mr H. Newman Bookseller at the Grashopper in the Poultrey.
> Mr Nett Bookseller in Pall.mall.
> Mr Mount Bookseller on Great Tower.hill near the Postern.
> Mr Robinson Bookseller at the Golden.Lyon in St. Paul's Church-Yard.
> Mr Freeman Bookseller at the Bible near Temple.Bar.
> Mr Place Bookseller at Furnival's Inn.gate in Holbourn.
> Mr Colier Bookseller on London-bridge under the Gate.
> Mrs Hope Bookseller at the North Entrance into the Royal Exchange,
> Mr Smith Bookseller at the Three Crowns in Cornhill. […]
> Mr Sam. Clark Bookseller in George-yard.

It is quite interesting to note that among the retailers of this remedy there is also a "Mr Atkinson Teacher of the Mathematicks at Cherry-garden-stairs in Redriff", evidently an intellectual who did something else beside teaching to make ends meet.

The "Elixir Magnum Stomachicum" (C112f9[17]) alone was sold in 37 coffeehouses, from "Peter's Coffee-House in Charles-street, Covent Garden" to "Lloyd's Coffee-House in Tower street", from "Linty's Coffee-House near Charing Cross" to "Hamett's Coffee-House, on London-Bridge, near the Draw-Bridge" and the Marine Coffeehouse in Birching Lane, i.e. all over London, even though the majority of the coffeehouses mentioned were in the City (see Appendix B for

---

> carriage back; for no body can think the profit great: therefore a Penny must be sent for every Parcel. From one Glass to six, makes a Parcel.

The passage testifies the extension of the postal service, and of the already started procedure of adding 'shipping costs' to the value of the merchandise. On the role of communication transport networks, especially in the first half of the seventeenth century though, see Joad Raymond, *Pamphlets and Pamphleteering* (2003), esp. pp. 124 and 171–72.

19 The first coffeehouse opened in London in 1652 (see Edward Forbes Robinson, *The Early History of Coffee Houses in England* (1893), pp. 85–91; see also Blanche Elliott, *A History of English Advertising* (1962), pp. 39–40).

an attempt at locating them on the basis of their addresses, albeit imprecise, and Fig. 14). Since most empirics' handbills are undatable, but considered to date from the last decades of the seventeenth century, after the Great Fire, we must imagine the renewed buildings and the widened streets designed by the rebuilders, and especially the presence of brick houses instead of timbered ones. Actually, a few coffeehouses mentioned in the bills are still visible in later London maps, where the Marine Coffeehouse in Birching Lane, for example, is observable as one of the places burnt down or damaged by another fire in 1748 (see Fig. 4).[20]

20 Fig. 4 also shows how dense coffeehouses were in this part of London in the mid-eighteenth century: there are fifteen in the Royal Exchange area circumscribed by Cornhill, Lombard Street, Pope's Head Alley and St. Michael's Alley. Besides the Marine Coffeehouse, the other venues surviving from the seventeenth century are: Jonathan's and Garraway's in Exchange Alley, John's at the corner of Swything's Alley, Cock Alehouse (transformed into Cock Eating House) and the Jamaica Coffeehouse in St. Michael's Alley. The last mentioned venue was very probably exactly there where the first coffeehouse stood in 1652.

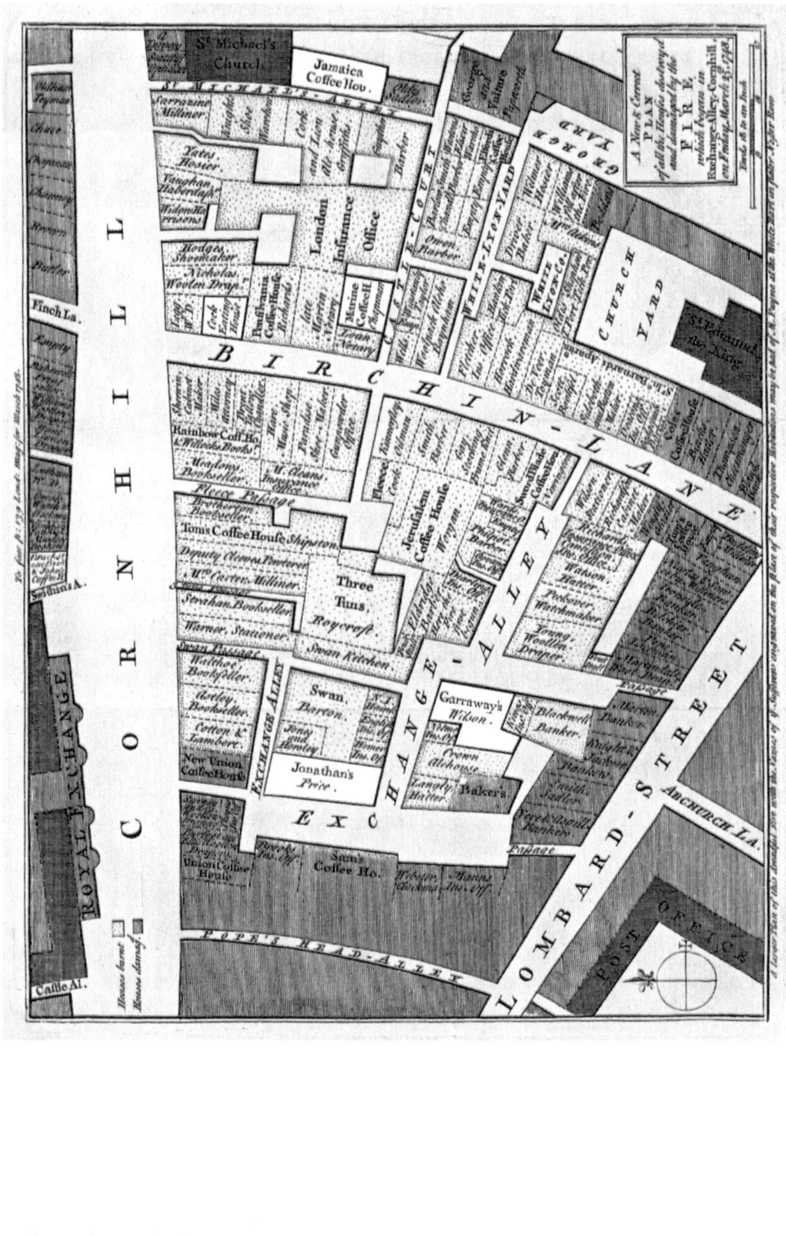

Figure 4: "Plan of the Houses destroy'd by the Great Fire in Cornhill", *The London Magazine*, March 1748, p. 139. By courtesy of the University of Michigan Library (spotlighting applied)

Among curious places where nostrums were sold there are also toyshops, although they represent a real minority: the same "Spirit of Scurvy Grass" mentioned above could be bought at "Mr William Giles a Toyshop nigh the Inner-Temple-gate"; "That Famous Friendly Pill, Electuary, and Balsam of Balsams of Dr George Jones of Hatton Garden" could be purchased from, among other "trusty friends", "Mrs Banbury within Westminster-Hall-gate, on the right hand, a Toy shop" (C112f9[8]); while "CLARK's Compound SPIRITS of Scurvey-Gras" (551a32[63]) was obtainable from "Mr Foster Toyseller, at the Hospital Gate in West Smithfield". A possible explanation for this might be that practitioners relied on parents' visits to this kind of shop, where objects to cheer up children, but also medicines for child care could be found.

Stationers and Others

After booksellers and coffeehouses, as already mentioned, the other venues where unofficial medicines were mostly sold include grocers, stationers, and cheesemongers. Among the second category Mr Thomas Lac(e)y represents a clear example of a retailer who served several practitioners. Actually he is mentioned in eleven handbills as selling diverse medicines of different provenance: the "Famous Friendly Pill, Electuary, and Balsam of Balsams of Dr George Jones of Hatton Garden" (C112f9[8] and [105]), the "GRAND BALSAMIC: Or, the Health-Procuring and Preserving Pill" (C112f9[24]), "the Incomparable EXTRACTUM HUMORALE, Called also PANARETON" (C112f9[48] and [137]), and the "Excellent Pill, Of the Late Eminent and Worthy Doctor Trigg, Of Tower-Wharf, called by him, The Golden VATICAN-PILL" (551a32[18]). Evidently Mr Lacy was also a reliable and long-term seller of "BATEMAN's Famous SPIRITS of SCURVY-GRASS", since his name appears in four different handbills advertising this medicine (C112f9[16], [54], [90] and [102], plus copies of some of them). The comparison of the addresses printed on the sheets, according to which Mr Lacy lived:

> at the Golden Lion near St. Thomas's Hospital (C112f9[8])
> at the Golden Lyon near the King's Head in Southwark (C112f9[16])
> at the Golden Lyon in Southwark (C112f9[24], [48], [137]; 551a32[18])
> at the Golden Lyon near the Kings Head-Inn, Southwark (C112f9[149]

shows that the shop was always the same, since St. Thomas's Hospital was in Southwark, where still nowadays there is a Kings Head Yard in the same area, just near Guy's Hospital (which replaced the old institution in the nineteenth century).[21]

21 Another Mr Thomas Lacy is mentioned in C112f9[79], as the seller of the "Famous Lozenges [...] of Mr Theophilus Buckworth of Milend-Green", but the address given

The sellers, whatever their profession, were generally men, but women had shops as well and some of them sold nostrums. The gender title 'Mr' occurs 1200 times in my corpus, whereas 'Mrs' only 210, but these data cannot be considered as meaning that women sellers were about one sixth of men, because both titles are also used to mention testimonials of the efficacy of the various cures offered by quacks. From the concordances, though, some interesting results can be drawn: among women workers, Mrs Ward had a coffeehouse, Mrs Osgood was a potter (both in C112f9[1]), Mrs Walker a stationer (C112f9[3]), Mrs Jefferson a slopseller, Mrs Pamor a chandler, Mrs Fort a cutler (all three in C112f9[8]), Mrs Yard a milliner (C112f9[16]), Mrs Taylor a fruiterer (C112f9[18]), Mrs Garland a grocer (C112f9[24]), Mrs Alkin a confectioner, Mrs Pierson a distiller (both in C112f9[33]), Mrs Atkins a midwife (C112f9[34]), Mrs Yates a seamstress (C112f9[53]), Mrs Hughs a perfumer (C112f9[55]), Mrs Jones an alehouse keeper (C112f9[119]), Mrs Tyler a servant (C112f9[160]), Mrs Bartleme an apprentice (551a32[21]), Mrs Noth a butcher (551a32[64]), Mrs Mores a salter (551a32[124]), Mrs Kennet a school-mistress (551a32[155]). Mrs Bainam sold coats, Mrs Collard cheese, Mrs Gylesand women's attire (all three in 551a32[116]); Mrs Watts worked in a periwig shop (C112f9[102]). In spite of the irrelevance of this list on a purely quantitative level in order to count the ratio of women as retailers of quacks' medicines, as stated above, it may be of interest at least to verify the ample range of women's trades in early modern London in the period under analysis.

Were these women also 'old' or 'cunning women', i.e. could they be counted among the "doctresses" and "Medicastra[s]"?[22] Certainly midwife Mrs Atkins

---

does not correspond to Mr Lacy the stationer's: this "Lozenges man" had his shop "against Pentioners Ally in Kings Street, Westminster, next the Myter Tavern". Since no particular profession is stated for this Mr Lacy, one can surmise that the latter was simply a homonym of the former.

22 The collection shelfmarked BL Harley 5931 contains a bill by "the [illegible] Wonderful Doctress" ([218]), who sells her services for the cure "of the most desperate Diseases of the Female Sex". It is dated 1677. The term 'doctress', though, is not used only by this self-advertising lady: it does not appear in the other two collections under scrutiny, but as early as 1577 it was used by Barnabe Googe in his translation of Conrad Heresbach's *Foure bookes of husbandry*: when describing the herb called *Scabious*, Googe wrote that "This hearbe being sodden with white wine, and drunke, doth helpe the Plurisie, against which diseases, the women of the countrey, that many times take vpon them to be great *Doctresses* in Phisicke, doo stil the water thereof in May" (Heresbach, iv, fol. 191v). The anonymous satirical author of *A Bold Challenge to the Whole Colledge of Physicians* (1740[?]), included both "Doctors, and Doctoresses" among those practitioners he pretended to defend. 'Medicastra' is the Italian

was in charge of some women's health care, but for the others no further information is available.[23]

Addresses

From the addresses printed in the bills it is not difficult to note that naming places (and reaching them) in late seventeenth-century London was not very easy, because the modern house numbering system did not exist as yet (it was introduced only as late as 1765). Mr Lacy's mentioned stationery shop, actually, was relatively reachable, since it was linked to the name of the Golden Lion, very presumably a well-known tavern at the time. But many other houses were really hard to find, so as to compel writers or speakers to explain their whereabouts in very detailed ways. Many irregular practitioners therefore used to give very meticulous information in order to direct their customers. Some examples will suffice to show how elaborate a procedure it was to give one's own address.

The self-appointing "Doctor James Tilborgh, Famous through Germany, and Holland, Brabant, France and Italy, for Curing the FRENCH POX, and all Venereal Distempers" declares he lives "at present at the Black-Swan in St. Gile's in the Fields, over against Drury-Lane End, where you shall see at Night three Lanthorns with Candles burning in them upon the Belcony" (C112f9[7]). Lanterns were also used as a sign by others (but not very frequently: there are only 9 occurrences in the corpus), for example, by a Dutch physician who specifies that patients can speak with him

> [f]rom his House in the Strand over against the May-pole, on the left hand coming from Temple-Bar, at the Sign of the Golden Cross, between a Sword-Cutlers and a Milliners Shop, the Sign of the Sugar-Loaf and the Barbers-Pole, within four Doors of the Mitre-Tavern; Where you may see a large Red-colour'd Lanthorn, with Eleven Candles in it, and two Candles, and his Picture in the Entry coming in; and a white Sign, written upon with Red Letters, DUTCH DOCTOR, Licensed by His Most Excellent Majesty: and a long Entry with a Hatch, and a Knocker on it. (C112f9[51])

And another foreign physician

word used by John Oberndorff with a clear contemptuous and dismissive value for a woman who boasted of her medicine in the presence of university physicians (*The Anatomyes of the True Physition* (1602), p. 28).

23 About the role of women in early modern health care see Chapter 6 below and the bibliography inserted there. See also Margaret Pelling, "Compromised by Gender?" (1996).

> who liveth over against the May-pole in the Strand, Six doors from Sommerset-house, is to be spoken with every day from Nine in the Morning till Nine at Night, where you will see Six Candles burning in a coloured Flag Lanthorn of Orange, white and blew, with this Subscription under neath. Gonsal Gerardts, A Dutch Doctor, No Cure no Money. Which Lanthorn hangs between the White Flying Horse, an Habbadasher of Hats, and the Coffee Sign. Also these Printed Bills pasted over in the long Entry, where you may privately come in. (C112f9[63])

The two former addresses share some details, but this does not allow one to think that Dr Gonsal Gerardts and the anonymous "Dutch doctor" were the same person. Rather, the coincidences may lead us to imagine that the Strand area hosted foreign practitioners who vied for patients, if not otherwise, through the number of candles lit up in front of their doors. The former Dutch doctor, furthermore, adds – at the bottom of his handbill – that "You are much desired to keep this Bill, that you may not mistake the House", evidently quite conscious of the difficulty people might have in arriving at a specific address.

Another particular surfaces from the sum of indications: first comes the information about the general London area where the house was (the Strand in this case, towards the place where London's major maypole had been till 1672), then the side of the street or other details facilitating the search, such as a nearby inn, or shop, or famous building; third such visual signs as a lit lantern, plus something written (a placard with words). In this way, both literate and uneducated patients were guided safely to the point.

The names of the places where people lived (and consequently their addresses) did not always sound very fit for somebody who boasted of belonging to a medical profession: a remarkable case is "Anne Laverenst a German Gentlewoman", who proclaimed she was particularly experienced in curing women's diseases, among which "all Vices of the Matrix, and […] all the weak Faculties of the Body, by this means rendring a Woman capable of Conception, that before was Barren", living in Holborn "over against Southampton-Square, at the Coffin and Child" (551a32[31]), a place whose name certainly did not look very alluring for ladies willing to procreate, since it reminded them of the high rate of child deaths in town.[24]

24 All the addresses quoted in this paragraph contain the phrase 'over against' as an indication of place, meaning 'opposite'. For the use of this phrase up to 1765 when house numbering was introduced (but dealing nearly exclusively with eighteenth-century addresses), see Laura Wright, "Street Addresses" (2006).

Cures

From the data it emerges that the most common medicaments sold by irregular practitioners were pills (there are 652 occurrences for PILL* in the corpus; see Fig. 5): of course pills as cure-alls, or – as a practitioner wrote in his handbill – "PILULÆ IN OMNES MORBOS; or, Pills against al Diseases" (C112f9[57]). Likewise the "Noble Solar Antiscorbutick Pills" cured the scurvy but also a lot of other illnesses, which were simply considered as symptoms of the scurvy, in a crescendo up to "the plague itself":

> [symptoms] which are Pains in the Head, Inflammations of the Brain, Frensies, Madness, Megrims, Convulsions, Falling Sickness, Tremblings and Weakness of the Limbs, Rheumatick and Gouty Swellings in the Joynts, Dropsies, Agues, Feavors, Black and Yellow Jaundice; Obstructions and Pains of the Stomach, Liver, Spleen, Womb and Ureters, Leprosie, Laxative Gripings in the Guts, Costiveness, Drowsiness, Want of Rest, Black Loose Teeth, Putrid Gums, Pineings and Wastings of the Flesh, Driness in the Mouth and Throat; Superfluous Moisture, Weak Rheumatick Eyes, Discoloured Skin, Spots, Scurff, Tetters or Ring-Worms, Pustles and Blisters on the Skin, Kings-Evil, Ulcers, Cancers, Cankers, Fistula's; nay the Plague it self is but an high graduated Scurvey, as appeared in our last great Plague (551a32[27])

Figure 5: A selection of concordances for PILL*

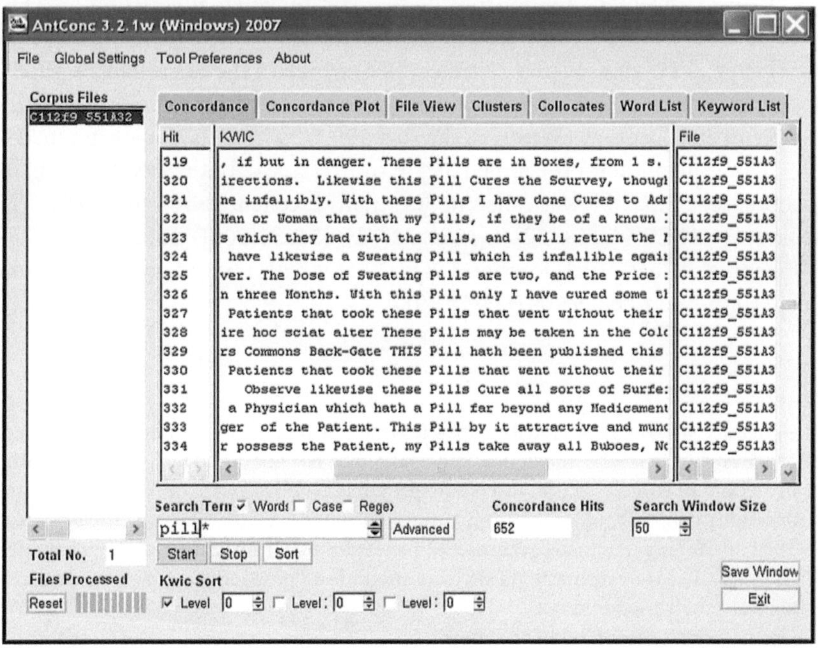

There were purging pills to solve all kinds of "obstructions", but also "antivenereal pills" advertised as "a Perfect, Safe and Private Cure for the CLAP" (551a32[34]), and "That Famous Friendly Pill" already mentioned, which was extolled as "giving Relief and Comfort to all Mankind: They cause all Complexions to laugh or smile in the very time of taking them" (C112f9[8]).

SPIRIT* has also a high frequency (269 cases), but while the singular form SPIRIT clearly refers to a liquid medicament, the plural one includes the 'vital spirits' of Galenic physiology. Therefore the real frequency of the word as a remedy amounts to only 228 occurrences, highlighting how liquid medicines were very widely offered for sale. Generally the term is accompanied by modifiers such as 'balsamic', 'volatile', 'cordial', 'purging", or by specifications of the illness that the spirit is said to cure ("spirit for the scurvy" and "spirit of scurvy grass" being the most frequent).[25]

ELIXIR (together with ELISIR) and POWDER present very similar numbers of occurrences (121 and 114, respectively).[26] ELIXIR is a widely used term to name drinks, whether or not connected to alchemical practices. In any case, since alcohol was a necessary ingredient, in the long run elixirs, spirits, and cordial 'waters' also became responsible for alcoholism (especially in women). The term 'elixir' was evidently so well understandable that John Russel, "Professor of Physick, and Oculist" 'invented' a verb from it, 'to elixirate', when advertising his "Elixirated Spirit of Scurvy Grass both Plain and Purging" (C112f9[1]). The more specific cluster 'elixir vitæ' occurs 12 times, 10 of which in the documents signed by the two members of an Italian family operating in London in the second half of the seventeenth century (Winter is the surname by which they made themselves known, in spite of their proclaimed origin from Naples), both 'Salvator' by name. Of course, such a drink was called no less than "excellent", but 5 times even "miraculous" (C112f9[9], 551a32[30], 551a32[32], 551a32[208]), since, according to its 'inventor', it "hath such force and vigor, that it hath revived great Numbers of People supposed to be dead" (C112f9[9].[27]

25 Generally speaking, by 'spirit' is meant either "A liquid of the nature of an essence or extract from some substance, especially one obtained by distillation; a solution in alcohol of some essential or volatile principle" (*OED*, 21.a.), or "a strong alcoholic liquor for drinking, obtained from various substances by distillation" (*OED*, 21.b.).

26 The concordancer actually returns 122 results for POWDER*, but 8 of them cannot be counted since they derive from such compounds as 'powder-man', 'powder-maker' or forms of the verb 'to powder'.

27 On the Winters, see Chapter 6 below.

Powders included once again cure-alls, but also the already mentioned "Superfine Sort of Jesuits Bark ready powder'd and paper'd into Doses" advertised by Dr Goodall (C112f9[28]) as an antipyretic and antimalarial, derived from the cinchona tree and imported from Peru, as well as beautifying and cosmetic products, such as the "Princesses Powder", said to have preserved Madame de Montespan's beauty, so that this famous lover of the French king Louis XIV "does not appear above eighteen or twenty years of Age, though she be above fifty five" (C112f9[19]).

Other medicines were sold as lozenges (32 occurrences), evidently tablets to be dissolved in the mouth while pills had to be simply swallowed. Another preparation was sold as a 'tincture' (the word occurs 20 times). The word's Paracelsian connections are relevantly clear in the two surviving handbills published by Dr George Jones's widow, in which a phrase from *Paracelsus his Aurora* (translated into English in 1659) can be found: Dr Jones's widow sells "the Tincture of the Sun" (C112f9[8]; C112f9[105]).

A particular 'medicament' deserves mention: necklaces, a term occurring 34 times in its various spellings. They were not jewels, but a chain for children to wear when cutting their teeth. They were supposed to ease teeth cutting, at least according to what "the great TRAVELLER Major J. C. one of his Majesties Chymists" assures us when advertising his "most and in a manner miraculous Necklaces":

> one of them being of no greater weight than a small Nutmeg, absolutely easing Children in breeding Teeth and cutting without pain, thereby preventing (by Gods assistance) Feavers, Convulsions, Consumption, Ruptures, Chincough, Rickets, & such attendant Distempers, to the Admiration of thousands in the City of London and Counties adjacent. (C112f9[87])

The full name corresponding to the initials is given as "John Chokes" in other handbills (C112f9[132] and [133]),[28] while some of the pamphlets in the two British Library Collections quote a different name of the necklaces' possible 'inventor': "Dr Paul Chamberlaine" (C112f9[169] and [169bis]). In Dr Perronet's booklet, though, whoever the inventor, necklaces are considered to be of no avail, at least according to the following witness's certificate:

> X. For a general Good I do hereby Certifie, That notwithstanding a pretended famous Necklace, and other Means, used for a Child of mine, violently afflicted with the hard Breeding of the Teeth, nothing availed, and Death hourly expected; yet, by the Blessing

28 With such a surname it is not difficult to imagine that initials were preferable for a practitioner selling necklaces.

of God, was immediately relieved and rescued from the Grave, by only rubbing this poor Sufferer's Gums with a Remedy I had of Mr Perronet, etc. Witness my Hand, Sarah Clark, (Widow of Thomas Clark, Watchmaker) living at Mr Callowes, Hatter, against the White Lion and Crown in Shoe Lane. (C112f9[162])

If pills, elixirs, lozenges and spirits were taken internally, balsams were typical external medicine. The lemma BALSAM occurs 50 times, nearly always accompanied by directions about where to 'apply' it, or which part of the body to 'anoynt' with it.

Dosages and Prices

Although instructions about dosages were contained in the "Books of directions" which practitioners proclaimed would be given to their customers when buying a medicine, a lot of information on how to use medicaments is contained in the handbills, too. The units of measurement for liquid medicines were either SPOONFUL or DROP. The former is used 47 times, while the latter 53. More generally, though, the bills resorted to the word DOSE (95 times). Apparently irregular practitioners were well aware that dosages had to be calculated taking the ill person's age into consideration; examples of such awareness are the following:

The way of taking it ["Mundus Sanitatis", sold by John Case], is iij or iiij Drops to a Child, and from xij to xx to elder Persons, in a Glass of Wine, Ale, Posset-drink, or any other convenient Vehicle. (C112f9[13])

Its [*sic*; "The true Compound Elixir of Scurvy Grass, and Horse Radish"] to be taken Morning, Noon and Night, 20, 30, 40 or 60 drops, either in Wine, Sider, Tee or Thea, Coffee, Ale, Water, or Water and Sugar; Canary that is neat and clean is best to take it in, but Water is better than bad Wine, etc.

Children may take it from 5 to 20 Drops according to their Age. (551a32[152])

The Drops [Lady Moor's Drops] are to be taken 5 in the Morning, and fast an Hour after, and as many at Night, in a Spoonful of Ale or Beer 9 Days together, then intermit 9 Days and take it again; but for a Child 5 Drops. (551a32[213])

Spoonfuls as units of measurement are suggested when larger quantities of a medicine or of other liquid substances had to be taken. In this case, instructions concerned the number of spoonfuls to be swallowed. When still selling his father Salvator Winter's Elixir Vitæ, Salvator Winter Jr attested that the right dose to remain alive and kicking was to drink "a spoonful thereof [the elixir] 4 or 5 times a day" (C112f9[9]). In order for the "Spiritus Vitæ Deauratus, or the Golden Spirit of Life" to be effective against fevers, patients were to take "a little before the fit comes two spoonfuls, and be covered warm to sweat a little" (C112f9[88]).

Actually the units of measurement used by physicians and apothecaries (such as ounces and drachms) seldom occur in the handbills: the lemma OUNCE is present only 26 times, and DRACHM is limited to one occurrence. The often quoted widow of Dr Jones offered her pills "for two shillings the Ounce, and twelve pence the half Ounce", while her balsam for "all Sores, Cuts, Ulcers, New and Old" was sold "for Twelve Pence the Ounce: If a Pound together, for Twelve Shillings" (C112f9[8]). The Italian "who never was any Stage-Quack or Mountebank" had "the Right Roman Orvietan, which he sells at Half a Crown the 3 Ounces, and 6 Ounces for Five shillings." (C112f9[150]). "A Sternutatory POWDER or SNUFF" was commercialised "at 2s. 6d. the Ounce" (551a32[17]).

The only occurrence of DRACHM – valuable in itself given its absolute rarity in the corpus – appears in a very particular handbill (C112f9[29]), published as a parody of and response to Dr Goodall's advertisement of quinine powder (his "Jesuits Bark"). The Collegiate Dr Charles Goodall offered his powder declaring it was available at the College itself. A commercial mentality is easily observable from Dr Goodall's concern about production costs:

> Whereas it hath of late been the Endeavour of several Members of the Physicians Colledg, to reform the Abuses of the Apothecaries, as well in the Prizes as in the Composition of their Medicines, This is to give notice for the Publick Good, that a Superfine Sort of Jesuits Bark ready powder'd and paper'd into Doses with or without Directions for the use of it, is to be had at Dr Charles Goodal's, at the Coach and Horses in Physicians Colledg in Warwick-Lane, at 4s. per Ounce, or for a Quantity together at 3l. per Pound; *for the Reasonableness of which Prizes* [sic], *(considering the Loss and Trouble in Powdering) we appeal to all the Druggists and Apothecaries themselves in Town,* (C112f9[28], my italics)

Actually it is precisely because of what he judges to be the exorbitant prices exacted by "a Member of the Colledg of Physicians" that Dr Goodall's 'respondent' launches his attack, and parodies Goodall's text by repeating part of it in his own phrase, "allowing for his great trouble and pains in Powdering it 1d. per Drachm" (C112f9[29]), thus accusing the doctor of greed.

In the passage quoted from Dr Goodall's bill POUND is used in its two meanings of a unit for solids and a monetary unit (expressed either as a word or with only the letter 'l'). It occurs 31 times altogether: 15 times as a weight measure, and 16 as money. It is worth noting that as money, it is used in five slightly different versions of the same bill (from the C112f9 collection: [15], [135], [136], [139], [144], the differences consisting mainly in the layout and the use of font types), not to specify the price of a medicament but to accuse physicians of greed, and advertise the present medicine as cheap:

> In short, these Pills should not have been made publick, but in favour that all may not Perish that have not five or ten Pounds to lay down for a Cure, but may here be Cured at a small Charge. (C112f9[15])

Actually, the prices charged for this practitioner's product appear much lower than the costs criticised in the handbill: "These Pills are in Boxes, from 1s. 6d. the Box, to 2s. 6d. the Box, and so to five Shillings".

Pills and lozenges were generally sold in boxes (sometimes tin boxes). The times when mountebanks threw back their wares wrapped in the handkerchiefs clients had thrown to them with the coins to pay for the medicine were evidently over by the late seventeenth century. Liquids were distributed either in bottles or in glasses: "Each Glass is sealed with the Bleeding Pelican" assured the writer of "A Catalogue of Chymical Medicines sold by R. Rotheram" (C112f9[80]).[29] Probably, however, the term GLASS as a container was simply a substitute for BOTTLE. Powders were sold in 'parcels', and balsams in 'pots'.

In the handbills the cost of each medicine follows the description and directions for its use. When a bill advertised more than one product, there were consequently differentiated prices in a single leaflet. Pills were sold by numbers, i.e. the price of a box of pills varied according to how many it contained. Balsams and liquids were sold by the ounce, or simply at a fixed price in their containers:

> at 1s. 6p. the half Box, and 3s. the whole Box, containing 36 Pills. (C112f9[12], a bill by J. Case)

> The biggest Box, containing 60 Pills, 5s. the half Box, containing 30 Pills, 2s. 6d. and the small Box, containing 12 Pills, for four Doses, 1s. (C112f9[89], "The Catholick or Universal PILL")

> The whole Box containing 46 Pills, is 3s. the half Box, containing 20 Pills, is 1s. 6d. each Box Sealed with Helmont's Head. (551a32[27], "ENGLAND'S SOLAR PILLS AGAINST THE SCURVEY")

BOTTLE as a selling measure occurs 109 times. Unfortunately, though, it is impossible to know the capacity of each container: only three times are quantities exactly stated – "half-pint" bottles occur twice (C112f9[12] and C112f9[100]), and a "quart bottle" once, (551a32[123]). Box is present many more times (around 200), which is a consequence of the fact that medicines in pills were by far the most widely sold ones.

From all the examples given it appears that prices were more or less aligned and accessible (with the exception of Dr Goodall's quinine), but there is also a case of "a Gentleman who had the honour to wait upon his Majesty at the general

29 Although the leaflet does not reproduce any "Bleeding Pelican", this was evidently the practitioner's coat of arms, or anyway the seal he used against counterfeiters. This handbill is one of the few which show the printer's name (Thomas James) and a date (1678).

Meeting of the Confederate Princes at the Hague" who sold his remedy at an incredibly high price on the grounds of its being "incomparable": "This Universall and now Incomparable Medicine I sell for Six Pound the Ounce, and three Pound the half-ounce." (C112f9[36]).[30] In comparison, John Piercy's lozenges, purchasable at 2s. 6d. "each paper containing a Quarter of a pound", were really cheap (C112f9[62]) and in line with Dr John Turner's selling the same quantity for 2s. (C112f9[151]).

When prices for different quantities of the same medicine are analysed, one might wonder whether practitioners followed a discount policy. It does not appear the case for most sellers, but a few handbills show that this policy was sometimes pursued: Dr Goodal, selling quinine "at 4s. per Ounce, or for a Quantity together at 3l. per Pound", actually reduced the price if the medicine was bought in a "Quantity" applying a 6.25 per cent discount; so did Dr Jones's widow, who offered her product "for Twelve Pence the Ounce: If a Pound together, for Twelve Shillings", with a 25 per cent discount (C112f9[8]). A discount was also applied to the buyers of whole boxes of "England's Solar Pills against the Scurvey", since – even if the price (3s. for 46 pills) was exactly the same as that of two half boxes together (each with 20 pills) – the number of pills one got is greater than twice the contents of a single half box.

Other Types of Information

What I think is most notable is how these very humble sheets of printed matter can open wide vistas on late seventeenth-century London life, and not only on the debatable activities of quacks and empirics. Much remains to be done about a lot of interesting lexemes (CHURCH for example, a word occurring 141 times when referred to actual buildings, might locate empirics' activities even better than the indications highlighted so far, taking into consideration also Christopher Wren's rebuilding of fifty churches burnt down by the Great Fire).[31] Besides, quite a complex map of London would emerge from tracing all the streets and alleys mentioned in the handbills (STREET occurs 476 times, ALLEY 101 times),

---

30 The king referred to was very probably William III, who attended the congress of the "Confederate Princes" in 1691.

31 The most frequently quoted church is St. Clement's, followed by St. Paul's and by St. Dunstan's in Fleet Street (St. Dunstan's-in the-West). The first two churches, as is well known, were destroyed by the Great Fire in 1666 and rebuilt in the 1680s. St. Dunstan's, on the contrary, escaped the fire but the original medieval church was demolished in the nineteenth century.

not to mention taverns and inns, even though many such premises are frequently not defined according to their social function (TAVERN presents 68 cases and INN 88). Three hospitals are mentioned in the whole corpus: St. Thomas's (twice), Bedlam ("old Bedlam" and "new Bedlam" twice each, i.e. 'old' and 'new' indicating the hospital for mental disorders before and after its rebuilding in 1676), and St. Bartholomew's in Smithfield. This latter, though, is quoted only as an institution near which there are some shops selling proprietary medicines.[32]

Handbills, in the end, together with the other main means of advertising (i.e. newspapers), seem to offer more than one opportunity to catch a glimpse of London life and of the foundation of advertising itself, when vendors progressed from the selling techniques of old to the attractive possibilities of the printing press, conscious – as at least some appeared to be – that advertisements had to be written in a captivating manner and include only relevant information, redundancy being an obstacle to selling:

> Because I intend such brevity, that what I print may appear to the Reader, at first sight, not likely to spend very much of his time to peruse: for I have often made it my observation, that what of this kind seems tedious, not one of twenty cares to read through. (C112f9[57])

But this aspect, concerning rather the pragmatics and the rhetorics of handbill writing than the direct factual information they offer, will be focussed on in a later chapter, while the next chapter will deal with one of the main topics of information retrievable from irregular practitioners' handbills: the diseases mentioned in the bills, their popular names, and other problems connected to healthcare.

32 Of course a great many details can be traced in such seventeenth-century London maps as Ogilby-Morgan's (1677) and Morgan's (1682): see Ogilby and Morgan (1992), and Morgan (2013).

3 Common Complaints in Corpora from the Medical Domain

A perfect Cure for Consumptions, Coughs, and all other Diseases of the Lungs, Rickets in Children, Gravel, the Stone, Pains of the Spleen, Dropsies, Jaundies both Black and Yellow, Agues, Feavers, Palsies; I have a perfect Cure for any that are Distracted. I seldom or never fail the Cure of Convulsion Fits, Falling Sickness, Mother Fits, Pains of the Head, Back, or Stomach, Pains or Lameness of the Limbs, also Pains of the Teeth, Ruptures, also Wens, Cancers in the Breast, Cankers, Ulcers, Fistulaes, &c.

(C112f9[84])

Madness in great ones must not unwatch'd go.
(William Shakespeare, *Hamlet*)

Words for Poor Health Conditions

To the loose generality of the signalled high-ranking stem CUR* in the semantic area of practitioners' actions there corresponds the likewise vague PAIN* (occurring 652 times in the corpus) on the side of ill people. This means that the targeted addressees of the bills were first of all spoken to with a very simple lexicon: the ill felt pains and the practitioners offered cures for them. After PAIN* comes DISEASE* with 635 occurrences. Table 3.1 shows the words indicating illness and symptoms in a very general way:

Table 3.1: General Terms for Health Problems

Rank	n. of Word Tokens	Word Type	Part of Speech	%/200,583
1	652	pain	noun	0.325
2	635	disease	noun	0.317
3	619	distemper	noun	0.309
4	256	patient	noun	0.128
5	154	sickness	noun	0.077
6	141	fit	noun	0.070
7	141	ague	noun	0.070
8	139	swelling	noun	0.069
9	135	fever	noun	0.067
10	132	consumption	noun	0.066
11	129	obstruction	noun	0.064

Rank	n. of Word Tokens	Word Type	Part of Speech	%/200,583
12	109	ache	noun	0.054
13	103	evil	noun	0.051
14	101	stoppage	noun	0.050
15	89	scab	noun	0.044
16	91	weakness	noun	0.045
17	76	ill	modifier	0.038
18	72	sore	modifier	0.036
19	51	sore	noun	0.025
20	50	infirmity	noun	0.025
21	49	weak	modifier	0.024
22	39	sick	noun	0.018
23	36	sick	modifier	0.019
24	31	inflammation	noun	0.015
25	21	infection	noun	0.010
26	21	malady	noun	0.010
27	20	bruise	noun	0.010
28	17	soreness	noun	0.008
29	11	illness	noun	0.005
30	9	painful	modifier	0.004

To read this table correctly, I think that a note is useful, first of all to explain that the ranking in the first column refers only to the terms included in the table itself, i.e. it does not correspond to the position an individual word type has in the global word list (for example, PAIN – here n. 1 – ranks in position n. 62 in the general word list of 200,583 word tokens, which is anyway a high place since most top positions are occupied by function words). Besides this, the word type column includes singular and plural forms under the same term, therefore presenting spurious, but nonetheless reliable, results: a justification for this procedure is that my interest lies in showing which words are used in the handbills, irrespective of their being singular or plural. On the other hand, though, entries are distinguished according to their grammatical function (e.g. SORE). A further detail: the percentages in the right hand column are calculated on the basis of all word tokens in the general word list, so as to show the relevance of each item in comparison with the total amount of words. Why 30 entries? There is no definite answer, but that I wanted to include in the grid both the most frequently used terms and some with a very low ranking, with the result that the modifier derived from the highest ranking word (PAIN) happens to gain the lowest percentage in the list. In spite of their common stem, as a noun PAIN was hugely used, whereas PAINFUL performed contrarily, superseded – as it were – by other modifiers such as SORE.[1]

Table 3.1 tells us that, for example, SICKNESS is a term much more widely used than ILLNESS; that FEVER (in its various spellings) and AGUE are equally distributed; that DISEASE and DISTEMPER are considered more or less synonyms and both attributed to human beings. As for these latter words, there are clusters that perfectly show their interchangeability: Cornelius à Tilbourn affirms that he will be available for patients to give them his judgement "according to the Nature of the Distemper" (C112f9[6]); Thomas Saffold, who claims to be "an Approved and Licensed Physician, and Student in Astrology", after casting a patient's urine, will give "an exact account of the nature of any Disease afflicting any part afflicted" (551a32[110]), while the same Cornelius à Tilburg (in this handbill the name is spelt differently from the previous one) again assures his prospective patients that the prescription of medicines will be "according to […] the Nature of the Distemper or Disease" (551a32[3]).[2]

Other terms meaning an indiscriminate pathological condition, but ranking much lower than those seen so far, seem to prefer particular usages: MALADY in the singular form generally appears in handbills (or sections of handbills) dealing with the "French pox" (syphilis), while its plural often co-occurs with DISTEMPER in the cluster 'Your Distempers and Maladies'. ILLNESS is used in 4 cases out of 11 by the author of four handbills which present variations in the practitioner's address and names of testimonials, in the phrase "These are to Advertise all Persons, whose Illness may require the help of a Physician, that […]" (C112f9[32], 551a32[12], 551a32[21] and 551a32[173]), but no particular usage seems evident. In other cases, a tooth-ache is called an "illness" (by David Perronet in 551a32[2]; the word is present three times in the same bill), or the term simply stands for any equivalent such as 'distemper' or 'disease'. One hypothesis for the very limited and personal use of ILLNESS can be that the word

---

1 There seems to be no explanation for this preference, unless one considers the Old English origin of SORE, and the Anglo-Norman one of PAIN, i.e. an older vs. a more recent word.

2 The interchangeability of the two terms is even more visible on reading the larger co-text preceding them: "At the Blue-Flower-Pot in Great-Lincoln-Inn Fields, […] liveth Cornelius à Tilburg […], who for several years past have cured many Thousands of People of the most dangerous, stubborn and chronick Distempers, by giving wholesome and faithful Medicines, according to the Strength and Constitution of the Patient, and the Nature of the Distemper or Disease" (551a32[3]).

was fairly recent in the seventeenth century, while all other terms had a longer history.[3]

EVIL represents a particular case, since its high frequency is due to the particular collocation 'King's Evil' for scrofula present in the corpus. Sometimes, though, the word is also used as a synonym for other unhealthy conditions (venereal diseases mainly, but also fistulas and epilepsy). The presence of the word in the list, therefore, is somewhat improper, since its ranking derives from the name of a specific illness, a category excluded from Table 3.1, and analysed separately in this chapter.

As for modifiers, the highest ranking one – ILL – is used both as a predicative and an attributive adjective, but also as an adverb. SORE mostly collocates with parts of the body: it is interesting to note that these are not limited to the collocate 'sore throat' as in contemporary usage, but it also combines with HEAD, EYES, LEGS, BREASTS, GUMS, MOUTHS, ULCERS. In some handbills it is also used as a collective noun, in the series "Of him the Poor, Sore, Sick and Lame, may have Advice for nothing", in a handbill in which Thomas Saffold advertises his cures for "either Men, Women or Children, of any Disease or Diseases afflicting any Body, whether inward or outward, of what Name or Nature soever (if Curable)" (551a32[97]). Sometimes this modifier occurs together with WEAK in the combination 'sore and weak'. The usage of WEAK is regular, as it were, and only in one case does it acquire a particular gender nuance, recalling "the weaker vessel" in 1 Peter 3:7 (King James Bible): in 551a32[231] a practitioner who calls his medicines no less than "transcendent", able to resolve all medical problems, also declares that "[h]e prevents Miscarriage, and Cures all those grievous Diseases happening to Women with Child; and also Easing all those Acute Tormenting Pains after the Birth". Towards the end of his handbill he explains the reason for printing his advertisement: "This I was resolv'd to Publish, not for any desire of gain, but in Compassion to that Tender Weak Sex, great numbers of which loose their Lives for the want of such a Preparative". As just mentioned, this is the only occurrence of the cluster 'weak sex' referred to women in the whole corpus.

SICK has also a 'regular' use, while PAINFUL with its very low number of occurrences seems to be linked mostly to the body's 'privy' parts: it actually co-occurs with 'standing of the Yard' and 'Piles' (3 cases each), and once with 'making water', whereas it is used only twice with TEETH.

3 See the *OED* for this and other terms.

These are but the very general terms with which practitioners mentioned what they were ready to cure. In the following paragraphs the most frequently mentioned illnesses will be discussed.

What the Londoners Suffered From

From the word list generated by the concordancer AntConc it results that the highest ranking illness mentioned in the handbills is SCURVY (in all its possible and creative spellings). It occurs 399 times, followed by POX. A partial list of the terms is collected in the Table 3.2, where only the first 60 items are inserted. A preliminary commentary is necessary in order to read the table properly: each ranking position does not correspond to the ranking of the relative term in the general word list, but it shows the place of a word in this particular table, i. e. POX is 89th in the total of 200,583 word tokens of the corpus with the same amount of occurrences, while here it ranks second. This is because a new set has been created and taken into account, listing only names of diseases and/or symptoms. Table 3.2, like Table 3.1, unites singular and plural forms of the same item under the same word type, but it also lists the commonest collocations (e.g. 'running of the reins', 'green sickness' etc.). Spelling has been modernised and made uniform, in order to avoid different entries for, for example, 'emrods', 'hemoroids', 'hemorroids', 'hemorrhoids', and unite their various rankings in one result. On the contrary, from the bulk of the occurrences of POX, which is nevertheless in the table, I have extracted two separate entries ('French pox' and 'small pox'),[4] because – especially – of the high frequency of the former and its social significance.

Table 3.2: Most Frequent Diseases in the Corpus

Rank	Word Tokens	Word Types or Collocations	%/200583
1	399	scurvy	0.199
2	290	pox	0.145
3	200	stone	0.100
4	192	dropsy	0.096
5	190	ulcer	0.095

4 Smallpox, although a very serious illness in early modern England, will not be dealt with in this chapter (it ranks at n. 36 in Table 3.2). Nevertheless, because of its disfiguring effects, it was socially deeply felt and it was also present in the literature of the time (see Raymond A. Anselment, *The Realms of Apollo* (1995), esp. Chapter 5, "A Double Death: Smallpox", and David E. Shuttleton, *Smallpox* (2007)).

Rank	Word Tokens	Word Types or Collocations	%/200583
6	168	worm	0.084
7	162	running of the reins	0.081
8	141	humour	0.070
9	139	swelling	0.069
10	125	rupture	0.062
11	107	venereal disease	0.053
12	96	French pox	0.048
13	92	cough	0.046
14	91	clap	0.045
15	88	jaundice	0.044
16	82	colic	0.041
17	81	melancholy	0.040
18	75	convulsion	0.037
19	72	griping of the guts	0.036
20	72	vomiting	0.036
21	68	green sickness	0.034
22	66	flux	0.033
23	63	breaking out	0.031
24	63	vapours	0.031
25	61	gonorrhea	0.030
26	60	itch	0.030
27	58	King's evil	0.029
28	54	cancer	0.027
29	53	deafness	0.026
30	51	bubo	0.025
31	51	falling sickness	0.025
32	50	barrenness	0.025
33	49	shortness of breath	0.024
34	48	rickets	0.024
35	47	spots	0.023
36	46	small pox	0.023
37	42	palsy	0.021
38	42	rheum	0.021
39	42	rheumatism	0.021
40	41	shankers	0.020
41	38	giddiness	0.019

Rank	Word Tokens	Word Types or Collocations	%/200583
42	38	miscarriage	0.019
43	37	cataracts	0.018
44	34	sciatica	0.017
45	34	French disease	0.017
46	33	lameness	0.016
47	32	fainting	0.016
48	32	pimples	0.016
49	31	fits of the Mother	0.015
50	30	phthisis	0.015
51	30	piles	0.015
52	30	redness	0.015
53	29	dullness	0.014
54	28	contraction	0.014
55	28	haemorrhoids	0.014
56	27	leprosy	0.013
57	26	morphew	0.013
58	25	hare-lips	0.012
59	25	madness	0.012
60	24	gripes	0.012

A quick glance at the table reveals that the relatively high ranking of both HUMOUR* and VAPOURS signals the still Galenic bases of handbills' writers, and – more relevantly – that illnesses are named according to a vernacular taxonomy which generally tends to use either popular forms or anglicised versions of old Latin terms. For example cases of HERNIA (a term present in the corpus 13 times) are preferably called 'ruptures', even if some practitioners also added the Latin definition – "Rupture, or Hernia Intestinalis" (C112f9[83]) – thus showing their knowledge, in particular to a literate public. Another such case is apparent with "Piles or Hemorrhoids in the Fundament", a phrase that uses the popular and the educated words, one explaining the other (even though the difference between the occurrences of the two terms in the table is very slight). Contrariwise, the discrepancy between the 3 occurrences of LUES and the 96 of FRENCH POX (to which the 34 cases of FRENCH DISEASE must also be added) constitutes a clear example of the practitioners' preference for popular names.[5]

5 Every time "the pox" is mentioned in the corpus, it is evident from the context that a venereal disease is anyway meant.

Another case is GONORRHEA, nearly always followed by 'or running of the reins'. The tendency of the writers is towards a simplification of their medical taxonomy in order to be understood by anybody, now and then also interspersing a higher-register word.

The Scurvy and the Pox

If the analysis is limited to the highest ranks, one sees that the sellers' major preoccupation was to offer remedies for the scurvy and the pox. The latter was also called "Morbus Gallicus" (ranking in 61st position with 23 occurrences), while the former, borrowing Gideon Harvey's title, might be called "Morbus Anglicus" because of its spread in Great Britain, at least according to the practitioners' care in offering remedies against this disease.[6]

The deficiency of vitamin C was particularly noxious to a seafaring nation like the British, but since in London not all people were sailors (or pirates), the main cause of scurvy was very probably malnutrition. The medicine sold to cure scurvy was made out of "scurvy grass" (Cochlearia), which actually contains vitamin C, but also "Horseradish": all but unique in the corpus, handbill 551a32[152] contains a recipe to prepare an elixir with the two herbs, "according to the Spagirick Art" (alchemy). "Scurvy was […] the archetypical disease of the late seventeenth century" writes Roy Porter, and adds: "It produced multifarious symptoms of malaise".[7] Indeed irregular practitioners' handbills tended to consider the scurvy as the cause of many other complaints, so much so that one of them, selling "ENGLAND'S SOLAR PILL AGAINS THE SCURVEY" (551a32[27]), collects a long and incredible series of symptoms in a climactic progression: the plague itself is but a manifestation of the scurvy.[8]

As evidence of the generalised ideas about the scurvy, a passage from another pamphlet – Dr Salmon's – will suffice:

> They cure the Scurvy, when it is grown so bad, as to become Scandalous, so as that many people think it to be the POX: for the Scurvy often causes great pains in the head and nose, shoulders and shin bones, with other pains all over the whole body, dulnesse and heavinesse, and redish or blewish spots and breakings out in the skin, weaknesse in the back and Loyns, a bad stomach, and sometimes losse of appetite, loosnesse and soreness of the teeth, throat, and mouth, a discoloured skin, with spots, stains, pimples, morphew

---

6 Gideon Harvey's book (*Morbus anglicus* (1666)), deals with many complaints, and mainly with tuberculosis.

7 Porter, *Quacks*, p. 199.

8 See the passage quoted above (Chapter 2, "Cures", before Fig. 5).

> and scurf, and a general weaknesse, and faintnesse all over the whole body, insomuch at last that it gets into the bones, and infects the very marrow of them; this cruel disease these Family-Pills cure at a few times taking. (551a32[222], seventh paragraph)

That the English considered the scurvy as a sort of national malady is clear from one of the pamphlets included in the other British Library collection, which actually mentions it as "that *Labes Britannica* or grand English Disease": the 'practitioner' was none but Alexander Bendo, the alias of John Wilmot, 2nd Earl of Rochester, who also adds

> And to say truth, there are few Distempers in this Nation that are not, or at least proceed not originally from the Scurvy, which were it well rooted out, (as I make no question to do it of all those who shall come into my hands, there would not be heard of so many Gouts, Aches, Dropsies, and Consumption: nay, even those thick and slimy Humours which generate Stones in the Kidneys and Bladder, are for the most part off-springs of the Scurvy. (C112f9[41], pp. 4–5)

This pamphlet will be analysed in a later chapter, but Rochester's satirical vein shines already through this passage, where the fake quack apes what many 'colleagues' of his proclaimed in their handbills.

By summing up the word tokens referring to Venereal diseases (given the number of occurrences of FRENCH POX, FRENCH DISEASE, MORBUS GALLICUS, GONORRHEA, CLAP, RUNNING OF THE REINS, and FOUL DISEASE with its 8 occurrences, and also the fact that THE POX – not listed separately in the table – occurs 86 times, clearly meaning a venereal disease) the major complaint dealt with in the handbills is syphilis in its various aspects (the tokens referring to it reaching the high number of 563, i.e. 0.280 per cent of the whole corpus). As Kevin P. Siena writes, though,

> It is impossible to say what individual patients 'actually' suffered from. Many probably suffered from syphilis, but it would be anachronistic to assume in every case that the early modern pox was the modern condition identified as syphilis. In fact, that term was hardly used in the period.[9]

As a matter of fact, the word never appears in the corpus, but there is quite an interesting euphemistic way to define it by understatement: the variously spelt French expression "à la mode" occurs 9 times in a collocate either with DISEASE or with DISTEMPER,[10] thus showing the cultural and social construction

9 Siena, *Venereal Diseases*, p. 14. To Siena's volume I refer readers interested in the medical (and historical) analysis of these issues.

10 These cases have not been included in the total 563 occurrences of tokens referring to venereal diseases; neither have such phrases as 'Venereal Disease' or 'Venereal

of the complaint, since the adjective FRENCH is substituted with a phrase which anyway refers to France (as the place where the disease was supposed to have originated),[11] but at the same time "à la mode" also implies the spread of the malady among the highest social classes (especially the so called "libertines" of whom John Wilmot, 2nd Earl of Rochester is certainly the most famous).[12] While it was widely thought that only men suffered from venereal diseases derived from sexual intercourse with already infected women, some handbills show a vague awareness of the reciprocity of contagion, i.e. that the cause was not always imputable to the female sex: this happens in 9 cases only (the usual phrase is "not alwaies got by Women, as some think", C112f9[45]).

The pox and its correlates were usually cured with very dangerous mercurial medicines that had a whole string of side effects, without being completely efficacious, so that many practitioners advertised their own remedies as operating "without Fluxing or letting of Business" (C112f9[10]) and "without salivation", actually the major effects of mercury. The "Doctor in Physick" who proclaims himself as "Twenty years since Fellow of Kings Colledg in Cambridg" explains that he is ready to cure

> THE POX, known by pains either in the Head, Shoulders, Arms, Legs, and sometimes by Scabs, and breaking out; sometimes only by a dulness and general indisposition of the whole Body, which he safely and effectually cures without fluxing, a Remedy that often proves worse than the Disease; for (besides that unspeakable torture the Patient endures in that way of Cure) the Mercury, if not timely and carefully expell'd, afflicts the Patient, with Aches in all parts of the Body. (C112f9[154])

Another practitioner appeals to a different aspect of the treatment of the disease, that is, the necessity for privacy:

> He hath a very secret and safe way for curing the Morbus Gallicus, called the French POX, the Running of the Reins, and all Venereal Distempers, without fluxing, so that a man shall not perceive it by his wife, nor the wife by the Husband, and none of their Relations shall take any notice of their distemper, to the admiration of the Patient. (C112f9[44])

Distemper' (21 and 26 cases, respectively). By adding them the percentage rises to 0.303 per cent.

11 In different European countries the disease had different names, based on its supposed geographical origin: it was 'Neapolitan' in Spain, France and England; 'French' in England and in Italy; 'Spanish' in Italy.

12 See Chapter 6 below for John Wilmot's activities as a mountebank.

The latter quotation reveals a very dangerous idea of privacy, especially if one considers the consequences of sexual intercourse between a healthy person and a "poxed" one, whether with one's spouse or with a prostitute.[13] As for the usefulness and success of non-mercurial medicines, many handbills stress that the cure offered, apart from being "speedy" (an adjective occurring 54 times in the corpus), does not hinder business, in this way revealing the "mercantile class" the advertisements targeted.[14] Discretion is also indicated in those complex addresses quoted earlier in Chapter 2: for example the practitioner who mentions that his house can be found by following instructions and by looking for "these Printed Bills pasted over in the long Entry, where you may privately come in" explicitly notifies his addressees that they can enter his practice safely and unseen, thus safeguarding their privacy (C112f9[63]).

Also women healers advertised cures for the pox. Their language, as Siena notices, was not different from their male counterparts'; for example the gentlewoman living "At a Potter's Shop in Russell Court, between Drury Lane and Bridges street" assures her patients that

> I cure the Morbus Gallicus, or French POX, with all its Accidents, with Ease, Speed, and Secresie. And for those that are so bad, that their Distemper requires a close Confinement, I have Conveniencies at my House to accommodate those that desire it, and require nothing for Diet, Lodging, or Medicines, till the Cure is performed. (551a32[214])

Even when not advertising directly, women also helped their husbands in their practice – many handbills declare that female patients could talk with the woman of the house if reluctant to speak to a male doctor – and this can readily be imagined in the case of 'pox'-infected ladies, whose privacy was more securely safeguarded when treated by somebody of the same gender.

The Green Sickness

Other high-ranking diseases would deserve at least a short comment here, but most of them can easily be identified in the twenty-first century, too. Other terms,

---

13 See Siena, "'The 'Foul Disease'" for a detailed study of practitioners' ads from this perspective. Siena, *Venereal Diseases*, pp. 22–27, offers a detailed picture of the effects of mercury, while Chapter 1 of the same volume also deals with privacy and discretion in case of venereal diseases. This is not the place where to discuss the relevance of venereal diseases in Restoration drama, but on this topic see Angelo Righetti, "Pox in Restoration Comedy" (2012).

14 Siena, *Venereal Diseases*, p. 46.

on the other hand, have either completely disappeared from the medical lexicon, or have changed their basic meaning. One of the former is 'green sickness'.

The 68 occurrences of GREEN SICKNESS in the corpus demonstrate that this disease was also a common ailment in early modern London. It was also called "the disease of virgins", being connected to female adolescence: green sickness "was a historical condition involving lack of menstruation, dietary disturbances, altered skin colour and general weakness once thought to affect, almost exclusively, young girls at puberty".[15] Also the more technical name of the complaint – chlorosis – is indebted to the physical appearance of the skin and not to more serious causes. In the handbills the collocate generally occurs either alone, or in a series of female illnesses.[16] Examples go from an attempt at defining the illness, like the following offered by "one M. Elmy, Operator":

> The Green Sickness is a Disease arising from the Obstructions of the Veins about the Womb, Liver, Spleen and Mesentery, causing various Symptomes in young Women, the course of Nature being stopt, producing a Cachexie or evil habit of the Body, alters the Complexion, sending ill Vapours to the Brain, causeth a Loathing of Meats that are good, occasion swellings in the Belly and Legs, with unwillingness to exercise, attended sometimes with difficulty of Breathing, and universally indispose the Body, so that most Distempers incident to Women may arise from it. (C112f9[131])

to a simple list of "distempers incident to Women", printed by a "High German Doctor" who

> also Cureth all sorts of Distempers incident to Women, viz. Hysterick Passion, the Green Sickness, Suppression, and unorderly Monthly Flux, &c. (C112f9[97])

It is also noteworthy that hysteria is here mentioned (one of the four cases in the corpus), whereas the most popular label for gynaecological ailments resulting in women's problematic behaviour – "Fits of the Mother" – occurs 31 times.

Another "High-German Doctor" even adds more pathologies to the previous list, among which the risk of abortion is noteworthy (especially because many practitioners were suspected of acting not to eliminate barrenness in women, but – on the contrary – to cause abortions), offering cures for

---

15 Helen King, *The Disease of Virgins* (2004), p. 1. See this volume for the medical and cultural history of the disease.

16 When using the term in *Henry IV, Part* 2 (IV.2.90), William Shakespeare finds it necessary to redefine it as "male green-sickness", applied as it is by Falstaff to young men with a sober life in the famous 'sack' speech. All Shakespearean plays, unless differently specified, are drawn from *The Complete Plays*, Electronic Edition (1989).

> Women and Maids of many Infirmities, as The Green Sickness, Stoppage or Overflowing of the Courses of Nature, He also helps the Whites and Weakness of the Back, and other Distempers of Women. He hath also a great Secret to help Conception; likewise a powerful Medicine to prevent Miscarriage, although you have Miscarried 5 or 6 times successively. (C112f9[2])

The operator selling "Rose's Balsamick ELIXIR" also highlights the positive results of his medicine, able to restore young girls to health and liveliness, thus connecting physiology to psychology. His medicine

> for Young Women, [...] helps all that are troubled with the Green Sickness to a Miracle, bringing to them what's convenient, causing a healthful Countenance and a lively Humour, keeping the Spirits in a true Temper. (C112f9[11])

In the early Renaissance marriage had been advocated as a possible cure for young vergins' medical problems,[17] but – since such a solution could not be 'sold' by practitioners or even by regular physicians – no handbill hints at this possibility, although the relationship between green sickness, melancholy and sexual activity was somehow felt. This because

> [g]reen sickness bears a certain affinity to lovesickness, and is increasingly associated with erotic melancholy in the early modern period. Called 'love fever' by the women of Brabant, it is linked explicitly to a lack of sexual activity, aggravated by strong sexual desire, and cured via coitus.[18]

Melancholy: A Disease of the Well-Off?

MELANCHOLY ranks even higher than GREEN SICKNESS in the corpus (81 occurrences) and should have been dealt with before, but is introduced only here as a separate and longer paragraph of this chapter because of the significance of this complaint in the early modern period and the role it played in British culture. Another reason for this is that melancholy is a disease which, although judged to derive strictly from disordered bodily activities according to classical medical theories, has deep effects on the psyche, so much so that George Cheyne's *The English Malady* (1733) hardly uses the word, preferring "nervous disease", or "nervous distemper" and "anxiety". The approach to this phenomenon is also slightly different, being grounded on the analysis of a multiplicity of corpora. What follows relies on a series of concordances based on three different corpora:

---

17 See Donald Beecher and Massimo Ciavolella, eds, *Eros & Anteros* (1992).

18 Lesel Dawson, *Lovesickness and Gender* (2008), p. 51.

a) the handbills; b) the EMEMT corpus;[19] c) one of the latter's sections (n. 3, "Recipe collections and *materia medica*"). It aims at analyzing and discussing the role of MELANCHOLY in the three corpora, so as to study the relevance of the term on the basis of its occurrences.

The Shakespearean canon has also been considered as the dramatic mirror of the "Elizabethan malady" – but kept in the background and not focused upon. According to Lawrence Babb,

> Melancholy was very much in vogue in the England of Elizabeth and the early Stuarts, especially among the intellectuals and would-be intellectuals. Elizabethan and early Stuart literature, consequently, abounds in references to melancholy and in melancholy characters.[20]

However, notwithstanding what the critic wrote in his seminal work on melancholy as a cultural phenomenon, this illness as such was actually nothing new, since it had been dealt with for centuries as a disease of the brain, even though it was Elizabethan and Jacobean society which saw an outburst of literary and medical works focused on this malaise, of which Timothy Bright's vast study on the disease *A Treatise on Melancholie* (1586), and Robert Burton's later (and more famous) *Anatomy of Melancholy* (1621) are the best known.[21]

In the excerpts from the medical texts included in EMEMT the word (as a lemma, in its various spellings both as a noun and an adjective) occurs 839 times out of 1,160,668 words,[22] equal to 0.072 per cent. The EMEMT subcorpus "Materia medica", which contains only collections of recipes for 'kitchen physic' and texts addressed to a more general readership than university physicians and educated people (consisting as it does of pamphlets containing recipes for self-cure and a series of practical medical advice), shows 97 occurrences of MELANCHOLY

19 In their introduction to the EMEMT corpus, the editors write that it "aims to be a representative sample of medical texts printed between 1500 and 1700", particularly stressing the concept of "representativeness" to which the selected texts adhere (Päivi Pahta and Irma Taavitsainen, "Introducing *Modern English Medical Texts*", p. 4).

20 Lawrence Babb, *The Elizabethan Malady* (1951), p. vii.

21 On Burton, among the most recent studies, see Angus Gowland, *The Worlds of Renaissance Melancholy: Robert Burton in Context* (2006), and Mary Ann Lund, *Melancholy, Medicine and Religion* (2010).

22 These are the word tokens making up the texts in which MELANCHOLY is to be found, i.e. corresponding to the total of 152 extracts containing the term (not the total of the EMEMT corpus).

in a corpus of 204,292 words, corresponding to 0.047 per cent.[23] In the handbills corpus, as touched on above, the term occurs 81 times out of 200,583 words, i.e. 0.040 per cent, with the least frequency, then, of the three corpora. In the Shakespearean dramatic canon it is present 79 times in 1,077,322 word tokens, that is, with a much lower frequency (= 0.007 per cent) (see Table 3.3).[24]

Table 3.3: Frequency of MELANCHOLY

Corpus	Word tokens	Frequency	%
Bright, *Treatise**	10,067	84	0.834
Burton, *Anatomy**	9801	37	0.377
EMEMT (all items)	1,160,668	839	0.072
EMEMT (Materia medica)	204,292	97	0.047
Handbills	200,583	81	0.040
Shakespeare	1,077,322	79	0.007

* In both cases only the excerpts from EMEMT are considered.

The four corpora (Shakespeare included)[25] obviously collect different text types, especially if one considers their addressees. The EMEMT subcorpus "Materia medica" and the handbills are the most similar: actually their target readerships are not very different, i.e. middle and lower social classes, even though this fact does not exclude the aristocracy from those who resorted to irregular practitioners for help.

23 Only 26 excerpts in "Materia medica" contain the lemma. Since the EMEMT corpus collects "shorter texts [...] in their entirety, and longer texts are represented by extracts of some 10,000 words" (Irma Taavitsainen and Jukka Tyrkkö, "The Field of Medical Writing with Fuzzy Edges" (2010), p. 57), any generalization concerning its 462 medical texts ought to be very cautious. Nevertheless the high number of texts in a certain way compensates for the incompleteness of some of them.

24 The texts of Shakespeare's plays in the Oxford University Press electronic edition (*The Complete Plays*) also include editorial words (and the stage directions), but certainly the editors' intervention does not affect the quantity of the occurrences of MELANCHOLY, while, if anything, slightly lowering the percentages. The text of *Edward III* is drawn from the Internet site "The Project Gutenberg", for it is not included in the electronic edition.

25 While in Table 3.3 there appear six corpora, here only the three non-Shakespearean corpora mentioned in the first paragraph are taken into account (i.e. the handbills, EMEMT and its section "Materia medica").

Of course the highest frequency of the word results from the EMEMT corpus as a whole, since the latter contains texts belonging exclusively to the medical domain and, furthermore, texts – such as Bright's and Burton's – specifically devoted to melancholy. In the excerpt from Bright's treatise in EMEMT (10,067 word tokens), for example, MELANCHOLY occurs 84 times (0.834 per cent), and in Burton's 9801-word piece 37 times (0.377 per cent): these – and other more general treatises – contribute to the high percentage of the word in the corpus as such. Certainly, as noted above, the values emerging from the "Materia medica" subcorpus and from the handbills are more similar to each other and nearly tally, while the result from Shakespeare is the most different one. This is not surprising for various reasons: first, the whole Shakespearean corpus has been searched, i.e. a totality of stage plays *versus* a selection of sources from the medical domain; secondly, the enormous difference between Shakespeare and the medical texts as text types must be taken into consideration, which would require a vast and in-depth study of the plays not to be attempted here. Because of all this, the results from Shakespeare are inserted in the table only as a reminder of the relatively high frequency of the term in the canon, but will not be analysed in detail. On the other hand, they also show that, in the end, Shakespeare was not so receptive to his time's 'malady', at least at the level of lexical choices, in spite of melancholy being 'fashionable'. The fact must be stressed, however, that MELANCHOLY has the highest frequency among the ailments present in the canon.[26]

Among the fairly homogeneous texts, MELANCHOLY occurs with least frequency in the handbills, i.e. in the socially lowest text-type, which targeted a wide series of social classes, literate and illiterate, and – at least supposedly – the poor. The rest of this paragraph will try to find explanations for this discrepancy.

Physicians about Melancholy

Melancholy – "which keeps his Court in the Spleen" according to Nicholas Culpeper's translation of Galen's *Art of Physick*[27] – is one of the humours of the body, on the basis of whose balance or imbalance a person is healthy or falls ill. Galen's

26 Actually, the word is used both as a noun and a modifier, with a roughly similar percentage. Only PLAGUE presents a higher frequency, but it is often used as a verb and with metaphorical value. These data have also been processed with the help of AntConc. I studied Shakespeare's medical language in "Shakespeare and the Words of Early Modern Physic" (2013).

27 Nicholas Culpeper, *Galen's Art of Physick* (1652), p. 6. This quotation and the following ones from other authors draw on the excerpts in EMEMT (later signalled in the notes).

theory held its ground well into the seventeenth century, and both university and popular medicine considered the human body as the place where the four humours (blood, flegm, choler, and melancholy, or black choler) mix, thus determining a person's health. When melancholy prevails – in itself a cold and sour humour which is considered to be particularly active in autumn – not only the body but also the mind suffers, since the vapours rise to the brain and affect it. Timothy Bright, in the first treatise devoted exclusively to melancholy in English culture, writes that the word 'melancholy'

> signifieth in all, either a certayne fearefull disposition of the mind altered from reason, or else an humour of the body, co~monly taken to be the only cause of reason by feare in such sort deprаued. [...] whereby the vnderstanding is obscured;[28]

His more famous successor in the field, Robert Burton, when presenting his own work on melancholy, tends to read the signs of the disease as the consequence of man's sinful behaviour:

> wee, as long as wee are ruled by reason, as long as we correct our inordinate appetite, and conforme our selues to Gods word, are as so many liuing Saints, but if we giue reines to Lust, Anger, Ambition, Pride, and follow our owne wayes, wee degenerate into beasts, transforme our selues, ouerthrow our constitutions, provoke God to anger, and heape vpon vs this [disease] of Melancholy, and all manner of incurable diseases, as a just and deserued punishment of our sinnes.[29]

In spite of that, though, Burton is always very attentive about identifying the physical symptoms of man's illnesses, and about madness, the most violent of the "diseases of the brain", he observes:

> Madnesse is therefore defined to be a vehement Dotage, or rauing without a feuer, farre more violent then Melancholy, full of anger, and clamor, horrible lookes, actions, gestures; and troubles the Patient with farre greater vehemency both of Body and Minde, without all feare and sorrow, with such impentuous force, and boldnesse, that sometimes three or foure men cannot hold them. Differing onely in this from Frensie, that it is without a Feuer, and their Memory is most part better.[30]

From the previous quotations it is evident that both melancholy, frenzy, and madness are taken into consideration and studied by the theologian-physician. Some decades later Thomas Brugis touches again on the same aspects of the distemper, particularly stressing the consequences of the illness, which makes "men sad,

28 Bright, *Treatise*, p. 1 (from EMEMT).
29 Burton, *Anatomy*, p. 8 (from EMEMT).
30 Burton, *Anatomy*, p. 12 (from EMEMT).

harsh, constant, froward, envious, and fearefull",[31] while Gideon Harvey, in his above mentioned *Morbus anglicus*, also highlights something that had already been stressed by Bright, i.e. that people affected by melancholy may be subject to sudden bursts of laughter: "many Melancholiques and Splenetick persons are of an exceeding merry and cheerful disposition".[32]

My analysis cannot be devoted to the long-studied phenomenon of the presence of melancholy in early modern English culture, focussed on by many specialised scholars to whom I refer the reader.[33] Here I would like to analyse, through some concordances resulting from the medical corpora mentioned above, whether melancholy was perceived as a widespread disease with a significant social weight, and whether (and how) the various texts foregrounded or, on the contrary, disregarded the disease while dealing with other illnesses of greater social urgency.

Concordances

As defined in the Preface, a concordance is a list of strings of key words in context. Like so much of my study in this volume, the search for MELANCHOLY in the various corpora has been carried out through a concordancer and the results it yields, since I think it is worth analysing the many strings in which the term occurs both in 'my' medical corpus and in the EMEMT "Materia medica", so as to be able to compare the outcomes and see how much concordances from the medical domain have in common with data resulting from the irregular practitioners' handbills.

The methodology followed for this phase consisted in searching the "Materia medica" section, through the EMEMT software, in order to create a list of the clusters containing the selected term (Table 3.4).[34] After that, the handbills corpus was processed with the help of the AntConc concordancer, in order to find

---

31 Thomas Brugis, *Marrow of Physicke* (1640), p. 34 (from EMEMT).

32 Harvey, *Morbus anglicus*, p. 37 (from EMEMT). The reference to Bright is to Chapter XVII of his *Treatise*.

33 On this issue see, among many others, Babb, *The Elizabethan Malady*; Alexander Brownlee, *William Shakespeare and Robert Burton* (1960); Carol Falvo Heffernan, *The Melancholy Muse* (1995); Jeremy Schmidt, *Melancholy and the Care of the Soul* (2007).

34 Table 3.4 is a selection of the results processed by the software offered by the EMEMT CD ROM; the numbers in the left hand column reproduce the original ranking (chronologically ordered as visible in the right one). Therefore each entry keeps its original rank, so as to show the extension of the choices and, at the same time, the cuts I have made.

out the occurrences of MELANCHOLY in it, which were also searched with the cluster function of AntConc (Table 3.5).

Concordances of MELANCHOLY in EMEMT, "Materia medica"

From the concordances deriving from "Materia medica" there is evidence for what has often been claimed, i.e. how early modern medicine still relied on Galen's theory of humours.

Table 3.4: Concordances of MELANC* in EMEMT, "Materia medica" (a selection)[35]

1	ense flewmes/ and humours of	melancoly.	Also it hath vertue to	1526_GreteHerball
3	keth an oyntement [}For	melancoly.	I}] This oyntement d	1526_GreteHerball
5	clenseth the blode of humour	melancolyke.	}Agaynst stra~gury	1526_GreteHerball
6	yeres. It purgeth flewme and	melancoly.	}For feuer cotidian..	1526_GreteHerball
9	he blode and taketh away the	melancoly,	and it heleth the brai	1550_Bacon_WatersArtyfyciall
17	cions/ the pensiffenesse and	melancoly.	is dryuen out/ and th	1561_Braunschweig_HomishA
24	urs, as bloud, choler, flegme	melancholie,	& such like, yet risin	1580_Bright_SufficiencieOfEn
27	ses of Urine, it taketh away	Melancholy,	and all infirmities co	1580_Monardes_IoyfvllNewes
29	e natural partes, it purgeth	melancholy	blood, it comforteth	1597_Langham_GardenOfHeal
41	for Pills to purge choler or	melancholy,	electuary of the juic	1649_Rondelet_CountreymansA
44	d Pearmain, help to dissolve	melancholly	humours, and to pro	1652_Culpeper_EnglishPhysici
45	to procure mirth, and expell	melancholly.	The oyntment called	1652_Culpeper_EnglishPhysici
46	s the heart merry, drives away	melancholly,	quickens the spirits	1652_Culpeper_EnglishPhysici
48	h Avicen) as to expell those	melancholly	vapours from the spi	1652_Culpeper_EnglishPhysici
52	or a Cordial. [}Against	Melancholie.}]	Take one spoonfull	1653_Grey_ChoiceManual
57	perfluities, and purge forth	melancholy	blood: from whence	1658_Porta_NaturalMagick
65	the Heart-burn, and purgeth	Melancholy	and Flegm; it expell	1673_Woolley_GentlewomansC
67	and Spirits, and to suppress	Melancholy.}]	TAke of the juyces	1679_WM_QueensCloset
69	rt, and expelleth Phlegm and	Melancholy.	}For a Noli me tang	1679_WM_QueensCloset
72	mforts the Heart, and expels	Melancholy:	It cleanses the Lung	1694_Pechey_HerbalOfPhysical
73	, and the Birth, and removes	Melancholy.	Baulm, in Latin Mel	1694_Pechey_HerbalOfPhysical
74	he Cordial-Herbs. It removes	Melancholy,	and cheers the Hear	1694_Pechey_HerbalOfPhysical
77	lieve the Faint, chear the	Melancholy,	and purifie the Bloo	1694_Pechey_HerbalOfPhysical
80	comforts Nature, drives away	Melancholy,	making merry and p	1700_Salmon_PharmacopoeiaB
81	d against Sickness at Heart,	Melancholy,	and pernicious Vapo	1700_Salmon_PharmacopoeiaB
86	ation, sickness of Heart and	melancholy	habit and disposition	1700_Salmon_PhylaxaMedicinæ
91	preserves health, represses	Melancholy,	causes chearfulness	1700_Salmon_PhylaxaMedicinæ
92	's, Quartan Agues, and other	Melancholy,	cold and moist disea	1700_Salmon_PhylaxaMedicinæ
94	to attenuate Atra bilis and	Melancholy.	And in all deplorabl	1700_Salmon_PhylaxaMedicinæ
97	ce, Quartans, hypochondriack	Melancholy,	Herpes, Scabs, Itch,	1700_Salmon_PhylaxaMedicinæ

35 All texts mentioned in the table derived from a search in the EMEMT corpus, unless discussed below, are listed only in the Bibliography.

From the first case in Table 3.4 (an anonymous *Grete Herball* translated from French and published in 1526, which offers the collocate "humours of melancholy"), to n. 24 (Timothy Bright's *Sufficiencie of English Medicines*, 1580, listing all the four humours), and so on to the end of the concordances, there appears no particular change in the medical analysis of the disease. William Salmon's *Phylaxa Medicinæ* (1700, n. 92 in the Table) still connects MELANCHOLY to the determiners COLD and MOIST (typical of the Galenic theory). For nearly two centuries, then, melancholy was considered as a humour that, with its vapours, contaminated the blood and could be eliminated in various ways, as can be seen from the verbs used in the quoted concordances.

Given the nature of "Materia medica", a certain amount of remedies are to be expected, since all the various authors try to offer solutions for the sick. The cures suggested for melancholy do not seem to be very different from what is usually offered for other diseases (so much so, that MELANCHOLY is embedded in lists including heterogeneous illnesses). Melancholy is considered a disease that must be 'cleansed' (n. 5), 'purged' (ns 6, 29, 41, 57, 65), 'taken away' (ns 9, 27), 'dissolved' (n. 44), 'expelled' (ns 45, 48, 69, 72), 'driven away' (n. 46, 80), 'suppressed' (n. 67), 'removed' (ns 73, 74). 'repressed' (n. 91), but can also be simply 'attenuated' (n. 94), or even 'cheered' (n. 77).

What appears to be the most frequently prescribed cure, then, is purging, while the "oyntement" present in n. 2 (once again from the *Grete Herball*) sounds quite strange. Its larger co-text reveals that the ointment is made of "Apium risus or crowfote layde in wyne and oyle to rotte and than strayned medled with waxe" and that

> [it] dooth grete ease to sekenesse of the splene caused of mela~coli and therfore it is called Apiu~ risus for it wasteth the melancolyke humours co~mynge of habundaunce wherof foloweth heuynesse and his absence lessed foloweth y~ co~trary that myrth and by consequence risus that is laughter & therfore it is sayde Splen ridere facit. The mylte causeth to laugh for it clenseth the blode of humour melancolyke.[36]

As early as this text a clear connection is made between melancholy and the spleen, and – even if indirectly – being melancholy is interpreted as being afflicted by sadness, therefore in need of laughter. To what extent an ointment containing buttercups ("crowfote") could be of help remains, of course, unknown.

In her *Choice Manual or Rare and Select Secrets in Physick* Elizabeth Grey, Countess of Kent, describes another recipe to cure melancholy:

---

36 Anon., *Grete Herball*, fol. A5^{v} (from EMEMT).

> Against Melancholie.
> Take one spoonfull of Gilliflowers, the weight of seven barley corns of Bezer-stone, bruise it as fine as flour, and so put it into two spoonfuls of Sirrup of Gilliflowers, and take it four hours after supper, or else four hours after dinner, this will cheer the heart.[37]

Grey mentions a particular ingredient of medieval magical and popular medicine – bezoar – considered to be a powerful antidote against all poisons, and cloves, with which to make a syrup. So, both an ointment and a syrup were considered to be good medicines in case of melancholy. What is peculiar in Grey's receipt is the stated effect of the drink, i.e. it serves to cheer the heart, whereas there is no mention of the brain. This shows a radical shift in – or rather, the mixture of – the organs affected by the specific humour: melancholy troubles man's heart (i.e. human feelings), rather than the brain.[38]

Actually, some other entries in Table 3.4 offer receipts for drinks and potions against the "heart-burn" and other diseases, among which melancholy itself. For example, John Pechey's *Herbal* suggests a potion containing basil, because "It comforts the Heart, and expels Melancholy",[39] and also a decoction made of borage, since its "distill'd Water, and the Conserve of the Flowers, comfort the Heart, relieve the Faint, chear the Melancholy, and purifie the Blood" (Pechey, p. 22). William Salmon advises a "Water of Clove-Gillyflowers" (with various ingredients) as a panacea for a series of distempers: "it is an admirable Stomatick, and wonderful good against Sickness at Heart, Melancholy, and pernicious Vapors from the Spleen, Reins and Womb".[40] The same positive effects, Salmon recommends, also derive from his "Tincture of Coral Compound", "against diseases of the stomach and heart, as indigestion, want of Appetite, Loathing, Vomiting, Fainting Swooning, Palpitation, sickness of Heart and melancholy habit and disposition of Body".[41]

What has just been mentioned constitutes another interesting aspect emerging from these concordances, i.e. the lists of other diseases (or, rather, symptoms)

---

37 Elizabeth Grey, *A Choice Manual* (1653), pp. 2–3 (from EMEMT). See Table 3.4, n. 52.

38 Lady Grey (1582–1651) was not a quack, of course, but – like many noble women – practiced medicine to help her household and the neighbouring poor. See Elizabeth Spiller, *Seventeenth-century English Recipe Books* (2008).

39 John Pechey, *The Compleat Herbal* (1694), p. 14 (from EMEMT). See Table 3.4, n. 72.

40 The text quoted here is the translation made by William Salmon of George Bate, *Pharmacopoeia Bateana* (1700), p. 7 (from EMEMT). See Table 3.4, n. 81.

41 William Salmon, *Phylaxa Medicinæ*, p. 10 (from EMEMT). See Table 3.4, n. 86.

juxtaposed with melancholy.[42] Brunschwig (or Braunschweig) links the disease to "straunge thoughtes and imaginacions [and] the pensiffenesse", all symptoms to be cured so that "all wycked thoughtes are forgetten", "and the braynes get agayne theyr force or strength and are encreased".[43] By Brunschwig headache is also associated with melancholy,[44] while other authors connect the latter to "deafness",[45] or even to "Green-sickness, Dropsie, Jaundice, Consumption, Asthma, Pleurisie [...] Ulcers, inward and outward, Scabs, and other Breakings out".[46]

What may surprise modern readers is that bodily and psychological ailments are so closely linked, as to be undifferentiated and simply put in an apparently unconnected series.

Concordances of MELANCHOLY in the Handbills Corpus

What has just been highlighted about the EMEMT corpus is decidedly more visible in the handbills (see Table 3.5). This feature is particularly observable in the long catalogues of very different illnesses, which mix bodily and mental or psychological diseases without any discrimination. One of the longest of these lists (if not the longest) can be found in the four-page pamphlet issued by 'Doctor' Salmon (the writer of *Phylaxa Medicinæ* quoted above) to advertise his "Pills, Drops & Balsam". The pills, in particular, cure

---

42 In the chapter devoted to "Diseases", Andrew Wear underlines that in early modern times, both for learned physicians and laymen. "the symptoms were often the disease" (*Knowledge*, p. 108).

43 Hieronymus Brunschwig, *A Most Excellent and Perfecte Homish Apothecarye* (1561), fol. 9^{v} (from EMEMT). See Table 3.4, n. 17.

44 The Comments to Brunschwig's text mention "Toke~s of headache caused of Melancoly" (Brunschwig, *A Most Excellent and Perfecte Homish Apothecarye*, fol. 2^{v}. From EMEMT).

45 Culpeper, *A Physical Directory*, p. 10 (from EMEMT). Culpeper observes that his medicine "helps deafness coming of Melancholly and noise in the ears" (the quotation is not included in the table).

46 Salmon, *Phylaxa Medicinæ*, p. 11 (from EMEMT). This passage, too, is not included in Table 3.4. Both William Salmon and the previously mentioned John Pechey were famous in seventeenth-century London as quacks, even if the latter was a regular licentiate of the College of Physicians "turned Quack-doctor", while the former was an unlicensed practitioner who proclaimed himself "doctor" (see Thompson, pp. 125–37. Both practitioners are documented in the *ODNB*).

> the Headach. Megrim, giddiness or swimming Apoplexy, Lethargy, *Melancholy*, Frensy, Madness Dimness of sight, thickness of Hearing, pain and noise in the Ears, Distillation sore Throats, shortness of Breath, stinking-Breath, Green-sickness, want of Appetite, Vomiting, Pains and stoppages of the Head stomach, Liver, or spleen, pains in the sides, Plurisie, Wind Gravel, Stone, Worms in Children, Pain, stoppage and heat of Urine, pissing Blood Convulsions, Falling-sickness, Palsie, Lameness, Numbness, SCURVY, DROPSY, GOUT, Sciatica, Jaundice Kings evil Rickets, running of the Reins, Barrenness in Women (though of twenty years continuance) stoppages of their courses, and other Disease belonging to the Sex. They purifie, cleanse and sweeten the Blood, rectifie all Distempers of the Head, quicken the senses, clear the sight, add a good colour to the face, and make the Body able to withstand Diseases. (551a32[128], p. 1; my italics)

It is evident that nearly all possible diseases are listed in this long paragraph, but only some of them – "Megrim, giddiness or swimming Apoplexy, Lethargy, Melancholy, Frensy, Madness" – seem to belong to the family of the 'diseases of the brain', with possible psychological implications.

In the pamphlet the term MELANCHOLY occurs three times: the first occurrence is in the passage quoted above, where it is embedded in a series of diseases connected to the head (and the brain, supposedly), only that the string of words goes on citing quite different illnesses, which have nothing to do with these parts of the body. What the paragraph says at its end allows us to classify the medicine on sale among general tonics. The second occurrence appears in a later paragraph devoted to the pills once again, which

> purge by stool flegm, choler, and melancholy; they dispose old Ulcers, Fistula's, running sores, sore-Breasts, sore eyes, scald heads, kings-evil sores, tetters, ringworms, salt humours, scabs, or any other breakings out to a speedy healing, by purging away the evil humours which feeds [*sic*] them. (551a32[128], p. 3)

The cure offered against melancholy, then, is still based on classical medicine (Galen's theory of humours) and on the easiest curing method (a purge), and appears to be a real cure-all, in spite of the specificity of melancholy. The third occurrence confirms the writer's connection with Galenic physic and repeats his tendency to juxtapose items of the most various sorts.

Table 3.5: Concordances of MELANCHOLY in the Handbills Corpus (a selection)

1	sort of Sickness, when the	Melanchollу	is not cleans'd and taken away, it	551a32[31]
2	Teeth or Consumption. For	Melancholy	Persons inclining to distraction, or such	551a32[85]
3	Jaundice, Cachery, Hypochondriack	Melancholy,	Green-Sickness and most Diseases of	551a32[109]
4	Lier or Spleen, Hypocondriac-	Melancholy,	Worms, Stoppage of Urine, Convulsio	551a32[121]
5	Lacteal Veins, Hypochondriack	Melancholy,	Jaundice, Fevers, Agues, Stone, Sand,	C112f9[13]
6	Fevers, Religious and Love	Melancholy,	Fits of the Mother, Small Pox, Meazle	C112f9[29]

7	of Liver or Spleen, Hypocondriac-	Melancholy,	Worms Stoppage of Urine, Convulsion	C112f9[39]
8	Mouth-Scurvey, Hypochondraick	Melancholy,	and Agues, etc. They mightily procure a	C112f9[54]
9	have any Friends Distracted or	Melancholy	are desired to accept this: and they that	C112f9[72]
10	that have been sixteen years	Melancholy	in six Months: though some kinds of thi	C112f9[72]
11	from the rest, being altogether	Melancholy,	lame on one side, supposing her self to	C112f9[72]
12	It easeth the Hypocondriack	Melancholy,	and openeth the obstructions of the Mib	C112f9[88]
13	outh-Scurvey, and Hypocondraick	Melancholy;	It mightily procures a good Appetite, he	C112f9[90]

Leaving aside the pamphlets, which are not counted in the corpus, it is nevertheless interesting to observe that MELANCHOLY very often occurs in the midst of a muddle of other diseases, as well as in other cases seen so far. The identification of the illness as a culturally loaded one is not stressed (in the same way as the pox is, for example). Some handbills, though, seem to consider the specificity of the malady. Such an awareness, if feeble, surfaces in an advertisement issued by Anne Laverenst, the "German Gentlewoman" already mentioned, whose lines devoted to the illness read as follows:

> There is yet another sort of Sickness, when the Melancholly is not cleans'd and taken away, it occasions Grief and heavy thoughts, nay sometimes Ragings, and an ill mind towards themselves or others. (551a32[31], *verso*; Table 3.5, n. 1)

Laverenst at least separates melancholy from other ailments and demonstrates that she knows not only the major psychological symptoms of the illness, but also that it can provoke violent behaviour, thus verging on madness. The "Gentlewoman", though, soon after the quoted passage, adds: "I cure the Piles or Hemorrhoids in the Fundament, all Warts, Excrescences, or superfluous Flesh in the mouth of the Bladder or Womb", thus belying the positive impression of a careful and attentive physician.

A concerned and thoughtful attitude towards melancholy is also present in another handbill. A "Doctor of Physick" advertising his "private cure" offers much more than a pill or a syrup, although once again melancholy seems to be treated together with other diseases:

> For Melancholy Persons inclining to distraction, or such that are Consumptive and desire Cure, he hath a Large Country-house with Gardens, being excellent Air, within a mile of the Town, where the Doctor is daily to give advice, and what Physick is most necessary for recovery, at easie rates, and where more advice is needful he consults some of the eminentest of the Colledge. (551a32[85]; Table 3.5, n. 2)

Dr Goodall, who claims that his "Superfine bark" is sold at Physicians' Hall, after defending himself against the accusation of selling too expensive medicines, proclaims that his medicament also cures (as usual, among many other diseases)

"Religious and Love Melancholy", thus expressing concern about pathological forms strictly connected to the psyche, and not only to the combination of humours (C112f9[29], Table 3.5, n. 6).[47]

In the two British Library Collections from which the corpus has been built there is only one single-page document which presents more than one occurrence of the term MELANCHOLY. It is C112f9[72] (ns. 9, 10, 11 in Table 3.5), addressed to those "that have any Friends Distracted or Melancholy".[48] Furthermore, the writer introduces himself as "Faithful and Expert in these Distempers", the only one – so far and in the whole corpus – who does not seem interested in curing each and every disease, but cites as credentials just cases of mental illness (rather madness than depression or sadness, or heavy thoughts, though). The four cases he mentions occurred in the 1670s:[49] a woman who "was much given to Swear and Tear"; a man who beat himself and was "so void of Sense and Reason as not to know any thing that was said or done unto him"; a man who believed he was King Charles II; finally a woman who thought she was unable to stand properly because of a "Plaister that a woman had applied to her forehead". This specialist also mentions the London asylum, Bedlam Hospital (he is the only one to do so in the whole corpus, even if the term also appears in two addresses as mentioned in Chapter 2). From what he writes, therefore, this unknown practitioner could be considered an early psychiatrist, a specialized professional.

In the corpus there are 14 occurrences of the lemma HYPOCHONDRIA (especially in the form of the modifier HYPOCHONDRIAC) which collocates mainly with MELANCHOLY (10 times; see ns. 3, 4, 5, 7, 8, 12, 13 in Table 3.5). It may just be a surmise, but I think that this high-sounding adjective is one of the many strategies used by quacks in order to surprise and impress their readers.[50] In other words, the modifier does not add anything to the noun in these cases, since it simply refers to what was considered the main cause of melancholy (hypochondria, originating in the liver with its black bile, or in the spleen, or in

47 For a thoughtful panorama of the connections between melancholy as a physical disease and as the object of religious and theological concern, see Angus Gowland, "The Problem of Early Modern Melancholy" (2006), esp. pp. 100–11.

48 It is necessary to remember that, as stated at the beginning, the term MELANCHOLY has always been considered here as a lemma, and not according to the different parts of speech it can represent (noun or modifier).

49 This is one of the few handbills which include dates.

50 See Chapters 4 and 5 below.

the abdomen generally speaking). A very nice example of how hypochondriac melancholy was diagnosed in the seventeenth century can be found in the First Physician's speech in Molière's play *Monsieur de Pourceaugnac*,[51] in which this kind of complaint is painstakingly and pompously described as different from two other forms of the illness, because it

> procède du vice de quelque partie du bas-ventre et de la région inférieure, mais particulièrement de la rate, dont le chaleur et l'inflammation portent au cerveau de notre malade beaucoup de fuligines épaisses et crasses, dont le vapeur noire et maligne cause dépravation aux fonctions de la faculté princesse, et fait la maladie dont, par notre raisonnement, il est manifestement atteint et convaincu.

> [proceeds from some lower part of the abdomen, and from the inferior regions, but particularly the spleen; the heat and inflammation whereof sends up to the brain of our patient abundance of thick and foul fuliginosities; of which the black and gross vapours cause deterioration to the functions of the principal faculty, and cause the disease by which he is manifestly accused and convicted.][52]

On the title-page of his treatise, Cheyne declares he deals with "Hypochondriacal and Hysterical Distempers": of the two modifiers the former occurs twelve more times, including the title pages of the three parts into which the volume is divided, the table of contents and the intertitles of some chapters. It always co-occurs with 'hysterical', except once when it forms the cluster "Nervous, Hypochondriacal and Convulsive Fits, and Paroxysms", therefore never together with MELANCHOLY, which is rather only one condition in a range from "Lowness of Spirits" to "a compleat Apoplexy".[53] This supports the idea that the cluster 'hypochondriac melancholy' in the handbills is just a means on the writer's part to bolster up their rhetorical appeal to their readership.

Were it not pedantic (or were it inside a purely linguistic and lexicographic study of quacks' language) a more detailed analysis of the entries in the tables would reveal other interesting details about the language of handbills as a very

51 Molière, *Monsieur de Pourceaugnac* (1978 (1670), I.8, p. 169). The collocate 'hypochondriac melancholy' occurs only 8 times in "Materia medica", i.e. far less frequently than in the quacks' handbills (there are 7 occurrences in Salmon, *Phylaxa Medicinæ*).

52 See <http://www.monologuearchive.com/m/moliere_018.html> for the English translation of this passage.

53 Cheyne, *Morbus anglicus*, pp. 275 and 16, respectively. This search has been made possible by viewing the book at the archive.org website (see Bibliography).

particular medical domain. What can be deduced from the data – and not only those concerning 'melancholy' – for example, is the gendered way nervous disorders were treated differently according to whether the sick were men, or women, or young women (green sickness being, apart from the skin colour of the girls affected by it, a sort of melancholy attributed to young women). As for the former disease, its name sometimes appears together with MELANCHOLY in the handbills, but not in the "Materia medica" concordances: was it because handbills targeted a larger readership than short treatises and pamphlets, thus trying to list all possible symptoms and illnesses and 'seduce' greater numbers of prospective patients?[54]

Real madness and its symptoms have not been specifically addressed in this chapter. Suffice it to say that some handbills include MADNESS in the same lists containing MELANCHOLY, while the word appears to be much less frequent than MELANCHOLY itself in "Materia medica" (20 occurrences vs. 97). In the handbills corpus MADNESS occurs 25 times, 15 of which together with MELANCHOLY, meaning perhaps that no great or sophisticated distinction was made between the two. After 1680, though, all Londoners could see the strong relationship and the differences between the two ailments when entering – or just passing by – the New Bedlam Hospital, whose gates were adorned by the two figures reproduced in Fig. 6.[55]

---

54 Overall the "Materia medica" section of EMEMT has only 15 occurrences of GREEN SICKNESS, while there are 68 occurrences in the handbills corpus. In only six of the twelve pamphlets included in the two British Library Collections does the term occur (11 times altogether; in two pamphlets it is repeated three times: in 551a32[222] and in 551a32[128], which are two versions produced by the same irregular practitioner evidently on different occasions).

55 The statues representing Melancholia and Madness were sculpted by Caius Gabriel Cibber in 1680.

Figure 6: Statues of "raving" and "melancholy" madness, formerly crowning the gates at Bethlem [Bedlam] Hospital. Engraving by C. Warren, 1808, after C. Cibber, 1680. By courtesy of the Wellcome Library, London

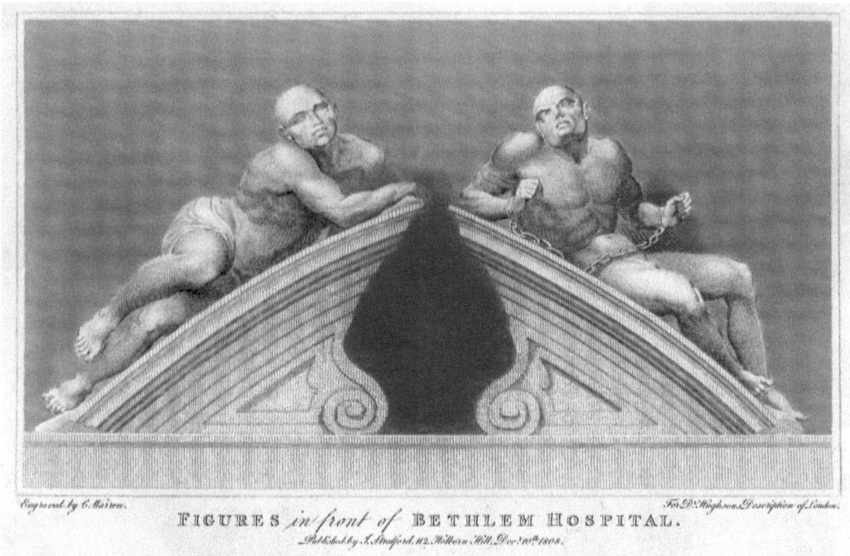

The present sub-chapter has shown that the disease of melancholy was much more the subject of official medical treatises than of medical printed matter targeted at larger social classes, such as both "Materia medica" and the quack doctors' handbills. Even if the percentages of these two corpora are not very far from each other, there are differences in the way the ailment is treated. "Materia medica" offers detailed cures and appears more interested in divulging receipts, while (on the contrary) the handbills only offer ready-made nostrums to be bought and not home-made. Furthermore, by listing melancholy together with a large number of other diseases, handbills do not appear to foreground it as a widespread ailment, as though their writers paid more attention to bodily illnesses rather than to mental and psychological anxieties, even if – as shown previously – MADNESS has a higher frequency in the handbills than in "Materia medica". Perhaps quacks' poorer customers had no time to pay attention to melancholy, busy as they were in surviving the very hard living conditions of early modern London, and when diagnosed as 'mad', they were chained in Bedlam rather than cured as people troubled by melancholy. It is no accident that the booklet attributed to Elizabeth Grey, Countess of Kent, hosts a special (and esoteric) recipe for melancholy: the affluent members of society had more leisure to devote to the cure of their psyche than the lower classes, who were certainly keener on taking care of their bodily health first. And the printed matter in the medical domain, especially (but not only) targeted at them, complied with this necessity, i.e. – paraphrasing Shakespeare – 'Melancholy in small ones can unwatch'd go'.[56]

56 The fact that melancholy as mental distress was a phenomenon linked mainly to intellectuals, aristocrats and upper middle-class people is also highlighted by Cheyne, who early in the "Preface" to his book observes that the "English malady" is also due to "the Inactivity and sedentary Occupations of the better Sort (among whom this Evil mostly rages)" (*Morbus anglicus*, p. ii). On Cheyne's volume see Schmidt, *Melancholy and the Care of the Soul* (2007), esp. pp. 176–84, and Roy Porter, *Mind-Forg'd Manacles* (1987), pp. 83–89. For melancholy as a complaint of the privileged see Michael MacDonald, *Mystical Bedlam* (1981), pp. 150–60.

4 How Quacks Addressed their Audience

> Here I might give you an account how he manageth a Stage to his advantage both in City and Country [...] How first his Buffoonries are exhibited in publick to attract the People, and having congregated a great many, *Mr Doctor,* who is in ken, comes and ascends the Stage, where having walkt to and fro very stately, and filling his hands with papers, and small vials, he then begins to disgorge the names of those diseases he not long since swallow'd, which, like vomits, will no longer be contain'd; he then tells you what excellent Pills, Plaisters, Powders, Spirits, Oyntments, Balsoms, Waters, and Elixirs he hath for all diseases that ever were, or shall be;
>
> (Richard Head, *Proteus Redivivus*)

Harangues, Handbills, and Title Pages

Up to now the activities of London irregular practitioners have been seen through what these people printed in their handbills, but as the information included in Chaper 1 shows, many of them were also mountebanks, i.e. they mounted a stage in order to offer their remedies from a material vantage point, a higher position when compared with the street or square level where their audience stood. It is not difficult, then, to visualise their scaffolds and to interpret them as real stages where trading performances took place. In this we are helped by the many visual documents – paintings and engravings – which are still extant. Therefore a modern approach to quacks' activities cannot but take the visual arts into consideration.[1] By so doing, we have ocular records to enable us to envisage them. What is so far missing in this picture is a sound track, so to say, that is, accounts of what they said, how they spoke from their stages in order to sell their medicines. The spoken word is ephemeral, unfortunately, but the social phenomenon of quackery was so relevant in early modern London society that quacks' oral performances did not go unnoticed to the point of becoming mythologised. Actually from the early eighteenth century anthologies were published containing quacks' speeches, even if their authenticity is now absolutely conditional, given that these collections also include literary and overtly satirical passages. One major example is given by the already introduced booklet *The Harangues or Speeches of Several Famous Mountebanks in Town and Country*, published without date, but – according to the *ESTC* – issued around 1725, and written by

1 For a rich collection of images I refer the reader to the London Wellcome Library.

a so far unidentified D. G.[2] With a view to demonstrating that the 'harangues' collected in it are mostly imitations of real speeches suffice it to remember that the last speech is that of "the Famous Scoto of Mantuano [*sic*]", i.e. a literal transcription (with Stage Directions included) of Volpone's oration in Ben Jonson's play, and that on pp. 23–35 there is Dr Bendo's, that is John Wilmot 2nd Earl of Rochester's, parodic speech taken from the brochure containing this fake mountebank's bill.[3] Furthermore, D. G. also drew from Restoration drama: "Lopus's Harangue at Madrid" is actually copied from Thomas Killigrew's play *Thomaso, Part 1* (IV.2), "The Harangue of Robert Wilmore" is nothing but an arrangement of Willmore's mountebank oration in Aphra Behn's *The Rover, Part 2* (II.1), and "Joseph Haines's Speech" is ascribed to the famous Restoration actor (therefore attributable to literary invention as well).[4] Nevertheless, since quacks' and mountebanks' authentic speeches have hardly ever been transcribed in print, this collection can also be usefully investigated as an imitation of public communication at the birth of English advertising. Therefore it is interesting to glean some information from this collection, since its writer (and editor) must necessarily have tried to imitate the real oral performances of his contemporary quacks, in order to sound at least credible. This is especially relevant to my purpose because my intention is to look for traits of oral communication in the handbills themselves, given that quacks addressed an audience either *in præsentia* by speaking to it, or *in absentia* by distributing handbills, but very probably using similar rhetorical strategies. My analysis, therefore, will try to find traces of orality in the written forms and special emphasis will be devoted to seeing whether and in what

---

2 D. G. actually does not appear as the writer, since he only signs a short dedication. However this work – the year 1700 being accepted as a reliable publishing date – is part of the EEBO Collection where it is identified as Wing/G7. As for the date, the volume has also been judged to have first been printed much later – in the 1760s – since the initials have been interpreted for David Garrick (see Katritzky, *Women*, p. 124). For a discussion of various editions of this volume see Chapter 5 below.

3 When not otherwise specified I will refer to this copy of the booklet (D. G., *Harangues*). Dr Bendo's speech was published "in various early editions of Rochester's poems. The earliest of these to appear seems to be that printed [...] in 1691" (Vivian de Sola Pinto, "Introduction" (1961), p. 11). For a reading of Rochester's adventure as a powerful satire, see Don Bourne, "'If I appear to any one like a counterfeit'" (2008); see also Chapter 6 below.

4 The three speeches occupy, respectively, pp. 48–54, 43–48 and 35–43 of the collection. On "Joseph Haines's Speech", see Chapter 5 below.

manner written and supposedly oral public discourses mirror each other,[5] underlining the pragmatics of both and keeping firmly in mind that printed matter was for private reading (even if sometimes read aloud to uneducated listeners) while oral deliverance was for an indeterminate audience.[6]

In order to attempt such an analysis, my research in this chapter will first compare some results from the handbills corpus with parallel ones deriving from a choice of forty-eight title pages of volumes and chapbooks from the medical domain. These latter have been chosen on the basis of their relevance to my work, that is, they are publications by or about irregular practitioners and about the early modern marketing of medicines. According to the *ESTC* all documents date back to the sixteenth and seventeenth centuries.[7] Both the handbills corpus and these titles have been searched in order to find the frequency of lexical words that are generally linked to evaluation, i.e. that have axiological value. I have, therefore, investigated the printed evidence focusing on high-frequency lexical words, since they are deeply revelatory as to the senders' persuasive strategies, but also on low-frequency words, because they seem to highlight individual linguistic uses meant to differentiate one's commercial offer from other vendors' products. Secondly, I will focus on terms which, in the written handbills themselves, may testify to the transposition of oral communication into the written medium. As well as this, a couple of harangues in D. G.'s collection will also be searched for authenticity markers and for traces of real orality. In a last phase, practitioners' attitudes towards their readers will be studied.

---

5 In an attempt to trace quacks' rhetoric, Carol Clark instead bases her analysis on fictional samples only: "To form an idea of mountebank rhetoric [...] we are obliged to rely on contemporary descriptions, and on imitations of the mountebank style by literary artists" ("'The onely-languag'd men of all the world'" (1979), p. 542). On this occasion I prefer to leave fiction aside and privilege authentic documents, when possible.

6 As already stated in Chapter 1, the unlettered often received information when they had access to people reading aloud (see Barry, pp. 78–85; see also Fox). As mentioned in many publications about early modern medical advertising, the use of the term 'audience' is quite legitimate for the addressees of quacks' speeches. Porter points out that "quackery is a one-way speech system. [...] the quack's patter is [...] like a monologue or soliloquy", thus underlining the tight correspondence between quackery and theatre (*Quacks*, p. 138).

7 By titles I mean the complete wordings as they appear in the *ESTC* (for untitled handbills they also include the first lines; for books the whole title page). As for the latter, Furdell states that "The title pages of published works [...] were 'advertisements in themselves'" (Furdell, *Publishing and Medicine*, p. 142).

In the relatively few studies about the language of quacks, what has been highlighted is the practitioners' power to deceive while promoting and selling nostrums. Roy Porter himself often writes of the "hyperbole of irregular medicine", even if he is always well aware that in early modern culture differences between professionals and 'popular' practitioners of medicine were not many:[8]

> Both orthodox and irregular medicine generated their own linguistic sub-cultures, whose vocabulary, tones and speech mannerisms, though somewhat distinct, played similar socially and even therapeutically active roles.[9]

But how did irregular practitioners attain their aims (both commercial and therapeutic) just by using words? What did their "linguistic subculture" consist of? First of all, let's try and investigate the possible discrepancies and similarities between oral and written discourse.

Speaking and Writing

Generally, the spoken word differs "in terms of structure, style and content from written mode", especially because the two channels of communication "primarily aural/oral and primarily visual/motoric" are separate.[10] But in the context of quacks' discourse, these channels seem to merge, revealing an interesting convergence of features, so as to show residues of orality in print. Walter Ong's early study of Tudor prose specifies what he meant by "oral residue", i.e.:

> habits of thought and expression tracing back to pre-literate situations or practice, or deriving from the dominance of the oral as a medium in a given culture, or indicating a reluctance or inability to dissociate the written medium from the spoken. Such residue is not especially contrived and seldom conscious at all.[11]

The speech-writing continuum seems to be particularly unbroken in quack literature, so that the immediacy of oral communication is also perceived in print. My hypothesis is that in the latter there remains much of quacks' oral activities in front of an audience that "may be compared to a demagogue's auditors, a preacher's congregation, or to theatre-goers". Quacks' words were part of a more complex ritual

---

8 As regards this point, Nagy (p. 2) writes: "Seventeenth-century medical practice in general was an untidy mixture of folklore, superstition, Galenic theory, herbal tradition, astrology and, eventually, chemical medicine. Into this mélange, both licensed and unlicensed practitioners indiscriminately dipped".

9 Porter, "The Language of Quackery", p. 76.

10 Rebecca Hughes, *English in Speech and Writing* (1996), pp. 11, 13.

11 Walter Ong, "Oral Residue" (1965), p. 146.

which appealed to the "public ear and eye",[12] a comprehensive routine including talking from a stage (or from horseback), being accompanied by a helper, often wearing particular clothes and displaying various animals and medical instruments. Like all peddlers and street vendors, quacks used language as an enchanting and persuasive tool of public communication, and relied heavily on its power to convince their audience. Unfortunately, as recalled above, we miss a proper 'sound track' of their enterprises to complement the many images of quacks' work,[13] but what happens now when reading quacks' handbills is very similar to the experience of reading the text of a play one has already seen performed at the theatre. One 'hears', so to speak, the charlatan's patter. Sometimes it is a sort of formulaic discourse typical of oral styles of communication,[14] sometimes it is a gesture made visible through the frequent use of deictics: in a way, charlatans' written traces resound with the dynamics of their lost oral performances.

Also the grammar of handbills echoes speech, in that informal structures pertaining more to orality than to written forms are present in them: asyndeton is often employed instead of subordination, simple polysyndeton such as 'and… and…' frequently occurs, and sometimes it is difficult to trace the correct reference because singular and plural pronouns blur the meaning. Some examples will suffice:

> These are to give notice to all His Majesties subjects, that Nicholas Culpeper late deceased […] a person generally approved of to be an eminent physician in his time, *and* by his indulgent care performed many excellent cures, *and* for the singular affection he owed to his said Majesties subjects […], hath prepared, composed, and made an excellent lozenge, and an universal pill […] You may give them to Men or Women, Old and Young, *and* Women with Childe, *and* to young Childrem […] *they* work very gently, *and* never *maketh them* sick at all: You may give a Childe a little Pill […] for there is no danger in *them*.[15]

> An approved antidote or cordiall medicine, that by Gods favour cureth the pestilentiall feaver […] *and that* at once taking […] *and hath* no tast nor smel: *and* the quantity at

12 Porter, *Quacks*, pp. 139, 137.

13 A great number of images of quacks and mountebanks are reproduced in Porter, *Quacks*, and in the following works: John M. McDowell, "Some Pictorial Aspects" (1946); M. A. Katritzky, "Marketing Medicine" (2001); William H. Helfand, *Quack, Quack, Quack* (2002).

14 See Walter Ong, *Orality and Literacy* (1982).

15 Richard Culpeper, *These are to give notice* […] (1668[?]). This handbill is not part of the three British Library Collections; a copy of the original is held by Harvard University (I quote from the EEBO Collection).

> one time to be taken is but 8 graines, *and* the vertue therof, will not decay in 40 yeares, *and* it is to be used as followeth[16]

As for the presence of deictics, an example from the speech entitled "The Quack by Thomas Rands" in D. G.'s anthology is of great interest:[17]

> Is there any old Women amongst **you**, who are troubled with the *Pimple-Pimplins*, [...] **See**, **here** is my *Antipamphastick Powder*, or my *Sovereign Carminick*, [...] Then **see**, **here** is my *Balsamum Stobula Swordum*, [...] Then, **here** is my *Unguentum Cataphon*, or an Ointment that's good against all *Strains, Sprains*, or *Bruises*.[18]

In this passage the direct address is worth noticing: from the inclusion of all the audience in the pronoun 'you' to the focus towards a specific sector of the spectators (old women), to the use of imperative verbal forms. What strikes one most are the fantastical names of the nostrums offered for sale: here the hyperbolic language of charlatans is at its best, mixing resounding English names with impressive-sounding Latin and dog-Latin forms. And, in order to verify whether D. G. copied from quacks' real-life activities, one has just to compare this passage with the title of a pamphlet – for example, *Smart's Aurum Purgans* – or with the heading of the handbill entitled *Elixir Magnum Stomachicum* (C112f9[17]).[19]

Axiological Communicative Markers

Catherine Kerbrat-Orecchioni defines objective discourse as characterized by the omission of any trace of an individual addressor's involvement, while – according to her theory – a discourse is subjective when the addressor is the explicit or implicit source of the evaluative information.[20] Affectivity and axiology are relevant factors as markers of oral discourse, and even if the "lexical density" of the written

---

16 Anon., *An Approved Antidote or Cordiall Medicine* (1650[?]). Neither does this handbill belong to the British Library Collections (quoted from the EEBO Collection). Italics mine.

17 Rands's speech simply reproduces, with small typographical variations, the twenty-fourth Chapter of this author's *Pax in Crumena* (1713). No information is available about Rands, therefore one can neither know whether his book circulated in manuscript before its print, nor use it to date D. G.'s collection.

18 D. G., *Harangues*, p. 2; boldface mine.

19 The *ESTC* simply attributes *Smart's Aurum Purgans* to "Smart, Quack doctor", and hypothesises that it was printed in London, around 1665 (quoted from the EEBO Collection).

20 Catherine Kerbrat-Orecchioni, *L'énonciation de la subjectivité* (1980), pp. 70–71: "lorsqu'un sujet d'énonciation se trouve confronté au problème de la verbalisation d'un object référentiel [...] il a en gros le choix entre deux types de formulation:

language cannot substitute the "grammatical intricacy" and the paralinguistic and interactional features of orality,[21] the following data will be analysed and discussed in order to see their relevance for a 'grammar' of quacks' language. To do this, only lexical items which present axiological nuances have been considered, i.e. nouns and modifiers that underpin a speaker's stance, because of their power to "express personal feelings, attitudes, value judgments, or assessments".[22] Or, to use Päivi Pahta's words, those terms that "[h]ighlight distinctions, at the same time signalling the author's involvement, commitment and point of view, including truth and value judgements".[23]

- Le discours 'objectif', qui s'efforce de gommer toute trace de l'existence d'un énonciateur individuel;
- Le discours 'subjectif', dans lequel l'énonciateur s'avoue explicitement ('je trouve ça moche') ou se pose implicitement ('c'est moche') come la source évaluative de l'assertion."

[when a subject of enunciation has to verbalise a referential object [...] they can generally choose between two types of expression: - the 'objective' discourse, which tries to delete all traces of an individual enunciator; - the 'subjective' discourse, in which the enunciator results explicitly ('I think it's ugly'), or implicitly ('it's ugly') as the evaluative source of the statement.]

Émile Benveniste's point of view about subjectivity in language, on the other hand, presupposes that each time somebody speaks (or writes) that linguistic act itself creates subjectivity: "Le langage est [...] la possibilité de la subjectivité, du fait qu'il contient toujours les formes linguistiques appropriées à son expression, et le discours provoque l'émergence de la subjectivité, du fait qu'il consiste en instances discrètes. Le langage propose en quelque sorte des formes 'vides' que chaque locuteur en exercice de discours s'approprie et qu'il rapporte à sa 'personne', définissant en même temps lui-même comme *je* et un partenaire comme *tu*" (*Problèmes de linguistique générale* (1966), p. 263). [Language is accordingly the possibility of subjectivity because it always contains the linguistic forms appropriate to the expression of subjectivity, and discourse provokes the emergence of subjectivity because it consists of discrete instances. In some way language puts forth 'empty' forms which each speaker, in the exercise of discourse, appropriates to himself and which he relates to his 'person', at the same time defining himself as *I* and a partner as *you*. (translation from *Problems in General Linguistics* (1971), p. 227)].

21 See M. A. K. Halliday, *Spoken and Written Language* (1989), pp. 63–80. For further characteristics of oral discourse such as fragmentation and interaction, see Douglas Biber, *Variations Across Speech and Writing* (1988), pp. 105–6; Nicholas Brownlees, "Spoken Discourse" (2005).

22 Douglas Biber et al., *Longman Grammar* (1999), p. 966.

23 Päivi Pahta, "*Ful Holsum and Profetable for the Bodi*" (2006), p. 210.

The Results from the Concordances

The quantity of axiological word types emerging from the handbills corpus is quite high, so that it is uneconomic to deal with them all here. From the tables I built for this research I extracted only the types which show the highest frequency and some with a much lower number of occurrences. An analogous search was carried out for the title pages. Then I chose the word types present in both corpora and compiled Table 4.1.[24] For the sake of brevity, I will limit the discussion on the one hand to the most frequent terms, on the other to those with a very scant occurrence.

Table 4.1: Lexical Words in Handbills and on Title Pages (a selection)

Word Types	Tokens in Handbills	% /200,583	Tokens on Title pages	% /3,770
All	1745	0.870	25	0.663
Any	1152	0.574	4	0.106
Many	699	0.348	8	0.212
Disease	635	0.317	25	0.663
Distemper	619	0.309	4	0.106
Medicine	538	0.268	18	0.477
Great	532	0.265	3	0.080
Most	505	0.252	19	0.504
Good	341	0.170	11	0.292
Physician	284	0.142	13	0.345
Remedy	268	0.134	4	0.106
Excellent	240	0.120	7	0.186
Doctor	228	0.114	14	0.371
Sickness	154	0.077	1	0.027
Virtue	150	0.075	9	0.239
Famous	138	0.069	5	0.133
Approved	90	0.045	6	0.159
Receipt	9	0.004	6	0.159

24 Because of their excessive length, the original tables have been drastically reduced to the selection presented here, i.e. this is a conflated table which is only designed to provide an immediate evaluation of the differences between the two corpora discussed (percentages are rounded up). Both singular and plural forms of nouns are calculated. Only the items from handbills are listed in decreasing ranking order.

High-frequency Words

Something must be said immediately about the different text types analysed here and featuring in Table 4.1, and about the total numbers of their word types, even if both aspects are self-evident: on the one hand there is a large quantity of handbills addressed to the public at large on a free basis, on the other a scant forty-eight title pages of books which had to be bought, with 'only' 3770 word tokens. The parallel function of both text-types, though, has already been stressed; in addition one has also to consider that most of the books are either collections of receipts or dietary regimens, therefore advertising the efficacy of their 'content' in their front pages, 'as though' the latter were advertisements. But there are differences, of course, which the table highlights very well. The most striking one emerges from the percentages in which DISEASE and DISTEMPER are used: in the handbills the two terms rank more or less together, while in the volumes the former is decidedly preferred to the latter. Furthermore, the percentage of mentions of DISEASE on title pages is twice that of handbills, whereas DISTEMPER occurs only for one third of its percentage in handbills. A possible explanation is that DISEASE is an older word, and therefore much more widely understood and at the same time more connected to the traditional medicine dealt with in the books, while DISTEMPER in the seventeenth century was still a sort of 'new entry', and possibly the writers of handbills wanted to appear as updated as possible in their lexicon.[25] A proof of this hypothesis is that the oldest word – SICKNESS (which has an Old English etymology) – is much less used in both corpora.

Another interesting remark can be made about the comparative use of PHYSICIAN and DOCTOR. The percentages diverge very clearly (the two terms are more present in the more 'learned' texts, but while they are more or less synonyms on the title pages with a slight prevalence of the latter over the former, in the handbills the prevalence is reversed: PHYSICIAN prevails over DOCTOR). A possible reason for this is again connected to the 'age' and usage of the two words: PHYSICIAN has Anglo-Norman origins, while the Latin DOCTOR sounds a more literate word, which acquired its meaning of 'doctor of medicine' only later, therefore fitter than its synonym to define the medical profession and the academic connections it implied. Besides this, book writers relied on a safe basis

25 See the definitions in the *OED*: DISEASE is an Anglo-Norman and Middle English word dating back to the fourteenth century; DISTEMPER is relatively more modern and used mainly in the seventeenth century.

for their success when proclaiming themselves 'doctor', thus implying the length of their education and the depth of their medical knowledge.[26]

All the words seen so far could be classified as objective, since they refer to the declared content of these texts. Apart from these, though, there are such words as ALL and ANY which cannot absolutely be considered neutral (or objective): actually they introduce a specific attitude of the sender towards the receiver. Readers or supposed listeners are prompted to accept the individual medical proposal because it is proclaimed to be good for everything and everyone, and therefore the two adjectives/pronouns acquire an evaluative trait and a perlocutionary force. ALL has a widening effect because its users stress the broadened efficacy of their remedies which work against "all diseases" (C112f9[19]), are addressed to "all gentlemen" (551a32[237]), hint at many testimonials since the specific remedy is "commended by all people" (551a32[159]), are successful for "all the degrees" of a mentioned sickness (551a32[180]), are profitable to "all that travel by sea",[27] give explanations for "all food" and "all herbs",[28] and are recommendable to "all families".[29]

ANY very often has a similar effect, suggesting that a particular remedy is efficacious against "any [...] chronick distemper" (C112f9[89]), works "upon any occasion" (C112f9[74]) and in "any time of sickness" (Ponteus). Sometimes, though, the adjective/pronoun implies quite a different meaning, for it is employed in order to extol a product (or a person) above any other, in this way praising its referent with a linguistic strategy bordering on the superlative. This is the case with phrases like "far beyond any medicament yet ever known" (C112f9[144]) and "that never yet any has done" (551a32[198]). ANY is much more present in handbills than on title pages, thus highlighting its use rather as an immediate indication of the reliability of a product or of a healer: handbill readers/listeners had to be caught in a very direct way by words, albeit simple ones, suggesting the fame and the efficacy of what was advertised.

Other terms with a good ranking are GREAT and MOST.[30] GREAT appears to be used in handbills with a percentage that is more than three times that of books,

---

26 The *OED* identifies the first occurrence of DOCTOR as late as Chaucer's *Canterbury Tales*, whereas PHYSICIAN had been in use since the *Ancrene Riwle*.

27 B. A., *The Sick-mans Rare Jewel* (1674).

28 John Archer, *Compleated with an Herbal* (1673).

29 John Ponteus, *The True Every Man & Woman their Own Doctor* (1676).

30 A linguistic analysis similar to the present one is to be found in Susan Kermas, "From Herbal to Advert" (2006), but it is mainly applied to ads in eighteenth-century newspapers; furthermore the author does not specify the quantitative weight of the terms she points out.

but it is not only a question of numbers, because in the handbills corpus the writers often capitalise on the connotative and axiological semantics of this modifier, as in the following examples: a "Famous and experienced High-German Doctor" "has a great Secret for the Curing of the Kings-Evil" (C112f9[4]); the Latin "Elixir Magnum Stomachicum" is rendered in English as "the great Cordial Elixir for the Stomach" (C112f9[17]); a "gentlewoman" is said to have "performed great Cures in Old and Young" (551a32[13]). Such usage is not present on title pages, which limit themselves to a simple denotative meaning. As for MOST, besides occurring in the regular formation of superlatives, it is used to augment the evaluative weight of other adjectives such as EXCELLENT in Turner's handbill to sell "his most excellent Lozenges" (C112f9[151]), in Salvator Winter Jr's for his "most Excellent Famous Elixir Vitæ" (C112f9[9]), and in the translation of Lanfranco's *Chirurgia parva* (1565) praised as "A most excellent and learned vvoorke of chirurgerie".[31] In comparison with the handbills, title pages often use MOST just to mean 'nearly all' (that is, MOST + pl. N.), therefore excluding the specific structure of MOST + Adj, which expresses feeling and subjective opinion, when MOST substitutes VERY as an intensive superlative. EXCELLENT itself is used with nearly similar percentages in both corpora: this shows that the strong positive meaning of this modifier was well understood and capitalised on by the authors. Something similar can be said for the noun VIRTUE, rich in strong positive semantic prosody, but the data reveal that its much higher percentage on title pages than in handbills seems due to the necessity to extol certain products in a few words, certainly fewer than in a long-winded handbill.

APPROVED and FAMOUS appear to behave like VIRTUE, their percentages being higher on title pages than in handbills. It is clear that they transmit their evaluative meaning simply through their semantics: they serve to exalt the individual operator, in the same way as 'virtue' implies the beneficial effects of a certain cure. Title pages – then and also now, although with different rhetorical and visual strategies – had to impress their readers and possible buyers in a more conspicuous, immediate way: these terms, actually, transfer a sense of certainty, authority and competence to their referent, in other words they serve to dignify a person (or an object). Therefore, they – present as they are in ephemeral printed products such as a popular broadsheet –appear even more on title pages, adding to the latter's intrinsic dignity. This issue seems to partially contradict

31 In the handbills individual adjectives, however, are generally used with lavishness, sometimes reaching a *crescendo* as in "A most infallible, and sure, cheap, secret, safe and speedy cure", which also calls attention to itself through its internal rhyme and alliteration (C112f9[14]).

the usual judgment about quacks' boastful and hyperbolic discourse: the results from Table 4.1 point to an analogous and even heavier use of positive modifiers and nouns by writers and/or printers of other material. In other words, advertising resorted to a lexicon aiming at impressing the addressee anyway, whether a medicine or a book was sold.

Low-frequency Words

As mentioned above, there are some words which appear very infrequently in my corpora. In spite of their low frequency, though, I think them relevant, since they occur in various texts to astound the reader with staggering terms and to "grab attention through surprise".[32] These are either incredibly hyperbolic modifiers or far-fetched, outlandish and bizarre terms, the latter used mainly to name extravagant medicines, in Latin or in English. CATHOLICK, with its possibly hidden religious meaning in Restoration London, occurs three times in the handbills: once to advertise a "Purgative and Diuretick" (C112f9[50]), twice (followed by its English translation) in a handbill advertising a pill of "universal" positive effects (C112f9[89]). The single occurrence of PHILOSOPHICAL in volume titles appears in Winter's chapbook for his "petza or plaister".[33] "Aurum purgans" is extolled in Smart's pamphlet (Smart 1665[?]); "medicus absolutus" is the first phrase of Maynwaringe's book against "the imposture of empericks".[34] INFALLIBLE occurs only in handbills, whereas a "Panchimagogum Febrifugum" (a medicine to expel all harmful liquids out of a sick body)[35] and the "Pilulæ Antiscorbuticæ" are sold in two anonymous bills (551a32[200] and 551a32[128], respectively).

Curiously enough (or, rather, quite understandably) the terms QUACK, MOUNTEBANK and EMPIRICK are rare: they total 24, 6 and 3, respectively, in the handbills (i.e. altogether 0.01 per cent of all the tokens), and 3, 3 and 1 in the volume titles (equal to 0.18 per cent). Two of them appear together in the already mentioned bill where an "Italian doctor" denies being a "stage-quack or mountebank" (C112f9[150]), and the writer of C112f9[125] invites his readers to "Beware of

---

32 Guy Cook, *The Discourse of Advertising* (1992), p. 8. As for this point, Halliday's words relating to the general "weight" of a "lexical item of rather low frequency in the language" seem relevant: "For a systematic, formal investigation of lexical density in texts we should have to adopt some weighting whereby *lexical items of lower frequency 'scored' more highly than common ones*" (Halliday, p. 65; my italics).

33 Salvator Winter, *Directions for the Use of my Elixir* (1664), title page.

34 Everard Maynwaringe, *Medicus Absolutus* (1668).

35 I am grateful to my colleague J. M. I. Klaver for translating for me a Dutch reference to this medicine.

Quacking, Cheating Mechanick Mountebanks". Both practitioners, evidently, and all those inserting the word in their handbills, wanted to keep their distance from the (other) despised charlatans. Even if generally scantly present, these words are to be found more on title pages, due to the satirical flavour attached to these terms. So, Merret's volume attacks "the frauds of the quacking empirick",[36] and cheaters and deceivers in all fields, whereas false physicians in particular are mainly referred to: there are "English", "French" and "Skilfull" mountebanks,[37] while the anonymous *Character of a Quack-Doctor* and *The Quacks Academy* also focus on such generic quacks.[38] It is evident that quacks did not employ these words unless they wanted to differentiate themselves from "pretenders" and that, given the negative meaning of the word, none of them named him/herself as such. On the contrary, book titles use both QUACK and MOUNTEBANK with all their negativeness because many of their authors generally belonged to the College of Physicians, which was the main antagonist of the irregular practitioners of medicine, as often said.

Orality in Harangues or Speeches

In D. G.'s collection there is a dedicatory letter "To Mr William Winter" (signed by D. G.), in which the author justifies his work in these words:

> The following Sheets are exactly fitted for you, they treating of what you us'd to divert your self with in *Moorefields, Covent-Garden, &c.* And as it has afforded you some Laughter to see the gaping Crowd be gull'd by the enchanting Tongues of *Quack* and *Zany*, who would unlock their Ears, and steal a Passage, by a magick Pill, into their Pockets, and so send them away with a small Apothecary's Shop, either to kill themselves or their Neighbours: So I hope they will revive your former Mirth in the reading them. (D. G., *Harangues*, fol. 1^{r-v})

From what D. G. writes, then, one is entitled to surmise that special care was taken in the reproduction of the features of quacks' oral communication. Therefore, although we must be wary about this pseudo-orality, it might be worth devoting particular attention to the writer when he was reproducing at least the main aspects of real quacks' performances. Thus, trusting D. G.'s imitative intention, what follows is designed to show analogies between a literary version of quacks'

36 Christopher Merret [?], *The Accomplisht Physician* (1670).

37 John Marriott, *The English Mountebank* (1652); Anon., *The French Mountebank* (1643); Joannes Baptista Lodovico Guardano puncto, *The Skilfull Mountebanke* (1638), respectively.

38 For an analysis of *The Character of a Quack Doctor* see below, Chapter 5.

language and authentic documents (such as the handbills analysed so far). In relation to this, a speech from the same *Harangues* collection will be examined.

The often reproduced engraving entitled *The Infallible Mountebank, or Quack Doctor* includes a speech in forty-five short rhyming lines pronounced by the quack in the picture.[39] The text is the same as appears in Motteux's play *Farewel Folly* (performed in 1705), a comedy that contains the musical interlude "The Mountebank" in which the eponymous character sings the words reproduced in the engraving.[40] It is clearly a literary invention, but some of its turns sound familiar by now:

1. SEE, Sirs, see here
2. A Doctor rare,
3. Who travell'd much – at home.
4. Here take my Bills:
5. I cure all Ills,
6. Past, present, and to come;
[…]
13. Thousands I've dissected,
14. Thousands new erected,
15. Spoilt and long neglected,
16. And such Cures effected,
17. As none e're can tell.
[…]
44. Read, Judge and Try,
45. And, if you Dye,
46. Never believe me more. (Motteux, pp. 56–57)

Some words have already been seen in handbills and title pages: this character calls himself a "doctor", has travelled extensively (but, self-ironically, only "at home", l. 3), affirms he is able to cure "all Ills" better than others (ll. 5, 17). The satirical touch in l. 3 is repeated at the end, when the mountebank implicitly confesses to

39 See the bpi1700 (British Printed Images to 1700) website for the image and its history (in Motteux the song has 46 lines). The speech is also in D. G., *Harangues*, pp. 11–12 and reproduced in Thompson, pp. 76–77. The collection Harley 5931 includes the engraving with its text, unnumbered but dated 1707. Because of the tentative numbering of the objects in this collection, it is impossible to give a univocal collocation to this broadside; suffice it to know that it is preceded by n. 174 and followed by a series of unnumbered items.

40 Peter Anthony Motteux, *Farewel Folly* (1707).

making people die. What is particularly interesting is l. 44 "Read, Judge and Try" because it partly reproduces a formula – "Read, try, judge, and speak as you find" – present in five of the late seventeenth-century handbills studied here (C112f9[25], 551a32[91], 551a32[110], 551a32[129] and 551a32[176]). Evidently Motteux the playwright copies from reality and his dramatic fiction sounds verisimilar. Besides, he makes his character sing words which are part of a previously written commercial text: perhaps this could be evidence of the strong orality of quacks' handbills, i.e. their performability, in other words their capacity to be read/pronounced on a stage with the corresponding "retinue" of varying "tones of voice, facial expressions and gestures",[41] according to the sequence consisting of street selling→ handbill→ drama→ theatre.

After this purely fictional speech, let's see one of the ten harangues included in D. G.'s collection: I have chosen "The Harangue, or Quack Speech of T. Jones at York" because I have not been able to trace it back to a literary antecedent.[42] It does not even contain absurd proclamations such as "It was I, cur'd Prester John's Juggler's wife" as in the speech of Thomas Rands partially quoted above (D. G., *Harangues*, p. 5). In other words, it sounds realistic and verisimilar enough. Furthermore, the name of the person to whom this speech is attributed is a very common one, thereby suggesting anonymity and, paradoxically, helping to authenticate the text as speech.

This relatively short text (609 tokens) immediately addresses its mixed-gendered audience with vocatives, later recalling their attention four times in the same way. The patter goes on, touching some topoi already seen in the other written texts, to which the speaker adds, from the very beginning, the price of his product. These formulaic topoi are the following: the speaker denies being a

---

41 Cook, *The Discourse of Advertising*, p. 71. Motteux's lines also have a purely theatrical flavour, given the deictics and the imperative forms with which the mountebank claims his audience's attention, thus contextualizing the scene and connecting the words to ostensive onstage action. The already mentioned harangues of Lopus, Wilmore and Scoto of Mantuano – i.e. passages taken straight from Killigrew's *Thomaso*, Behn's *The Rover*, and Jonson's *Volpone*, respectively – feature a rhetorical complexity and stylistic accuracy that reveal their literary origins. For a study of the recurrence of medical practitioners in seventeenth-century drama see Herbert Silvette, *The Doctor on the Stage* (1967) and Anat Feinberg, "Quacks and Mountebanks" (2000). The most famous quack in Restoration drama features in William Wycherley's *The Country Wife* (1675); this character, though, only serves to trigger the plot and as such has no relevance to the present research.

42 D. G., *Harangues*, pp. 19–22. The transcription of T. Jones's harangue is in Appendix D to this volume.

charlatan and using difficult words (which he lists, though) to enchant his listeners; proclaims his title; brags about his many years of travelling; boasts of the spread of his fame in the world (and relatively near home!).[43] He then attacks those practitioners who offer a single medicine for all diseases, but soon afterwards presents his remedies which – he says – cure all. As for the recurrence of certain terms, ALL is used 13 times in the text (1.96 per cent), therefore a percentage even higher than, but comparable to, the occurrences of the same modifier in handbills and on title pages; DISTEMPER, together with its synonyms DISEASE (1) and MALADY (1), is present 4 times (0.60 per cent); VIRTUE appears twice (0.30 per cent), whilst highly evaluative modifiers (WONDERFUL, INCOMPARABLE, UNPARALLEL'D, ADMIRABLE and RADICALLY) occur once each. There is also a string of simpler axiological adjectives ("a perfect, sage, and speedy Cure")[44] which relies, at least partially, on alliteration and isometry for its effect. A lot of diseases are named, thus parallelling handbills. In spite of Jones's denigration of 'hard words', he calls his "Cordial Pills" the "Tincture of the Sun" and his "most useful medicine" "Pulvis Cathartichus", thus employing a phrase in dog Latin.[45] The speech ends with the speaker's address (a usual indication in handbills), also adding where and when people may go for consultation.

The orality of the whole is suggested by vocatives and by the use of deictics which accompany the ostension of the various medicines: "this my packet" and "this my *Pulvis Catharticus*". Of course, the action of a quack can well be imagined on these two occasions and elsewhere, as, for example, the beginning when Jones reveals the price of his remedies to be bought "here". Redundancy and *copia* surface in the list of diseases and places, and as such are a good marker of orality.[46] There is also a closing sentence ("And so I wish you Health and Happiness") which marks the end of the harangue and, in its simplicity, confers a

---

43 Jones mentions Berwick upon Tweed, a town just south of the Scottish Border where there was a famous hospital for the sick and the poor, thus pointing to a 'reliable' medical place, very probably known to the people of York.

44 'Speedy' acquires an evaluative nuance, since it is used to underline the efficacy (the 'virtue') of a particular remedy.

45 'The Tincture of the Sun" of Paracelsian origin is present in three bills (twice in C112f9[8], once in C112f9[105]); see Chapter 2 above. There is also a touch of fantasy in the mention of the improbable Unicorn's Horn, a term rarely found outside texts on magic and still highly reputed in magical thought.

46 See Ong, *Orality*, p. 40. Redundancy, a conspicuous feature of many handbills, is a strong marker of orality, where it is used "to counterbalance the adverse effects of noise on comprehension" (Khosrow Jahandarie, *Spoken and Written Discourse* (1999), p. 142).

certain flavour of authenticity on it. Therefore, in spite of some aspects which might make one consider this text simply a parody of quacks' real harangues, it can be read as true, or at least very near the truth.

As if it were a Summary

What emerges from the analysis of "quackspeak" is that this language is very similar in both its written and purportedly oral expressions, since also handbills resound with the "reliance on the 'formulary'" typical of orality, so that we can read the majority of handbills as if we were listening to them being pronounced and performed aloud, because they belong to a "preliterate mode of expression" – that of the market place and of the fair – where traditionally quacks looked for and met their clients.[47] The "affective role" of the spoken word and "its strong association with emotion" surface from the printed texts here examined, in both handbills and the supposed transcription of a quack's speech.[48]

Things are slightly different when we look at title pages. The comparable results from Table 4.1 show that on title pages some lexical items such as DOCTOR, GOOD, MEDICINE and FAMOUS occur with a much higher percentage than in handbills, while ANY and MANY are less frequent. This, however, does not invalidate the general observations about the similarity of the vocabulary used in these two media. The differences mainly reflect the respective senders' 'intentions' and their specific targets. Indeed, in the sixteenth and seventeenth centuries, when book titles were still so lengthy and full of words as to resemble tables of contents, books written by, or against, quacks seem to rely on the same rhetorical strategies and lexical choices as shorter and more popular printed matter, even if they lack the prosody and the paralanguage of their humbler companions.

Quacks to their Readers

The Use of Pronouns

Second person pronouns are quite frequent in the handbills: although YOU ranks 33rd with 774 occurrences in the general word list, together with its derivative possessives it reaches 1027 cases, thus ranking 24th. It is not by chance, since the writers, given their specific purposes, address their possible readers very directly.[49]

---

47 Ong, "Oral Residue", pp. 150, 153.

48 Cook, *The Discourse of Advertising*, p. 58.

49 The second person singular pronoun THOU ranks extremely low, with only 2 occurrences, THEE occurs 4 times, THY 7 times, while there is no THINE. Evidently the

In spite of these numbers, though, the word READER occurs only 42 times in the handbills corpus (0.02 per cent), thus manifesting that irregular practitioners, while interested in communicating in writing to somebody, seldom named their targets as people able to read. Even within these 42 cases, the term does not always work as a direct address: for example Cornelius à Tilbourn, after 'youing' his addressee, writes that "I could mention a great many more which I have cured, but the Paper being too little, and not to trouble the Reader too much, I omit them" (C112f9[6]), without involving his readers too closely. In the same way, even if the reader is more than blandished in the passage, the seller of the "Pilulæ in omnes Morbos, or Pills against all Diseases" begins his bill with an intriguing but not exactly a closer-getting move:

> Before I make good what is promised in the Title [*A Brief Account of some Wonderful Cures*], give me leave to request him that reads thus far, to deal so fairly by me, (and also to do himself that right) to read, and throughly consider this Paper before he otherwise Disposes of it, and if the matter contained in it proves Satisfactory, I shall conclude he will not think himself much injured in his Expence of three or four minutes time, to peruse it.
>
> The next thing note-worthy, is, to present the Reader with a short view of some remarkable Cures, wrought by this incomparable Medicine, and in these, the **judicious** Reader may plainly see, are comprehended almost all diseases incident to Mankind. (C112f9[33], my emphasis)

Whenever the term READER is used, the practitioners' persuasive speech act becomes stronger and the illocution is still more evident, although the simple fact of distributing handbills in the medical marketplace is in itself an overall persuasion, enriched with a strong perlocutionary force (i.e. 'read and buy!'). The bills try to persuade "the favourable Reader" (C112f9[36]), "the judicious and discreet Reader" (C112f9[50]), "the ingenuous and unprejudic'd Reader" (C112f9[58]), a "Loving Reader" (C112f9[61]), a "Courteous Reader" (C112f9[66]; C112f9[84]; 551a32[27]; 551a32[218]]; 551a32[122]), a "Beloved Reader" (C112f9[138]), a "Kind Reader" (551a32[34]), or – simply – a "reader" in most cases.

Usually, readers are implicated in the course of the texts, but there are two handbills which address them straight from the beginning, thus trying to build a closer relationship with them. This is the case with handbill C112f9[138], written by Willemina Sasbout van Soeburgh, a Dutch healer:

---

pronoun and its possessives were already considered very old-fashioned and the YOU forms were preferred.

> Beloved READER,
> Being but lately come into this Kingdom, I do according to my duty, make my self known unto you all by this present Paper, which without the same, might otherwise be many years before I be known.

And with another woman's, who opens her bill with

> Loving Reader,
> God Almighty hath not created Man for himself, neither for his own ends, but hath given him a natural affection for to love his Fellowes, and loving them, to cure them by all means; and whereas I have many Sciences and Mysteries of Nature, as likewise particular Experiences, new Inventions, natural secret Arts for to cure many and divers great and dangerous accidents, as well as internal and external, specially for Women and young Maidens, could I not forbear to cause these to be printed for to make me known unto every one; without which it would be too long before I should be known. (C112f9[61])

Towards the end of this bill, the writer reveals her name, declaring that the print is due to "me Sarah Cornelius de Heusde, Widdow of Dr Sasbout, and Grand-mother of the Doctor that had his Stage upon Great Tower-Hill, and did so many Cures before the Fire." The detail about Dr Sasbout's stage being "upon Great Tower-Hill" is very interesting, since very few irregular practitioners mention this outdoor part of their activity (only 6). Sarah's surname makes a modern reader doubt the authorship of the two bills: did the latter come from the same person who used two different names, or was there simply an undeclared family connection between the two women? As for her address, Sarah "liveth at the Sign of the Red Lyon by the Postern Gate, in George Yard, between Great and Little Tower-Hill", while Willemina's house was "in Exeter street, at the Golden Ball behind the Exchange." This does not differentiate the two ladies completely, since it is well-known that quacks often moved from one place to another and that it is impossible to date the majority of handbills so as to judge which was printed earlier, but it allows us to think of a family activity: maybe Sarah was Willelmina's mother, besides being Dr Sasbout's widow. Both Sarah and Willelmina would thus be the heirs to Dr Sasbout's practice.[50]

Apart from the family connections behind these two bills, it is interesting to notice how both ladies justify their resorting to handbill printing: advertising by handbills helps make themselves known in their new and foreign country. Other writers apologize for using their readers' time (as is already discernable

---

50 Since both women claim to be particularly competent in women's diseases, their cases will be more widely treated in the last Chapter. See there for family business as well.

in Tilbourn's bill quoted above), sometimes with a subtle pragmatic strategy, as in the bill by the "Licensed Physitian" who lived "At the Golden-Ball and White-Horse in Water-Lane near Fleet-street". While showing his concern for his addressee, he boasts of his own healing powers and quality, thus performing a double illocutionary speech act full of negative politeness:[51] "I will not trouble the Reader with any more of the many hundreds I could name, were it proper, that I have cured, of all the Distempers that afflict Mankind." (C112f9[119]).

Nearly the same pragmatic feature can be found in the handbill printed by "a physician" who lived "At the Heart and Star, at the Dyers-Arms, next to John's Coffee-house, in the Great Old-Baily", but this practitioner is not so refined as to adhere to his programme of *brevitas*; actually, after declaring that "It would be tedious to insert the many Cures he hath performed, and therefore shall trouble the Reader only with these few following", he proffers a 297-word list of people cured by him, including all their addresses (551a32[204]).

As can be seen from the passages quoted above, sometimes practitioners used the first person singular pronoun, sometimes the third, sometimes the two together inside the same text. The former allows a more personalised form of communication, while the latter objectifies the speaker distancing him/her as an absent 'narrator' from the 'protagonist' of the narration itself. The formulaic *incipit* "This is to advertise" or the bill's title "Advertisement" are followed by the information about a newly arrived practitioner, his/her address and qualifications: all this uses the third person pronoun, but soon afterwards the text resorts to the first. Some examples will suffice:

> Nihil absque Deo. Try the Preserving of Health.
> These are to Advertise all Persons, whose illness may require the help of a Physitian, That there is come to this Place an experienced Artist, who (by the Blessing of God) performs the Gift of Healing, and Cures most Distempers incident to the Bodies of Men, Women and Children. [...][52]
>
> He cures all Rheums and Tumours in the Eyes or Weakness in the Sight, to admiration, in a short time. [...]

51 On the concept of positive and negative politeness, see Penelope Brown and Stephen Levinson, "Universals in Language Usage: Politeness Phenomena" (1978).

52 It is particularly relevant here that the writer refers to himself as an 'artist' able to 'perform' cures. The verb and the noun do not necessarily hint at theatrical performances, though, but simply at 'doing' cures, even if one might be reminded of the spectacular selling strategies used by mountebanks (see also the 'Conclusion' to this volume). Actually, the verb TO PERFORM occurs 171 times in the whole corpus, thus showing its very general use.

> I have, under God, and [*sic*] infallible Remedy in destroying all Worms in Children, of what Kind Nature and Quality soever they be: And likewise restore the Deaf to perfect Hearing. (551a32[12])

> ADVERTISEMENT.
> At the Crown and Golden-Ball, next door to Old King Charles's-Head, between great and little Turn-stile in High-Holborn, Liveth Doctor Peter Maris, an Experienced and able Physitian.
> Who has oft with good success remov'd these distempers following, [...]
> He hath likewise an Incomparable Eye-Water, for Curing all Distempers in the Eyes, and for Strengthning and restoring the decayed Sight of People, of what Age soever; You may have this Excellent Water of him, and no other, from Five Shillings a Bottle, to what Price you please.
> I perfectly cure the Morbus Gallicus, or French Pox [...] (551a32[29])

It is evident that the grammatical and logical consistency of the whole was not striven for, so that the general effect when reading most handbills is that of a double sender: first a crier who makes an announcement, or a presenter who introduces somebody or something in a show, then the protagonist who takes his/her turn and starts 'speaking'. On considering irregular practitioners' dual means of public communication (from a stage *in præsentia* and from handbills *in absentia* as already noted) – especially the fact that when on a stage quacks had helpers and stage-hands at their disposal as many pictures testify (the so called Merry Andrews), and that this feature goes back to the Italian *ciarlatani* and their *zanni* – this apparent irregularity and inconsistency in the use of pronouns seems to mirror in print what actually happened on a public stage. This feature, which corroborates the idea of similarities between practitioners' speech and writing, presents therefore the following schedule: the 'principal actor' starts his part only after being introduced, and the potential readership becomes an enlarged audience.

How to Appear Pious and Charitable

Some of the examples quoted have already shown how quacks relied on their readers' religious beliefs in order to have themselves accepted as devout people, i.e. judged as reliable and far from deceiving their neighbours. The blessing of God is often invoked (the term GOD occurs 320 times, 0.16 per cent; BLESSING has 164 occurrences, 0.08 per cent) as a guarantee of individual practitioners' medicines (it is the case of Salvator Winter Jr, who stresses the efficacy of his remedy "Seeing the great and wonderful Success it hath pleased Almighty God to bless this my Elixir with", C112f9[9]), but mainly as a pre-emptive defence against future accusations of inefficacy of a certain medicament. For example, Thomas Saffold informs "the Sick" that they can have

> of him good Medicines cheap, with directions how to use them, by which, and God's assistance, he is able to cure any disease either inward or outward, of what name or nature soever, if curable. (C112f9[100])

In other words, if God does not assist, no medicine can cure the sick; or, rather, this wording seems to forestall and reduce any blame for a possible failure of the medicine. The bill publicising "Major John Choke's most Virtuous Necklace" (C112f9[133]) which was supposed to ease teeth cutting "without pain, thereby preventing (by Gods Assistance) Feavers, Convulsions, Consumptions, Ruptures, Chin Coughs, Rickets, and such attendant Distempers", clearly assigns to the deity a major power to save children from many ailments, but at the same time paradoxically almost invalidates the healing effects of the necklace by submitting them to God's will. Both examples, therefore, far from perceiving the self-destructive irony of their phrasing, seem to prefer the positive public image such wording favours in the readers, rather than worrying about style and subtle rhetorics. On the whole, theirs is a strategy that pragmatically is part of a positive politeness process, when the speaker seeks in-grouping in order to be accepted by the interlocutor, and not seen as an intruder.[53]

On other occasions, God's blessing is referred to as a special gift bestowed on the healer, who, because of this, indirectly proclaims him/herself particularly valuable. It is the case of James Tilborgh (very probably a relative of Cornelius'):[54]

> This is to give notice by these Papers, That there is a very expert famous outlandish Doctor, and Citizen of Hambourgh, who is lately arrived here in London, and hath brought by God's blessing, a wonderful Art with him (C112f9[7])

And of Dr John Case, who claims that "after much Pains and great Cost in the said Art [alchemy], [he] hath at length, by the Blessing of God, Attained a most noble Universal Medicine" (C112f9[13]).

The common belonging to Christianity signalled by the appeal to God is reinforced by the formula "The Poor may have Advice for Nothing",[55] used to

53 See Brown and Levinson, pp. 112–17 for the in-grouping strategy as part of the process of positive politeness.

54 See Thompson, pp. 90–92.

55 In the handbills there is no hint of religious differences even if the texts under scrutiny date to the second half of the seventeenth century, i.e. a time with strong divisions among residual Puritans and Anglicans, but also obsessed by the fear of a prospective Catholic king before the Glorious Revolution.

emphasise the charitable attitude of the bill's writer, thus complying – in a way – with King Henry VIII's "Quacks' Charter", issued to combat physicians' and surgeons' greedy fees. Those practitioners who adopted this exact phrase are only 19 in the corpus; some of them hasten to add "and proper Medicines at reasonable Rates", though, as in C112f9[25], or "And approv'd remedies at reasonable rates" (551a32[168]), thus limiting the range of their supposed Christian charity.

A Question of Professionalism

In order to delete any morally negative shadow from their professional status, and to highlight that they were no greedy profiteers of mankind's illnesses (one of the major accusations addressed to them), many practitioners introduced the following formula into their handbills: "No Cure No Money". It meant simply that they required to be paid only after a patient's recovery.[56] What is found in the London handbills does not correspond to what Gianna Pomata has studied about the laws issued by the medical authorities (the Protomedicato) in early modern Bologna, since in this Italian city itinerant medical professionals obtained licences to practice according to very different procedures from those followed in London, and also because in Bologna the agreements between a healer and a patient were very strict and anything but indulgent towards the doctor. In fact, they defined the duration of the cure and the fees, but also the details of the contractual obligations of the healer who was prosecuted by the Protomedicato judges in the event of non-compliance: "in other words, patients were to pay only if they had been healed, and not otherwise".[57]

London irregular practitioners who had the phrase "No Cure No Money" printed in their handbills were not subject to any authority on that issue, simply because their words had no legal value beyond what could be considered morally fair. In spite of this, they did write that phrase as a declaration of fairness, indeed, and as a warranty of their commitment and obligations. However, the ferocious satires against the "horse quacks", i.e. practitioners who performed on horseback only to be readier to run away in case of failure of the promised cure, are famous and testify to the disloyal behaviour of many false physicians.[58]

56 This formula might also echo a statement asserting a principle of negotiation on a patient's part. However, in the corpus there is no trace of this specific meaning.

57 Gianna Pomata, *Contracting a Cure* (1998), p. xvi. See the "Appendix" in Pomata's volume for some documents attesting these contracts. On the Italian licensing system in early modern times, see Gentilcore, *Medical Charlatanism*, pp. 118–51.

58 See Chapter 5 below.

Some handbills try and explain what the phrase "No Cure No Money" meant. For example, a

> most Renowned Doctor, whose Great Skill, and good Success in Curing all Venereal Distempers, [and who] hath been most Eminently approved at the Hospital in PARIS, and at the LAZARETTO, the Hospital in VENICE

maintains that

> Now for to let the World know his Integrity, and upright and honest dealing, he maketh this Agreement, That he will not have any Money for his Pains and Medicines until half a Year after that the Patient hath been perfectly Cured: That is to say plainly,
> No Cure, No Money. (C112f9[51])

Another, even more detailed case, is represented by a H. Lippen, who definitely states fees and times for his cures, in order to convince his readers of his complete honesty:

> He would not have you think he aims at high Prices, or makes it his business to get great store of Money: No, in truth, he is none of those; he will give you to understand his Terms, (which are very reasonable) before he undertakes you, that you may not be cheated.
>
> This is the Agreement with all his Patients that are afflicted with the abovesaid Distempers; He takes no money for his Trouble or Medicines till a quarter of a Year after the Cure is perform'd, and they have left off their Trusses or Bands: And then as a reward for the same, requires the sum of Fourty shillings, for those who are not able Thirty shillings. And for those that have no money, and desire it for Gods sake, he will cure Gratis. (551a32[46])

In both cases the use of the word AGREEMENT has to be underlined, because it resounds with its commercial usage: if, on the one hand, it shows the healer's will to appear straight and law-abiding, on the other it manifests the commodification of health, the cure of which can be contracted in the market square.

As I have tried to discuss in this chapter, the marketing of medicines, which spread later into the mercuries and journals and which had already appeared in almanacs,[59] relied specifically on the sellers' voices, on what John Donne calls

---

59 See E. S. Turner, *The Shocking History of Advertising* (1952), and Juanita Burnby, "Pharmaceutical Advertisement" (1988). Regarding the presence of advertisements in almanacs, Louise Curth writes: "[they] have three unique benefits. In the first place, almanacs were the first true British mass media which were printed in their hundreds of thousands every year and which began to carry advertisements in the late sixteenth century. The first advertisements in newspapers, on the other hand, are generally agreed as appearing in the 1620s. Secondly, advertisements in almanacs had a long

the "Mountebankes drugtongue" ("Fourth Satire", l. 41), in the double version of oral delivery and printed advertisements. The authors of both demonstrate that they are fully conscious of the persuasive possibilities of their means which, in spite of being often accused of naivety and ingenuousness, they refined to a high level of complexity, thus anticipating future theories of advertising discourse and showing a thorough, practical understanding of the power of their medium.[60]

Theirs was a form of public communication full of subjective markers, axiological force and evaluative words because quacks had to conquer their addressees by getting them to feel individually included among the 'happy few' so privileged as to meet such healers. The affectivity emerging from this type of documents is targeted at the readers' and listeners' bodily needs, the necessity of curing the widespread diseases which even expensive academic medicine could not cope with as yet. And quacks succeeded in that, at least judging by the acrimony of the College of Physicians' attacks and legal prosecution against them, and – to quote a literary source – by Sir Politic Would-Be's fascination at listening to Scoto of Mantua's art of speaking, when the knight, charmed and taken in by Volpone's disguise, exclaims "Is not his language rare?" (Jonson, II.1.112).

---

life span, for unlike handbills or newspapers they would remain in use for an entire year. This meant that individual advertisements might be seen a number of times by the same reader, which is an important tool in creating both demand and brand awareness for commercialized medicines. Finally, the distribution of almanacs meant that their advertisements had the potential to reach a local, regional, national and even international audience." ("Medical Advertising in the Popular Press" (2006), p. 31). For an analysis of the language of eighteenth-century advertising in newspapers, I refer again to Maurizio Gotti' articles.

60 Besides what has already been suggested about advertising discourse, see Geoffrey N. Leech, *A Linguistic Study of Advertising in Great Britain* (1966), esp. pp. 25–31.

5 Quacks and the Media

> [I]t is incredible, and scarce to be imagin'd, how the Posts of Houses, and Corners of Streets were plaster'd over with Doctors Bills, and Papers of ignorant Fellows; quacking and tampering in Physick,[…] with such flourishes as these, (*viz.*) INFALLIBLE preventive Pills against the Plague. NEVER FAILING Preservatives against the Infection. SOVERAIGN Cordials against the Corruption of the Air. EXACT Regulations for the Conduct of the Body, in Case of an Infection […]
>
> (Daniel Defoe, *A Journal of the Plague Year*)

> "What is the use of a book", thought Alice, "without pictures or conversation?"
>
> (Lewis Carroll, *Alice's Adventures in Wonderland*)

This is not the place to discuss the development of periodical printing as a medium in English culture because much has been studied by specialists,[1] and, even more importantly, because up to now the fact that irregular practitioners used print in a functional way has always been stressed. When newspapers and journals started to circulate, their advertisements found an appropriate home in the new medium, but – at least during the first decades of the eighteenth century – such ephemera as handbills and broadsides continued to be distributed.[2] A feature present in handbills, though, tended to disappear in the columns of the periodical print, that is, images.[3] It is true that not all the handbills in the two British Library Collections under scrutiny have pictures (only *c.* 15 per cent of them all have an image, although many others are decorated in a simpler way with borders), but the fact that a good percentage of them presents illustrations testifies to the practitioners' consciousness that the use of a dual medium (images

---

1 See, among others, Joad Raymond, *The Invention of the Newspaper* (2008), and *Pamphlets and Pamphleteering.*

2 Harley 5931, which also includes cuttings printed in red ink, has fewer illustrated quacks' handbills than the other two collections, while accumulating various and sundry items concerning different fields (theatre bills, announcements of spectacular shows of wondrous people or artifacts…). Because of the small size of many of these advertisements, one is tempted to consider them rather cuttings from newspapers than handbills (there are real handbills, though, as can be evidenced by comparing them with copies existing in the other two collections).

3 The 'conversation' invoked by Alice was necessarily absent from handbills, even if the 'dialogue' between writers and their prospective patients remained open, as the use of the second person pronouns (outlined in the previous chapter) clearly shows.

and written language) enhanced the memorability of their stuff.[4] In this chapter some illustrated handbills will be analysed on the one hand, and, on the other, one of the harangues present in D. G.'s anthology will be read together with the images that happened to accompany it, as a testimony of the use of print also by the opponents of quackery.

Capitals, Italics, and Images

In the famous passage printed as the first epigraph to this chapter Daniel Defoe – writing his *Journal of the Plague Year* still at a time when quacks 'swarmed' in London and when the satire against them was at its most ferocious, furthermore relating a specific historical moment when irregular practitioners flowered in the city soon after the Restoration – summarises the impact of quacks' handbills on a population struck by the deadly pestilence in 1665, and shows a profound perception of the visual techniques used by such medicasters (1722, p. 36). Defoe's first printers reproduced in the novel the series of capital letters present in many handbills so as to help the reader visualise the bills, besides capturing their flavour by using hyperbolical adjectives.

So far in this book the language of quacks, apart from some passing references, has been analysed only from the verbal point of view, while here I would like to focus on paratextual features such as typographic fonts, formats, and images.

Fonts

Roy Porter claims that the format and layout of seventeenth-century handbills were simple and naïve, so to say: "The maximum possible number of words was crammed on to the sheet [...] the paucity of eye-catching illustrative material is noteworthy".[5] This is only partly true, because there are examples of ingenious woodcuts in some handbills, and printers (mostly anonymous) showed they were able to catch the eye of the reader, often simply by using diversified typefaces.[6]

---

4 Memorability is one of the categories Leech interprets as necessary for an advertisement to be efficacious, together with Attention Value, Readability, and Selling Power: "Advertising has to make a lasting impression if it is to affect buying behaviour" (Leech, p. 28).

5 Porter, *Quacks*, p. 165.

6 "The printers of these items [handbills] are not normally identified on the page, but were likely the owners of small workshops or corner presses, the term for a business with one press run by a printer who was also a designer and printseller." (Furdell, *Publishing and Medicine*, pp. 143–45).

Joseph Addison, writing *The Tatler* n. 224 (for September 12–14, 1710), dwells on advertisements in general, noticing their position in a paper and their social and personal function ("they are instruments of ambition", he says, because "a man that is by no means big enough for the *Gazette*, may easily creep into the advertisements"). They also serve "to inform the world where they may be furnished with almost everything that is necessary for life".[7] Later, he extols "the great art in writing advertisements", which

> is the finding out a proper method to catch the reader's eye; without which, a good thing may pass over unobserved, or be lost among commissions of bankrupt. Asterisks and hands were formerly of great use for this purpose. Of late years, the *N.B.* has been much in fashion; as also little cuts and figures [...] I must not here omit the blind Italian character, which being scarce legible, always fixes and detains the eye, and gives the curious reader something like the satisfaction of prying into a secret. (p. 151)

What appears particularly noteworthy is that the principle outlined by Addison at the beginning of the eighteenth century ("to catch the reader's eye") is still the basis of our contemporary visual publicity.[8] Certainly it was what also guided the quacks of the previous century.

Maurizio Gotti points out that capitalization is a technique "skillfully exploited by 18th-century advertisers [...] Indeed, the non-capitalized words are semantically and pragmatically less important".[9] In seventeenth-century handbills, however, nearly all lexical words are capitalized according to coeval printing conventions, so that in addition to initial capital letters other devices are used to stress certain words or phrases. The passage from Defoe's *Journal* shows one of these devices, that is total capitalization, thus highlighting the habitual way of medical publicity of catching the reader's attention with something pre-verbal, i.e. an appeal to the reader's sight with printing stratagems, one of which being the very dimension of printing fonts. Even undecorated handbills employ a great variety of fonts. An example is John Case's document selling a "**Cure for a Clap**", a phrase printed centre page in a blackletter typeface very similar in dimension to

---

7 Joseph Addison, *The Tatler* n. 224 (12–14 September, 1710), in *The Tatler* (1898), IV, pp. 148, 150.

8 The already mentioned steps for an advert to be successful – "1 attract attention; 2 arouse interest; 3 stimulate desire; 4 create conviction; 5 get action" (Vestergaard and Schrøder, p. 49) are the same as those also pursued by the effective, though perhaps ingenuous, seventeenth-century quacks.

9 "Linguistic and Stylistic Features" (2008), p. 377.

a modern 28-point font (C112f9[14]).[10] The cure is advertised as "*most infallible, and Sure, Cheap, Secret, Safe, and Speedy*" in a previous line printed in *c.* 14-point italics, a remedy good for the "**Running of the Reins**" in roman typeface, but bold and in a larger dimension (about 36 points), followed by "**FRENCH-POX**" printed bold and all capitalized, of the same size as the latter. It is evident that the crescendo strategy-through-letters fixes the reader's attention on synonyms of venereal diseases, which were unfortunately widespread in London society at the end of the seventeenth century, as already highlighted by the high frequency of word tokens referring to them in the handbills. The rest of the text, with the usual hyperbolic language of quacks, informs readers about various medicines sold by **John Case** ("an Approved and Licensed Physician, and Student in *Astrology*" he defines himself), whose name, occurring twice on the leaflet, uses blackletter once again (but smaller). The body of the text is in roman typeface, but here and there italics appear, especially for lists of diseases, and for the address of this irregular practitioner. No image is present, neither are there "asterisks and hands", but the impact of the whole is highly visual; words and their meanings (something socially relevant but confined by prudery to the private sphere) first of all engage the reader's sight, which is guided, as it were, by the provocative size and forms of the characters in construing further connotative meaning.

In order to realize how heedful printers (and quacks) were as to the layout of their handbills, suffice it to say that there exists another version of John Case's leaflet, which also uses blackletter for "**French POX**" (of the same size as "Clap" in the previously analyzed bill), eliminates the bold font for the "Running of the REINS" and at the same time reduces the dimension of the characters (C112f9[104]). But, as is visible from my attempt at reproduction, some relevant words are all in capitals. One might wonder why there are these two versions: we can only judge from our modern reaction to them, no witness of contemporary reception existing. Certainly the use of the same size or of the same facetype unites words, ordering them in one semantic field and creating meaningful links between them.[11] As for the use

10 The *ESTC* dates this handbill *c.* 1695. It is also collected in Harley 5931: it has no number, but is followed by a bill numbered 69.

11 A similarly careful use of fonts is present in E. M.'s handbill publicizing "The Universal Scorbutick Pills", printed in 1675 (C112f9[50]), and in Nathaniel Lomax, *Delaun Reviv'd* (1680[?]), a booklet of twelve pages extolling "Delaun's Pills" and offering some "receipts". But the use of different typefonts is a well spread habit also at the beginning of the century: an early seventeenth-century example is Jacobus Maximinus's handbill, advertising "Foure most strange and rare Artificiall Stones" useful for the cure of many a disease (*Whereas the Professor hereof, Iacobus Maximinus* (1622); in the EEBO

of blackletter, in itself less legible than roman typefonts, it certainly enhances the visibility of a word embedded in a differently printed passage, conferring on it an aura of antiquity and authority. William Caxton's *cedula* mentioned in Chapter 1 was necessarily, given the times, printed in blackletter, and so was Master Gervaes's decorated bill – the oldest surviving medical advertisement – probably printed by William Copland around 1550.[12] But when the roman type had become the most widely used, to decide to print a text, or parts of its, in blackletter acquired some specific meaning. Blackletter fonts were still widely used for the printing of ballads and, especially, to publicise government documents; therefore they were both familiar and authoritative, even though progressively substituted by roman typefaces.[13] Furthermore the use of italics, which according to Addison "gives the curious reader something like the satisfaction of prying into a secret", certainly attracts attention and arouses interest, connected as they are in this case to what makes one suffer.

Hands and Asterisks

As for the "asterisks and hands" mentioned by Addison, especially the latter, they are present in many seventeenth-century handbills.[14] But these were also used in longer types of publications, such as pamphlets containing directions to patients. For example, Lomax's *Delaun Revived* (p. 3) has a well printed hand with a pointing finger in a line introduced by "Note also", so that words and sign coincide and stress meaning reciprocally. 'Hands' are particularly frequent towards the end of the century (in 1710 Addison, actually, refers to them as "formerly of great use"): not all handbills, though, resort to this device – which is, in any case, a tool to embellish the print and make it more interesting from the visual point of view – so that the majority of quacks' production consists of a short title and a thick text in a small typeset. Given the extant documents, I would surmise that only successful

---

Collection). Here blackletter prevails and there is no large-sized character, the only decoration being James I's coat of arms at the centre top of the page.

12 Thompson dates it around 1525 (p. 27), while Furdell locates it ten years later (*Publishing and Medicine*, p. 142). It is held in the Royal College of Surgeons of England Library.

13 See H. E. Rollins, "The Black-Letter Broadside Ballad" (1919), and Fox, pp. 299–334.

14 Sometimes pointing hands added in handwriting by readers are to be found in printed matters, thus demonstrating that the use of 'hands' was a widely spread convention not only in advertising print, but also among readers desirous to mark a relevant passage in a book. Numerous examples are in John Cotta, *A True Discouery* (1617), pp. 12–17 (copy in the British Library).

and famous empirics used pointing hands; or, seeing things from another standpoint, only those who had enough money to pay more refined printers.

Cornelius à Tilburg is the clearest example of those quacks whose handbills present both asterisks and hands. The *Calendar of State Papers, Domestic Series* registers that on 2 October 1682 Cornelius, "practitioner in physic and chirurgery", asked "to be sworn one of the King's chirurgeons" because he had won King Charles II's trust by "taking 60 grains of auripigmentum and arsenic" and surviving after ingesting his own antidote.[15] The request resulted in Tilburg being honoured with the title of "one of his Majesty's chirurgeons in ordinary". He came from Germany, like many other empirics of the time, and also worked in London under King William. His extant handbills, always decorated with the royal coat of arms and – often – with phrases in Latin, display a rich variety of devices, from blackletter to italics, from asterisks to pointing hands. Of course, Cornelius à Tilburg is not the only quack to use hands in his bills: an anonymous "*Doctor* [...] who (by the Blessing of God) performs, with great Ease and Dexterity all manner of Cures and Distempers incident to the Bodies of Men, Women and Children" uses hands lavishly (551a32[21]). After the quack's self-presentation, the text of the handbill lists six cures on sale, the wording of each of which is preceded by pointing fingers (besides being printed in individual paragraphs, and therefore highlighted).

Images and Decorations

Even if the majority of surviving handbills have an inconspicuous appearance, thus conveying their writers' deep trust in the literacy of prospective buyers who were evidently supposed to be able at least to skim through the tight characters and understand what the whole thing was about, a good number of them have at least one decorative feature. This may be a simple woodcut frame, or the image of a shining sun,[16] or the coat of arms of the sovereign of the time. This last decoration is highly significant, since it implies either the writer's loyalty or a royal patronage, or both (this is the case with Cornelius à Tilburg's production after 1682, i.e. after he was appointed "one of his Majesty's chirurgeons in ordinary").[17]

15 *Calendar of State Papers, Domestic Series, of the Reign of Charles II: 1682* (1860), p. 450.

16 A sun is printed on Salvator Winter Sr's first handbill (Salvator Winter, *Nothing without God* (1647)), while Charles II's coat of arms is reproduced in other handbills of the Winter family (for the activity of the Winters, see Chapter 6 below).

17 Tilburg's bill selling his "True Orvietan, or Antidote" presents both the coat of arms of the English monarchy and a double-headed eagle, to denote the practitioner's new and old countries. A double-headed eagle, widely present in European heraldry,

In one case only, of all the bills of the two collections, has a royal coat of arms a preponderant position on the page: the anonymous handbill of the "Italian Doctor, *who never was any Stage-Quack or Mountebank*", printed on both sides of the sheet like most handbills, shows a huge Stuart coat of arms occupying two thirds of the printing area (C112f9[150]). The text follows on the rest of the page and on the *verso*, but there is no cramming of letters. Apart from commenting on the pride of the 'Doctor' in maintaining that no activity of his is similar to those of the so ferociously denigrated quacks, one can say that the enlarged size of the symbol of royalty may signify a statement of the deep loyalty of the foreign doctor to his new home.

The homage paid by the Italian 'Doctor' to his new country contrasts with the permanence of symbols connecting a practitioner to his/her foreign origins. For example, the handbill of Ann Laverenst, the already mentioned "German-*Gentlewoman*" who offered her services "To LADIES and All others of the FEMALE SEX", shows only a double-headed eagle at the centre top of the page, probably to advertise at once at a visual level her coming from abroad, before readers started reading (C112f9[26]).[18] This also happens in the handbill of a "most Renowned *Dutch* Operator", which has half of its front-page occupied by the Amsterdam coat of arms (C112f9[128]).

The most ambitious handbills reproduce other types of images: vignettes of the quack-writer's activities and instruments (like those discussed in Chapter 2), self-portraits, emblem-like pictures, and bodily parts. What follows will deal with some I consider among the most striking examples.

John Russel, Professor of Physick

John Russel, active in London about 1680, had at least three handbills printed with a central text surrounded by illustrations which, although they may seem artless woodcuts, show in a very clear way the practice of this self-appointed "Professor of Physick" (C112f9[1], C112f9[148]).[19]

---

might also be associated with the Byzantine Empire and with the Russian kingdom, but the most immediate interpretation leads to the Holy Roman Empire and to many German cities.

18 For women's handbills, see Patricia Crawford, "Printed Advertisements" (1984). I am grateful to Margaret Pelling for pointing this article to my attention and sending it to me; the presence of this image in Ann Laverenst's handbill is not commented upon, though, by Crawford.

19 See also John Russel, *J. Russel, Physician and Ocultist* [Oculist], *at the two Blew-Posts* (1680[?]), in the EEBO Collection. In this handbill the practitioner's face looks older

Figure 7: John Russel's handbill (C112f9[1]). By courtesy of the British Library

The frame (always the same in the three different versions) includes Russel's portrait at the top centre, with instruments for distillation on both sides, to connote that this practitioner – perhaps a iatrochemist – prepared by himself all (or most of) the medicines advertised on the verso of the leaflet (Fig. 7).[20] All the other images – with plenty of crude and terrifying details – represent individual operations the 'professor' claims to be able to do. Each vignette has a short caption whose function, it seems, is just to reinforce the visual meaning, or to remove any ambiguity. Russel does not conceal that his operations are painful: in spite of some faces showing no suffering, others have tears in their eyes, while drops (of blood) mark the point where the surgeon is working. Each image presents surgery 'in fieri', as it were: apart from one detail without any sign of the 'agent' ("A Rupture cured" at the top left corner, diagonally and symmetrically opposite to "A Rupture Cutting" at the bottom right corner), all pictures show one or two operating hands, detached from the body of the surgeon. The focusing on the patient's body (on the afflicted and suffering bodily part) must have been very efficacious in communicating the ability of this 'doctor' and might be considered equivalent to our modern recordings of surgical operations given to patients when they leave the hospital. Prospective patients, interpreting these images, were enabled to see what they would not see when being operated. The reassuring effect of the images is only twice impaired by the tears flowing from two women's eyes (there are no tears on the men's faces), women being traditionally considered less brave than men. The surgeon's disembodied hands look like

than in the other two handbills; besides Russel has a moustache. The last but one line of the front text reads: "I should have forborn Publishing Papers if I had not been Reported Dead, etc." This wording may be interpreted as due to the real necessity to let people know that he – although old – was still working, but also as a communicative device in order to regain the market at a time of scant business. A similar bill is in Harley 5931, but its text is completely different; apparently the illustrated frame was used by a Tho. Craven "who married the widow of those two famous Physicians [Dr Russel and Dr George Jones]" because of its complexity and (perhaps) fame. Some pictures are changed and some captions are replaced: the overall look is that of an old and worn-out typographical mould. (It appears to be unnumbered, but is preceded by a n. 72 bill, and followed by n. 79.)

20 A practitioner's portrait is also in the handbill of "Doctor *James Tilborgh*" (as previously hypothesized, a relation of Cornelius à Tilburg). It shows a richly dressed man with a chirurgical instrument in his right hand (and two others lying on a table behind him). He is holding something with the tool: either a stone extracted from a patient's bladder, or a cyst. The text, however, deals only with cures for the French pox (C112f9[7]).

a popular surviving memory of the hands so often portrayed in emblems in the sixteenth and early seventeenth centuries, only that the metaphysical or esoteric aura of emblems has here yielded to a very physical meaning and everybody could read the rest of the picture in its omitted details: the hands belonged to the doctor. What is interesting is that the pictures are somewhat at variance with the main text which, although partly different in the three versions, does not describe the images. It is clear, then, that these pictures are something added to the words, a pictorial shortcut to summarise ideas and avoid long explanations, while passing information efficiently.[21]

Venus and the French Pox

Both dated around 1700 by the *ESTC*, there are two particular handbills advertising cures for venereal diseases. They differ from the many others of the same tone (among which the "Cure for a Clap" mentioned above),[22] because they use the etymology of the disease itself to introduce their texts. *Venus with her Crown* is anonymous (C112f9[142]), while *A Caveat to the Unwary: Or, Venus Unveil'd* is by "T. Clark, M.D.", who declares himself the son of "one of Charles I's Chief Physicians" (C112f9[179]). Both practitioners use an image of the goddess of love to illustrate their advertisements. "*VENUS* with her CROWN" is addressed to "all Persons […] that hath been sporting in *Venus* Garden", thus making use of metaphors in order to connote both sexual activity and its results. The goddess is on a chariot driven by Cupid, who is on the point of darting one of his arrows (Fig. 8).

21 A layout similar to Russel's is to be found in *The Famous Water of Talk and Pearl* (C112f9[126]), a handbill publicizing cosmetic products and datable around 1670. The images here – all of them of instruments for distillation with burning fires and alembics – point at the representation of the sophisticated production process of the waters and ointments advertised by the printed text, not a word of which, though, refers to chemistry. Images, though, qualify the products as highly reliable *because* technologically guaranteed (see Chapter 6 below).

22 Because of the dangerous spread of venereal diseases in London, the handbills promising adequate cures are the majority in the collections here analysed (more than 50 per cent of the total; see Siena, "'The 'Foul Disease'", p. 204).

Figure 8: *Venus with her Crown* (C112f9[142]). Detail. By courtesy of the British Library

Venus, with a crown on her head, is holding a threatening-looking spear. The figure floating in the air and flying towards Venus, possibly a roughly designed Mercury, carries a caduceus (or a rod of Asclepius), meaning the protection of medicine against the dangerous "sport of Venus".[23] The connection between image and text is very close: the "Right Medicine Master […] High Renowned Operator, Artist, Master, or Traveller", as the writer calls himself, has arrived in London because he "is informed that many Thousands of people are troubled with these distempers & symptoms [those relating to syphilis]". The text of the handbill is also linked to the image by a caption in rhyming couplet: "The sight hereof will make you for to think; | But the blessing of God, we after hint.": the parallel between the emblem tradition and this late and popular interpretation is thus reinforced.

---

23 Here Mercury also signifies the substance which was at the basis of so many (dangerous) cures against the French pox.

The other handbill making use of an image of Venus is quite different: in a leafy frame a woman is portrayed lying in bed, her body disfigured by scales and spots (Fig. 9).

Figure 9: *A Caveat to the Unwary: Or, Venus Unveil'd* (C112f9[179]). Detail. By courtesy of the British Library

A bearded and horned (?) man is raising a sheet, so as to make the woman visible by 'unveiling' her. Probably the male figure is Mercury once again, and his 'horns' are what is left of the winged cap he usually wears in many ancient images.[24] At the foot of the bed kneels Cupid, his hands concealing his sorrow at the sight, while his bow hangs on the wall. Instead of the triumphing and menacing goddess of the previous handbill, here the results of that 'triumph' are grimly represented. The pessimism of the image goes hand in hand with the title of the bill: "A Caveat to the Unwary: Or, VENUS Unveil'd" (Latin is used also for a short phrase – "In maximis meis Doloribus" – attributable to the suffering Venus, and printed in the space between the male and the female figures). Doctor Clark, evidently, aimed at

24 The horned man might also represent a devil or, rather, a satyr (especially if what shows behind him is interpreted as the mythological figure's horse- or goat-tail), thus being connected to the wanton and licentious life leading to venereal diseases.

scaring his prospective customers (the "Martyrs to Venus"), even if he claims to have issued "this Bill as a Precaution".[25] To patients affected by venereal diseases he offers, though, his "singular Skill" which he contrasts with any "Medicastors[']". The image may also be interpreted as a staged display of the words of the title: the lying figure speaks (Latin) and the drapery with its curtain and part of a bed canopy reminds the reader of a theatrical scene representing a heroine's death. For the position of the female body, the death of Cleopatra in William Shakespeare's *Antony and Cleopatra* would be the most obvious analogue, were it not that the canopy strangely resembles the decoration of Imogen's bed during Iachimo's deceit in the engraving preceding the text of *Cymbeline* in Nicholas Rowe's edition of Shakespeare's plays.[26] Very probably either sleeping Imogen or dying Cleopatra were in the mind of Clark's anonymous printer, who reproduced a theatrical moment on his cheap page, using a type of decoration which Rowe's publisher also found appealing shortly after. Doctor Clark, who claims to be a regular practitioner, seems to address a variegated audience: certainly all those affected by the French pox, but among them a more sophisticated sort of patient: people with a little Latin, those who were conversant with paintings representing Cleopatra's death, and theatregoers.

The cases discussed here, together with the comments to figures 1 and 2 in Chapter 2, show that authors (writer and printer) of the few fully decorated handbills understood the power of the interaction of image and word. Sometimes images proved even more efficacious in transmitting the essential meaning of the words to follow (certainly they caught the reader's eye sooner and much more effectively than the verbal text), and smaller devices such as asterisks and pointing hands guided the very act of reading. Practitioners and printers seem to have been very conscious of the paratextual implications of all this, i.e. that the 'look' of print is a "lieu privilégié d'une pragmatique et d'une stratégie, d'une action sur le public" [a privileged place for pragmatic strategies, for an action towards the public].[27]

Print and Anti-Quack Satire

As seen in Chapter 1, attacks against irregular medical practitioners started quite early in English culture, whether they were simple mountebanks or physicians

25 'Venus' occurs 38 times in the handbills corpus, mainly in the cluster 'sporting in the Garden of Venus', i.e. a euphemistic way of mentioning dangerous – but pleasurable – sexual activities leading to venereal diseases.

26 *The Works of Mr William Shakespeare*, 6 vols (1709), VI.

27 Gérard Genette, *Seuils* (1987), p. 8.

who had graduated outside England. Such vitriolic assaults were generally embedded in thick volumes dealing with problems connected to the medical profession in general: it is the case, for example, of John Securis's *Detection and Querimonie of the Daily Enormities and Abuses Committed in Physick* (1566), but also of John Cotta's *A True Discovery of the Empiricke* (1617) and of Dr Primerose's *Popular Errours* (1651).[28] No such lengthy work as Sonnet De Courval's *Satyre contre les Charlatans et Pseudomedecins Empyriques* (1610), though, was ever devoted by an English writer to the phenomenon. Neither was a treatise like Giovanni Domenico Ottonelli's *Della christiana moderatione del theatro libro, detto L'ammonitioni a' recitanti* (1652), which – as seen in Chapter 1 – mixes the condemnation of medicine vendors with the author's barbs against booth-stage players. In the second half of the seventeenth century, anyway, criticism intensified especially in the pamphlet format, that is, in publications of a limited number of pages and of smaller size (some of the works whose titles have been used in Chapter 4 testify to this fact). Irregular practitioners, especially in London, more and more often became the target of satires both because of some extravagant behaviours of theirs, and – mainly – because of the danger they represented for the Collegiate Physicians. But, as the dedicatory letter to Mr William Winter in D. G.'s *Harangues* demonstrates, they also became popular as sources of entertainment. Writing to his reader, D. G. declares his hope of procuring mirth by "treating of what you us'd to divert your self with in *Moorefields, Covent-Garden, &c.*", thus documenting that quacks were 'comedians' and caterers of entertainment (*Harangues*, fol. 1^{r-v}). These two aspects, virulent satire and recreation, seem actually to be joined in many short publications of the period (including broadsides), while the fashion for writing about and against quacks really burst out at the turn of the seventeenth and in the first decades of the eighteenth century. Ned Ward's *The London Spy*, Part I, was first published in 1698 (the first publication in book form was in 1703, which also included Part VI with the attack on quacks and on horse-quacks in particular); the anonymous *Modern Quack* (possibly attributable to the physician Daniel Turner) appeared in 1718, later reprinted with variations and a slightly different title in 1752; its 'continuation', so to say, *A Bold Challenge to the Whole Colledge of Physicians* was issued around 1740.[29]

---

28 See also John Cotta, *A Short Discouerie* (1612).

29 Both *The Modern Quack* and *A Bold Challenge* were printed for J. Roberts in Warwick Lane, that is, in the same street where the College of Physicians had its headquarters, thus corroborating the hypothesis that both works came from Collegiate physicians (in spite of the ironical full title of the latter publication: Anon., *A Bold Challenge to the*

It is this cultural frame that can explain the success of a single-face broadside which, as I hope will be clear at the end of this chapter, had a very long history (and a long story to tell).

Waltho van Claturbank: A Labyrinth of Dates and Data

If one looks up 'Waltho van Claturbank' in the British Library Catalogue, one soon finds that it is the name of somebody who wrote (?) an eighteenth-century broadside entitled *Pharmacopola Circumforaneus, or the Horse Doctor's Harangue to the Credulous Mob*, only that Claturbank is a pseudonym, and no real person seems to correspond to it.[30] The first question arises, then, about the identity of this individual. Actually the name is mentioned for the first time as the speaker of a harangue with the above mentioned title in D. G.'s collection (whose first date of publication, as stated elsewhere, is very uncertain, ranging from 1700 to the 1760s).[31] The uncertainty about the publication date is analogous to everything concerning Waltho's speech and is the keynote of its subsequent editions. Indeed, almost certainly for its strong satirical content, this speech was often reproduced in broadsides (these, too, of uncertain date) and in the various reprints of D. G's collection.

The British Library also possesses another edition of the booklet which constitutes a uniquely peculiar object, it consisting of the original text interspersed with images and ephemera deriving from sundry sources.[32] Most ephemera are quacks' handbills and newspaper cuttings advertising proprietary medicines; some are engravings of social scenes focusing on quacks' activity; some are broadsides. One of these is a two-column print entitled "Quack Doctor's Speech", with no illustration, which reproduces Waltho van Claturbank's words

---

Whole Colledge of Physicians: or, a Defence of those Practitioners in Physick Commonly Call'd Quacks (1740[?]). It is interesting to notice once again that the title of the latter work later mentions female practitioners as *Doctoresses*, a rare word which – according to the *OED* – was first recorded in English in 1577.

30 Christopher Merret (*The Accomplisht Physician*, p. 40) translates "pharmacopola" as "seller of præpared Medicines". The whole phrase "pharmacopola circumforaneus" is used by Cicero for a charlatan selling medicines in a square (*Pro A. Cluentio Oratio* (1920), XIV, p. 40).

31 I am quoting here, as above, from the EEBO copy, corresponding to the BL shelfmark 1038.g.46. I also accept the EEBO dating (1700[?]), while the *ESTC* attributes it to 1725. In it the "Pharmacopola" speech occupies pages 13–19.

32 The tentative date provided for this item, shelfmarked 12330.k.121, is 1725[?]

verbatim.[33] D. G.'s work reappears anonymously in another version, bound with other items in a volume which starts with William Shakespeare's *Julius Caesar*. This clearly dated edition (1762) has a slightly different title: *The Harangues or Speeches of Several Celebrated Quack-doctors, in Town and Country* [...] *By Various Hands*. This version, printed in a smaller typeface than the original, does not respect the page division of its 'forefather', and presents some changes (there are added "several merry receipts, and three mountebank songs"; the last speech in D. G. is omitted, while a new one is added at the beginning).[34]

Besides the above mentioned broadside, though, Waltho's speech is also published in other extant documents: one, printed in Dublin, is cited in the *ESTC* with its *Pharmacopola Circumforaneus* title and presents a three-column lettering;[35] another, similar to the previous one but without title, belongs to the British Museum;[36] a third is identical to the Dublin one, but its engraving is signed "T. Slater, sculp." (Fig. 10).[37] The fourth – simply entitled *The High German Doctor's Speech* – is also datable around the 1730s/40s[?], printed for T[homas]. Kitchin, but there is no entry for it in the *ESTC*.[38] Its lettering is in two columns of elegant italics and the engraving is totally different from that in the previously quoted broadside (Fig. 11).

33 Waltho van Claturbank, *Quack Doctor's Speech* (1760[?]). The edition of the speeches accessible in the ECCO Collection appears to be similar to D. G.'s version, but there are some images added (most of them present also in BL 12330.k.121), whereas the text starts only on p. 11 with the speech of "The Infallible Mountebank, or Quack Doctor", therefore cutting the first pages which include the dedicatory letter and the first two speeches of the original edition.

34 This edition is included in the ECCO collection as a separate item.

35 Waltho van Claturbank, *Pharmacopola Circumforaneus* (1737[?]).

36 This image, printed in London for J. Bowles, has the same engraving as Fig. 10 in this volume; see it at The British Museum Collection online website (according to the web page, it is a "late impression of a print first published in 1713". The date of this reissue is *c.* 1770). The Bodleian Library, Oxford, also has a copy of the speech, without any title (it is reproduced in Katritzky, "Marketing Medicine", p. 139). Other broadsides, similar to van Claturbank's *Quack Doctor's Speech*, continued to be published in the eighteenth century, and at least one of them was also attributed to John Wilmot, 2nd Earl of Rochester ("Supposed to be spoke by the famous Lord Rochester" reads the subtitle of an end-of-century print of the *Quack Doctor's Speech*. In ECCO).

37 T. Slater, *Pharmacopola Circumforaneus* (1700–1750[?]).

38 Anon., *The High German Doctor's Speech* (1730–40[?]). For the date, see the bpi1700 website. This simplified title may cause some confusion because in D. G., *Harangues* there is another speech attributed to a German doctor ("The High German Doctor and the English Fool", pp. 8–11), but the two texts are quite different.

Figure 10: *Pharmacopola Circumforaneus*... By courtesy of the Wellcome Library, London

Figure 11: *The High German Doctor's Speech*. By courtesy of the Wellcome Library, London

THE HIGH GERMAN DOCTOR'S SPEECH.

Gentlemen and Ladies, I Walthe Van Claturbank High German Doctor, Chymist and Dentifricator, Native of Arabia Deserta, Citizen and Burgomaster of ye City of Brandipolis, Seventh Son of a Seventh Son, Unborn Doctor, of above 60 Years Experience; having Studied over Galen, Hypocrates, Albumazar and Paracelsus, am now become the Esculapius of this Age: Having been Educated at 12 Universities, and Travell'd through 52 Kingdoms, and been Counsellor to the Counsellors of several Monarchs, Natural Son of the Wonder working Chymical Doctor Signior Hanesio, lately arriv'd from the farthest Part of Utopia, Famous throughout all Asia, Africa, Europe and America, from the Suns Oriental Exaltation to his Occidental Declination: Out of meer Pity to my own Dear Self, and languishing Mortals, have by ye earnest Prayers and Intreaties of several Lords, Earls, Dukes and Honourable Personages, been at last prevail'd upon to oblige the World with this Notice ....

That all Persons, Young and Old, Blind or Lame, Deaf or Dumb, Curable or Incurable, may Know where to repair for Cure, in all Cephalalgia's, Paralytick Paroxysms, Palpitations of the Pericardium, Empyemas, Syncopes and Nasieties, arising either from a Plethory or a Cacochymy, Vertiginous Vapours, Hydrocephalus, Dyssenterys, Odontalgic or Podagrical Inflammations, Iliac Passions, Icterical Effusions, Exanthemata, ye Hen Pox, the Hog Pox, the Whores Pox, and ye Small Pox, ye Ascites Tympanites, Anasarca, and ye entire Legion of Lethiferous Distempers.

Imprimis, Gentlemen, I have a never failing Styptic, Corroborating, Odoriferous, Anodinous, Balsamic Balsam of Balsams, made of dead Mens Fat, Rosin, and Goose Grease; which infallibly Restores Lost Maidenheads, Raises Demolish'd Noses, and by its Abstersive, Cosmetic Quality, preserves Superannuated Bawds from Wrinkles. Item, I have the True Carthramophra of the Tripple Kingdom, my never failing Heliogenes, being ye Tincture of ye Sun, deriving Vigor, Influence, and Dominion from ye same Light: It causes all Complexions to laugh or smile, at the very Time of Taking it: Is 7 Years in preparing, and being compleated, secundum Artem by Fermentation, Cohobation, Calcination, Sublimation, Fixation, Philtration, Circulation and Quidlibitification, in Balneo Mariae, Crucible and Fixatory, the Athanor, Cucurbita and Reverberatory is the only Sovereign Medicine in the World. This is Natures Palladium, Healths Magazine, it Works 7 manner of Ways, in order as Nature, her self, requires, for it scorns to be confin'd to any particular way of Operation; so that it effecteth the Cure, either Hypnotically, Hydrotically, Cathartically, Poppismatically, Hydrogogically, Pneumatically, or Synechdochically: it Mundifies the Hypogastrium, wipes off abstersively, those tenacious conglomerated sedimental Sordes that adhere to the Oesophagus and Viscera; Extinguishes all Supernatural Fermentations and Ebullitions, and in fine Annihilates all Nosotrophical Morbific Ideas of ye whole Corporeal Compages. A Dram of it is worth a Bushel of March Dust: For if a Man chance to have his Brains beat out or his Head chop'd off, 2 Drops (I say) 2 Drops Gentlemen, seasonably apply'd, will recall the fleeting Spirits, reinthrone the deposed Archeus, Cement the discontinuity of the Parts and in 6 Minutes restore the lifeless Trunk to all its pristine Functions, Vital, Natural and Animal: So that this believe me Gentlemen, is the only Sovereign ... Remedy in the World. I have the chiefest Antipudenda Gragran Specific in Venus's Regalia, which infallibly Cures the French Pox, with all its train of Gonorrheas, Bubo's and Shankers, Carnositys, Phymosis, Paraphymosis, Christalline, Priapismus, Caudalomata, and Ragades, without Baths and Stoves, and that with as much Pleasure as the same was contracted: so that its worth any Persons while to get the modish Distemper once a Fortnight, if it be to be had for Love or Money, to enjoy the Benefit of so Diverting a Remedy. I have the Panchymagogon of Hermes-Trismegistus, an Incomparable Spagyric Tincture of ye Moons Horns, which is the only infallible Antidote against the contagion of Cuckoldom. Besides my Vermifugus Pulvis, or Antivermatical Worm conquering Powder, so famous for destroying all ye sorts of 'em, incident to humane Bodies, breaking their complicated Knots in ye Duodenum, and dissolving ye Phlegmatick Crudities that produce these Anthropophagous Vermin: it hath brought away Worms by Urine, as long as the May-Pole in ye Strand, when it flourish'd in its Primitive Prolixity, tho' I confess not altogether so thick. Look ye Gentlemen, I have it under the Hands and Seals, of all yt Greatest Sultans, Sophys, Bashas, Viziers, Chams, Serasquires, and Muftis, &c. in Christendom, to verificate ye Truth of my Operations, that I have actually perform'd such Cures, as are really beyond human Abilities.

I Cur'd Prestor John's Godmother, to the great Admiration of all the Court, of a stupendious Dolor about ye Os Sacrum, so that the good Old Lady really feared the Perdition of her Huckle Bone; I did it by fomenting her Posteriors, with a Mummy of Nature, alias call'd Pilgrims Salve, mixt up with the Spirit of Mugwort, tartaragraphated thorow an Alembick of Christalline Transfluency ......

Thence was I sent for to Sultan Gilgon, Despote of Bosnia, who was violently afflicted with the Spasmus, He came to meet me 300 Leagues in a Go Cart: But I gave him so speedy an Acquittance of his Dolor, that the next Night I caused him to dance a Saraband, with Flipflaps and Somersets ....

I Restor'd Virility, and the Comforts of Generation, to above 150 Eunuchs in the Grand Seignior's Seraglio, and by a Pair of Prolific Pills lately caus'd a Vintners Widow, who had been Barren all her Days, to conceive of a Man Child in the Twelfth Lustre of her Age, without the Help of her Husband ....

I Cured likewise the Dutchess of Boromolpho of a Cramp in her Tongue, and the Count de Rodomontado Corrept wth an Iliac Passion, contracted by eating butter'd Parsnips ....

I also Cured an Alderman of Grand Cairo, who had been sick 7 Years of the Plague, in 46 Minutes: And by ye like Empyrical Remedies I lately Cur'd Duke Philorix, of a Dropsy, of wth he Dy'd.

Venienti occurrite Morbo. Down with your Dust ....

Principiis obsta. No Cure, no Money ....

Quaerend Pecunia primum. Be not sick too late ....

N.B. You that are willing to render your selves Immortal, buy this Pacquet, or else repair to the Sign of the Prancers in Vico vulgo dicto Rattlecliffero, something South East of the Templum Danicum, in the Square of Profound Close, not far from Titter Tatter Fair, and you may see, hear, and return, Re-infecta ....

Printed for T. Kitchin, at No. 59, Holborn Hill London.

Figure 10 represents "the doctor above named [Waltho] on horseback in a street, and attended by his zany; the former addresses a crowd of persons who are standing about him; some of them stretch forth their hands to receive papers which he is distributing. A boy with a monkey is in front; likewise a woman seated near a barrow full of fruit"[39], thus respecting the title-image correspondence. Figure 11 shows a mountebank on a stage, accompanied by two zanies, one of whom wears Harlequin's costume, while the other blows a trumpet. On the stage there is also another person, possibly a sick man, seated in an armchair, his right leg raised on a low stool. The mountebank holds a bottle (of medicine) in his left hand and is clearly addressing his audience, among which there are women, men and children.

Evidently, D. G.'s original collection of speeches was a great success: after what can be considered its first edition it was enriched with images, it was anthologized with other texts (no less than one of Shakespeare's plays), and – given the existence of broadsides with passages from it – it helped popularize a literary sub-genre, i.e. that related to anti-quack satire, which throughout the seventeenth century had been sustained especially by regular physicians' medical and polemical writings.[40]

The Anti-Quack Medical Literature

Even Desiderius Erasmus himself seems to have resorted to irregular physicians' medicines. In a letter dated 29 June 1517 the Venetian ambassador in London Sebastiano Giustinian wrote to him, who evidently had been ill, wishing "him better health than the quack medicines (*pillulæ illæ tuæ*) given him by a foolish empiric can procure" and trying to put him on his guard "against physicians, who make no difference in their treatment of horse and man, and sometimes use garlic for aloes (*allium pro aloe*)".[41] Just one year later King Henry VIII founded the College of Physicians of London, which was to become the absolute – and powerful – arbiter of public medicine in the capital. But London citizens (and the British in general) still used folk and popular medicine so that the College flexed its muscles against mountebanks and quacks from the beginning, attacking these irregular practitioners both on professional and on moral grounds. Suffice it to quote from Johann Oberndorff's *The Anatomyes of the True Physition,*

39 *Catalogue of Prints and Drawings in the British Museum Division I*, p. 152, n. 1406.

40 To the bibliographical information already provided, also Roy Porter, *Bodies Politic* (2001) must be added.

41 Sebastiano Giustinian, "Letter to Desiderius Erasmus", in *Letters and Papers, Foreign and Domestic, of the Reign of Henry VIII*, II (1864), n. 3414.

and Counterfeit Mounte-banke, translated into English in 1602. After presenting the "character of a true doctor", the author describes the "Manners and Conditions" of medicine sellers:

> For if a Man consider his [a quack's] Person, he shall finde him Lewd, Shamelesse, a Hater mortall of all Good Men, well seene and practiced in all Couzening, Legerde-maine, Coney-catching, and all other cunning Shifts, & Sleights, a cracking Boaster, Proud, Insolent, a secret Back-biter, a contentious Wrangler, a common Iester, a Lyar, a Busie-body, a Runnagate Wanderer, a Cogging Sycophant, and Trencher-Chaplaine, a covetous Exactor, and Wringer of his Patients: in a word, a Man, or rather Monster, made of a Mixture of all Vices. (Oberndorff, pp. 10–11)[42]

Some years later, the "Doctor in Physicke" John Cotta, who wrote in English "for facilitie of common reading", reiterated the condemnation of quack activities. These people, "vile" and "vnskilfull",

> [w]ithout restraint, make gainefull traffique by botching in physicke; and hereby (besides many wicked practises, juglings, cousinages & impostures, which maske vnespied under the colour and pretence of medicining) numbers of vnwotting innocents daily inthrall, and betray themselves, their liues and safetie, to sustaine the riot, lusts and lawlesse liuing of their enemies & common homicides.[43]

Moral and professional condemnation of quackery continued to be published by physicians, but assaults became more and more satiric and the characters of mountebanks came to be the object of caustic descriptions based on social rather than medical grounds. Probably it was the diffusion of quackery in London, especially in the second half of the seventeenth century and after the plague in 1665, that favoured the production (and, evidently, the favourable reception) of pamphlets against mountebanks and empirics. These latter terms, to recall some information given at the beginning of this volume, had been more and more often supplanted by the word 'quack', used generally to mean somebody who pretended to a profession without being qualified for it, but, in a more precise sense, applied to false physicians or to practitioners who had not obtained a regular licence from the College of Physicians.

42 The physician John Securis had already censured "these sort of fellows which now a days almost in al places so rashly, so fondly and so wickedly do abuse the noble art and science of Phisicke", especially on cultural grounds, accusing them of lacking the necessary "knowledge of the tongues, of the liberall sciences, of Philosophie, of anatomie, of the simples, of the compound medicines, and of the temperatures of complexions" (Securis, fol. Avii^{r}).

43 Cotta, *A Short Discouerie*, fol. A3^{v}, and p. 8.

Among the extant pamphlets containing the term 'mountebank' or 'quack' in their titles, some of which are political satires or parodies of real quacks' books of cures, there is the already introduced *Character of a Quack-Doctor, or, The Abusive Practices of Impudent Illiterate Pretenders to Physick Exposed* which mixes both a physician's reprimand against mountebanks and a more generally satiric vision (1676).[44] Consisting of only six tightly printed pages, it first portrays – as the title announces – "the character of a quack-doctor" beginning with the definition of the term ("*A Quack-Doctor* is one of the Epidemical Diseases of this Age", p. 1), then goes on to describe a quack's behaviour. It is exactly at this point, when the anonymous writer's voice deals with empirics' handbills, that – at last – a possible origin of Waltho van Claturbank's harangue may be found.

The Parody of Quacks' Handbills

After writing about the "Angling Baits" of empirics, i.e. their use of boasts in extolling their nostrums especially when on a stage, the author of *The Character…* observes that the real "Draw-Net" is "a Printed Bill", which serves the false doctor to catch fish "in shoals". The fishing metaphor is very apt to describe the quacks' habit of distributing handbills (and broadsides in the most elegant cases) to advertise their stuff. The author, doubting the literacy of quacks, suggests that

> he [the quack] ingages some Friend that's *Book-Learn'd* to correct the false English, and sprucify the sence, and interlard it with *Proverbial Lattin* and *Crampwords* […] then to a confiding *Printer* he goes […] and then out comes a *Proclamation* of wonders, trickt up in some strange form, with abundance of Inviting *Capitals* and *Inticing Rubricks*, the *Tenour* commonly to this effect […] (p. 3)

thus also revealing his attention to the design of handbills and their paratextual apparatus.

The pamphlet continues with a long, articulated and high-flown passage, written in the third person singular through four paragraphs (as a clear imitation of a true handbill's structure), and in the first person singular in four others. What is transcribed in the Appendix E at the end of this volume is Waltho's speech from

44 The text is also included in Harley 5931[182–85]. From now on quotations from this pamphlet will be signalled in the text. The anonymous *The French Mountebank* (1643, fol. Aiv^{r}) uses the now common frame of a mountebank's speech in order to conceal a political satire when offering a "Cordiall for this languishing Kingdome" and proclaiming the effects of his medicine against the "Caterpillars of the Common-wealth". On the contrary, John Marriott's *The English Mountebank* is a parody of charlatans' books of cures, containing improbable recipes.

D. G.'s anthology, which has been compared with the anonymous parodic bill in *The Character*. The two texts match almost completely. This correspondence has never been noticed by critics, neither have bibliographers traced it when trying to date the broadside and D. G.'s collection of harangues. It is possible to say, then, that Waltho's future speech has more than a simple 'analogue' as early as 1676, and that – while it figures as a direct address, spoken by the "Horse doctor" to a "credulous mob", i.e. oral discourse targeted at a gathering of people – it had been originally invented as a parody of those handbills that quacks handed out at fairs and in London streets.

The lettering of D. G.'s text, and even more so that of the broadsides, uses capitals much more often than its direct source: the "inviting capitals" seem to have undergone, in the rewriting, a process of purposely burlesque inflation. The puffing and bombastic language is the same in the two documents; a lot of far-fetched and sometimes totally invented medical terms occur in both, building up series of alliterative and/or rhyming words in a grotesquely exaggerated accumulation; the satiric attitude is parallel, and the patients 'cured' by the two speakers/writers correspond. Some phrases are placed in a different sequence, but this does not alter the whole; there are, though, some changes worth mentioning. The most relevant one is the inversion of one of the proverbs at the end of the texts: the pamphlet reads "No Mony, no Cure", whereas the "Pharmacopola" speech has "No Cure, No Money". It is not just an inversion of arithmetical addenda, since the meaning changes radically. The former phrase, actually, underlines the quacks' covetousness (= they are ready to cure only if previously paid); the latter means that the irregular practitioner requests to be paid only after the patient's recovery, as has already been observed. In other words, the pamphlet is bitterer against quacks than D. G.'s collection and its derivative broadsides, which simply use a formula widely employed by real quacks in many still existing handbills in order to proclaim their honesty. One of the sayings cited in both works, though, is the Latin "Quærenda pecunia primum" which rather signifies avidity than generosity, thus letting readers glimpse the original meaning under the new word order.

Another significant change occurs in the adjective used for bawds in paragraph 3: *The Character* calls them "super-animated" while they are "superannuated" in the "Pharmacopola". The former adjective, not without poignancy in reference to the busy activity of bawds, might be a printer's mistake; the latter undoubtedly attacks the vanity of old ladies who try to mask their age.[45]

---

45 It is worthwhile noticing that while the source and the broadside use the phrase "modish Distemper" as a synonym of the French pox, the adjective has disappeared

The Haines Case

The first lines of the two texts differ widely from each other in the quack's presentation. The parodic handbill invented in 1676, after printing the address of this fantastic doctor, says that he is "the *Paracelsus* of this age, by name *Seignior Doloso Effrontero*, Native of *Arabia Deserta*, natural Son of the wonder-working Chimest Doctor lately deceased at the *Devils Arse*" (p. 3). The name, clearly reminding the reader of the negative meaning of both its parts, recalls those of Italian irregular practitioners, so frequent in seventeenth-century London, especially during the reign of Charles II. In D. G.'s *Harangues* and in the "Pharmacopola" broadsides deriving from it, on the contrary, not only is the name definitively Dutch and fictitious, but it is also accompanied by many different details and, exceptionally, by the name of a real person:

> Gentlemen, I *Waltho van Claturbank*, High German Doctor, Chymist, and Dentifricator, Native of *Arabia Deserta*, Citizen and Burgomaster of the City of *Brandipolis*, Seventh Son of a Seventh Son, Unborn Doctor of above 60 Years Experience, having studied over Galen, *Hypocrates*, *Albumazar*, and *Paracelsus*, am now become the Æsculapius of this Age. Having been educated at twelve Universities, and travelled through Fifty two Kingdoms, and been Counsellor to the Counsellors of several Monarchs, Natural Son of the Wonder-working Chymical Doctor Signior *HANESIO*, lately arrived from the farthest Parts of Utopia [...][46]

It is likely that the 'old' version from *The Character* was adapted to the new historical situation which, after the Glorious Revolution in 1688 with a Dutch king now on the English throne, saw a lot of Dutch physicians arriving from the Continent. Not only that; Waltho uses all the formulaic paraphernalia of previous and contemporary quackery in proclaiming himself "Seventh Son of a Seventh Son, Unborn Doctor", thus attributing special occult medical powers to his own person.[47] He also declares himself "Citizen and Burgomaster of the City of Brandipolis" and son of "Doctor Hanesio". It is these two very names – Brandipolis and Hanesio – which have prompted some critics to call this text "Joe Haines's

from D. G.'s text (and therefore is not reproduced in the Appendix). Was syphilis less fashionable at the beginning of the eighteenth century than before and afterwards? It does not seem so, at least according to the number of surviving handbills, the majority of which advertise cures against this disease, as often remarked.

46 D. G., *Harangues*, p. 13. My small caps.

47 See Thompson, p. 188.

Speech", connecting it to the Restoration comic actor Joseph Haines (or Haynes), whose name is Italianized as "Hanesio".[48]

Joe Haines, who was praised by Samuel Pepys as early as 7 May 1668 as an "incomparable dancer of the King's House [Theatre Royal, Drury Lane] and a seeming civil man" and a good singer, died in April 1701.[49] In 1702 the satirist Thomas Brown published his *Letters from the Dead to the Living*, reprinted the following year and, later on, as part of Brown's *Works*, in which one of the correspondents from the nether world is Joe Haines.[50] Haines-the-character finds himself in Pluto's capital city, Brandipolis, where he hires a house and sets up as physician and fortune-teller under the name of Giuseppe Hanesio. Therefore the connection between Haines, Brandipolis and medical activities is in a way settled by Brown's work no earlier than 1702, above all because of the proclamation of Hanesio as "Signior Giusippe [*sic*] Hanesio, High German Astrologer and Chymist, Seventh Son of a Seventh Son, Unborn Doctor, of above Sixty Years Experience, Educated in Twelve Universities, having Travell'd through Fifty-two Kingdoms, and been Counsellor of several Monarchs", a long sentence that reoccurs at the beginning of the "Pharmacopola" nearly *verbatim*.[51] According to one of his biographers, at a certain time of his life – even if no date is given for these events – Haines "determined to turn mountebank, and set out with a retinue of tumblers, dancers, &c. for Hertford", where "great was his practice, and great his applause; the invalids and curious of all ages flocking to him".[52] Besides his theatrical activity, then, Haines appears to have tried a quack's life, and Thomas Brown to have linked the actor's real identity to his own fiction.

---

48 One of these is Robert Chambers, who plainly declares that "his [Haines's] burlesque speech was published as a broadside with an engraving representing his temporary stage" (*The Book of Days* (1864), I, p. 512). The engraving, printed on the same page, comes from the here reproduced Fig. 11, though, not from Fig. 10.

49 Samuel Pepys, *The Diary of Samuel Pepys* (1970–83), IX, p. 107.

50 Thomas Brown, *Letters from the Dead to theLiving, by Mr Tho. Brown* […] *From Jo. Haines of Merry Memory, to his Friends at Wills* (1702). "Brown's choice of his correspondent, the recently deceased 'Joseph Haines of Merry Memory', was both literally apt and commercially shrewd, designed to attract the attention of fashionable readers" (David Mazella, "Diogenes the Critic" (2006), p. 106).

51 Thomas Brown (1707 edn), p. 12. The *Catalogue of Prints and Drawings in the British Museum* asserts that "The text [of the broadside] appears to be a parody" of the proclamation itself (1873, II, p. 152).

52 John Galt, *The Lives of the Players* (1831), I, p. 38.

Figure 12: An itinerant medicine vendor selling his wares from a stage … ["Joe Haynes's Mountebank's Speech"]. By courtesy of the Wellcome Library, London

The attribution of the authorship of Waltho van Claturbank's speech to Haines would thus seem quite plausible, only that D. G.'s original anthology contains another harangue specifically named "Joseph Haines's Speech, High-German Doctor and Astrologer in Brandipolis", different from the "Pharmacopola", in spite of some common passages.[53] Furthermore there also exists an image entitled "Joe

53 D. G., *Harangues*, pp. 35–43.

Haynes's Mountebank's Speech", which differs from those recalled so far (Fig. 12).[54] The above mentioned passage from Thomas Brown, as can be seen by comparing it with the incipit in Appendix E, coincides with what most diversifies "Pharmacopola" from *The Character*. Other portions of Haines's speech seem to have migrated to Waltho's text, especially to the latter's paragraphs 4, 5, 7 and 9. These are exactly the parts shared by Haines's and Waltho's speeches in a relation of reciprocal dependence. D. G., then, has integrated *The Character* with passages 'usable' on various occasions. While paragraphs 4, 7 and 9 simply mirror (or are mirrored by) passages from Haines's harangue, in paragraph 5 D. G. shows his special jocular vein. The two speeches, actually, share almost the whole paragraph, diverging only for the funny series of alliterative and rhyming adverbs. These are juxtaposed in a breathtaking list by Waltho: "Hypnotically, Hydrotically, Cathartically, Poppismatically, Hydrogogically, Pneumatically, or Synechdochically",[55] and 'explained' by Haines as follows, in order to specify the multiple actions of his medicine, which works

> HYPNOTICALLY, by throwing the Party into a gentle Slumber, HYDROTICALLY; by their Operative Faculty, in opening the *Interstitia Pororum*, CATHARTICALLY, by cleansing the Bowels of all Crudities and tartarous Mucilage, with which they abound; PROPPISMATICALLY, by forcing the Wind downward; HYDRAGOGICALLY, by exciting Urine; PNEUMATICALLY, by exhilirating the Spirits; and lastly, *or* SYNECDOCHICALLY, by corroborating the whole *Oeconomia Animalis*.[56]

From the comparison of these two textual portions, the mirroring/sharing process emerges in a clear manner: when writing "Joe Haines's Speech" and "Pharmacopola" D. G. made use of interchangeable blocks of phrases, and, economizing on his own and his printer's time, he repeated them in both texts, thus adding to the original parodic bill from *The Character.*

The main question, though, remains: was Mr Haines's speech ever spoken? Or was Waltho van Claturbank's? And which is the source for the other? It is possible to hypothesize that the real Joseph Haines, when 'playing the mountebank', made use of the parody of handbills from *The Character* for his burlesque open-air speeches (or even for his theatrical ex tempore performances), inventing 'Waltho

54 The image is in the copy of D. G., *Harangues* shelfmarked BL 12330.k.121 and in the ECCO collection, but not in the one shelfmarked BL 1038.g.46. The engraving derives from Thomas Brown, *The Works of Mr Thomas Brown [...] In Four Volumes. The Fourth Edition* (1715 [-20]), II, p. 167: it is a variation of a slightly different previous image, dated 1691, reproduced as Fig. 6 in McDowell).

55 D. G., *Harangues*, p. 15.

56 D. G., *Harangues*, p. 37. My small caps.

van Claturbank' as one of his impersonations. D. G. – whoever he was – when compiling his little volume of *Harangues* may be supposed to have transcribed two satires of Haines's against quacks, one with the actor's name, the other with his *alter ego*'s. Or another hypothesis can be made: D. G. capitalized on the success of Haines as an actor on the one hand, and on the fortune of Thomas Brown's *Letters from the Dead* with its Brandipolis on the other, so as to compile two appealing and partly coinciding speeches for readers *à la mode*, to be printed together with such famous pieces as Scoto of Mantua's harangue. What is certain is that between the seventeenth and the eighteenth centuries a real fashion for quack parodies exploded, so that with or without images, these parodies were published (and pirated, I suppose) by many printers. The existence of at least five versions of Waltho's speech in broadside format testifies to a wide readership and to the posthumous fortune of what some anonymous satirist had written in the well-nigh forgotten source of all this, *The Character of a Quack-Doctor*, printed in 1676.

6 Three Case Studies: Men, Women, and a Courtier

> And your Playes are below the Dignity of a Mountebanks stage. *Salvator Winter* wou'd have refus'd them.
>
> (Thomas Shadwell, *The Sullen Lovers*)

> Loe here a *woman* comes in charitie
> To see the *sicke*, and brings her *remedie*.
> [...]
> But loe an *Angell* gently puts her backe,
> Lest such *erroneous* course the sicke doe wracke.
>
> (James Primerose, *Popular Errours*)

> Being under an unlucky Accident, which obliged him to keep out of the way; He disguised himself, so that his nearest Friends could not have known him, and set up in Tower-street for an Italian Mountebank, where he had a Stage, and practised Physick for some Weeks not without success.
>
> (Gilbert Burnet, *Some Passages of the Life and Death of the Right Honourable John Earl of Rochester*)

This last chapter will be devoted to three 'case studies', touching three different aspects of quacks' production. Firstly a family business will be studied, as it is documented by the Winters' bills and other publications: the two Salvator Winter (father and son had the same name) were of Italian origin and with their enterprise covered nearly all the second half of the seventeenth century, becoming so famous (or notorious) as to be mentioned by name in Restoration literature. Secondly a particular typology of products on sale will be touched, i.e. cosmetics as part of a more general offer coming from women practitioners, since many female handbills advertised both cures for women's diseases and "beautifying" remedies (although men, as well, sometimes specialised in this branch). Thirdly, the focus will be on Dr Alexander Bendo's adventure, i.e. on the self-imposed 'exile' John Wilmot, the second Earl of Rochester, resorted to when, because of problems at the court of King Charles II, he was compelled to leave it, and disguised himself as a quack, putting up a stage in Tower Street as his biographer states in the third epigraph to this chapter, and dubbing himself 'Dr Alexander Bendo'.

Once again the documents which are at the basis of the analyses in this chapter will be drawn from the two British Library Collections, with the addition of other coeval material.

Two Generations of Italian Irregular Practitioners

On the title page of *A Pretious Treasury: Or a New Dispensatory* published with the names of Salvator Winter and Francisco Dickinson, there is a curious woodcut reproducing a healer on a raised stage, while addressing a dense crowd assembled around, and a child (or young man) near him, who is also speaking to somebody in the audience (Fig. 13).[1]

Figure 13: Title page of Salvator Winter's *A Pretious Treasury.* By courtesy of the Wellcome Library, London

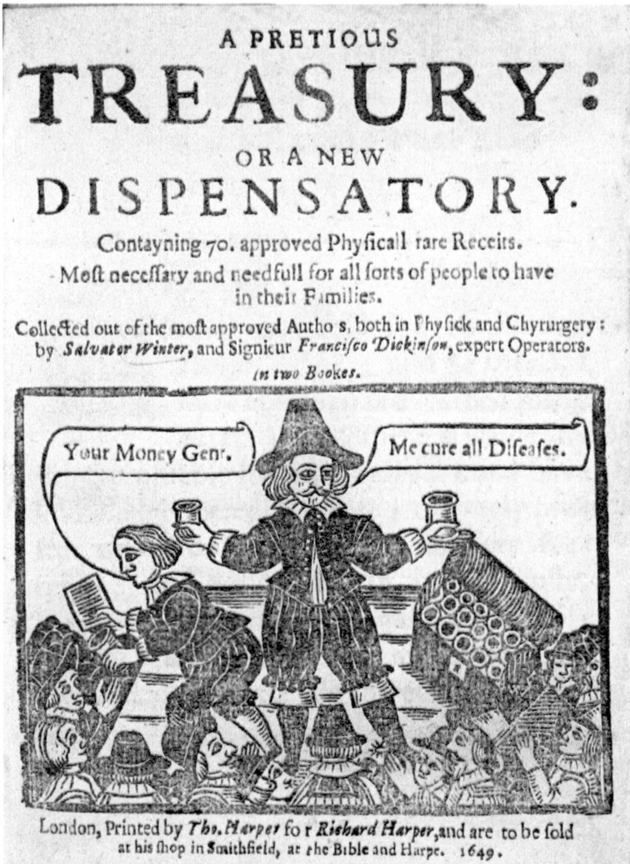
A PRETIOUS
TREASURY:
OR A NEW
DISPENSATORY.
Contayning 70. approved Phyſicall rare Receits.
Moſt neceſſary and needfull for all ſorts of people to have in their Families.
Collected out of the moſt approved Authors, both in Phyſick and Chyrurgery: by *Salvator Winter*, and Signieur *Franciſco Dickinſon*, expert Operators.
In two Bookes.

London, Printed by *Tho. Harper* for *Richard Harper*, and are to be ſold at his ſhop in Smithfield, at the Bible and Harpe. 1649.

---

1 *A Pretious Treasury* (1649). The booklet contains an address "To the Reader" by Winter himself. Both Winter's and Dickinson's parts appeared separately in the same

The man, richly dressed in a black doublet and a hose, with a white shirt, is wearing a high hat and holding two round jars; a scroll coming out of his mouth declares him a foreigner, given the incorrect use of the personal pronoun ("Me cure all Diseases"), and a quack in view of the meaning of his sentence (i.e. his boast of curing all distempers). Beside him the younger personage, clad in the same manner but without any hat so as to show his youth and/or his lower position, also has a scroll to his mouth ("Your Money Gent."). The older man's words proclaim him a healer, the younger one's his helper, in the act of asking their customers for money, while distributing a written sheet of paper. On the stage there is a large chest full of jars similar to those in the older man's hands, while the people around the platform raise their heads attentively to the whole scene. The picture would seem very similar to the diverse and sundry images of charlatans and mountebanks who swarmed all over Europe at the time, but it has something very peculiar: there is no ape, neither is there any Merry Andrew or Commedia dell'Arte Zanni in a multicoloured and patchy costume entertaining the crowd, nor any instrumentalist playing a violin or a trumpet,[2] while the only helper of the older man is a boy, perhaps of his own family. Very probably the image represents the healer himself, the principal author of the booklet, i.e. Salvator Winter, and his son, also named Salvator.[3] In other words, the title page supposedly

year (Salvator Winter, *A Nevv Dispensatory*; Francisco Dickinson, *A Precious Treasury of Twenty Rare Secrets*). Neither had a vignette. For an attempt to discuss the supposed overlapping identity of Winter and Dickinson, see John Ferguson, *Bibliographical Notes* (1896), I, pp. 25–27.

2 For a wide series of images relating to mountebanks, once again I refer to Katritzky, *Women*.

3 Salvator Winter's son is named John Baptista Quarenteni (for very strange and inexplicable reasons, since the two surnames are different) in *Nothing without God*, one of the two handbills with this title attributed to Salvator Winter Sr and dated 1669 by the *ESTC*. Neither is included in the British Library Collections, while there is another starting with "Salvator Winter, an Italian of the City of Naples, Aged 98 Years", 551a32[30], dated 1665 by the *ESTC*. They are available in EEBO. In two other bills, though, the writer is certainly "Salvator Winter Junior" and "Salvator Winter, Son of the late Ancient and Famous Physician Salvator Winter" (551a32[32] and C112f9[9], dated 1665 and 1665[?] by the *ESTC*, respectively), while the only handbill by Salvator Winter Sr contained in a British Library Collection is the already mentioned 551a32[30]. Actually, not only does the name "Quarenteni" sound strange when given to somebody whose father's surname is Winter, but also the surname "Winter" is strange for an Italian. From where had Salvator "Moretto" taken it? In the 1620s-30s there was in London a James Winter, apothecary and surgeon, who was fined by the College of Physicians for illegal practice (see Pelling and White, s. v.). Charles Goodall

represents the Winter family while working together, in the open air (a square or a street), as sellers of medicines, remedies and 'secrets'. They came from Naples, as Salvator Sr repeatedly wrote in his handbills and on the title page of the other, different, edition of the pamphlet.

The first piece of extant information about Salvator Winter dates back to a couple of years previous to the publication of the two booklets: an anonymous hand wrote "1647" at the bottom of a handbill sent out by "Salvator Winter Moretto, Neapolitane".[4] This, together with four others, and – when necessary – the two booklets and a series of instructions on how to use Winter's remedies, will be the corpus of authentic texts taken into consideration in this case study, in search of the permanence and variations of the Winters' 'family sayings' concerning their common profession of irregular physicians in London.[5]

Very little is known about the Winters apart from what is retrievable from their printed production, and a handful of facts recorded elsewhere. Certainly Salvator Winter Sr went through an alchemical phase, besides selling medicines as an irregular physician.[6] This is clear from the tone and the words he uses in his second handbill, where he mentions "Hermes" [Trismegistus?], and says, in a somehow confused way, that

---

includes James Winter, labelled first "Apothecary" and then "Surgeon", among the practitioners registered in the College's "Proceedings against Empiricks &c.". By the College Censors James Winter was fined £10 for malpractice (*The Royal College of Physicians of London* (1684), pp. 407, 419–20). Had Salvator Winter Sr been an apprentice of James's and taken his master's name?

4 Salvator Winter, *Nothing without God* (1647).

5 Salvator Winter, *Directions* (1664). This booklet is a pamphlet of eight unnumbered pages. All quotations follow the dating of the *ESTC*. For a possible new dating, see the discussion in this chapter, as a result of which – later in the text, the Bibliography and the tables – the suggested new dates are juxtaposed with those of the *ESTC* between square brackets.

6 It is possibly during this period that he got to know Sir Kenelm Digby (1603–65), a courtier, adventurer, alchemist and multi-faceted writer, who praised Winter's elixir (so much so that in the handbills posterior to 1669 the Winters rely on Digby's judgment to sell their own products): "The most Learned and Honourable Sir *Kenelm Digby* did highly commend it to the World […] styling it in his Book, *The Miraculous Elixir Vitæ*", boasts Mr Winter Sr at 98 years of age (551a32[30]). In fact, Winter's eulogy appears in Sir Kenelm Digby, *Choice and Experimented Receipts* (1668), i.e. in a book published after its author's death and compiled by G. Hartman (Winter's balsam and 'spirit' are mentioned on pp. 146–51: Winter's so-called spirit – the elixir? – is praised as "excellent", an adjective also used for the balsam).

> we [his son and himself] found out the Key for to open the door of Natures Cabinet; wherein Learning by which means Nature every day draws Supercelestial Virtue, we attained the Knowledge of the power and operations of that invisible *Magnes*, which shut up in that Point, which is the Center to the Trigon of another Center, weddeth Day and Night, Heaven and Earth with *Platos* golden Chain.[7]

What is relevant in this same handbill is that Winter invites the people to reach "this our Stage", that is, the raised platform which is his open-air shop.

What he writes in his pamphlet of directions (1664), where he declares that "I my self at this time am Four-score and three years Old", would mean that he was born in 1581 (or thereabouts).[8] From his subsequent handbill (551a32[30], oddly dated 1665 by the *ESTC* but possibly to be post-dated to 1679), we learn that he was still at work when he was ninety-eight years old (of course he attributes the reason for his continuous good health to his own "Elixir Vitæ, which he alwayes carries in his pocket adayes, and at Night under his pillow"). From Salvator Winter Jr's words in his second bill stating that his father lived "to the 99th year of his age" (C112f9[9]), one can deduce that he died the following year (1680). We also know, from the *Calendar of Treasury Books*, that Winter Sr received some money "as royal bounty" from Charles II on 20 October 1679, and that one of his apprentices was accused of stealing some bottles of his precious *elixir vitæ* (again in 1679).[9] This means that he was still alive in that year, when he is called "a very ancient Itallian Gentel man, who has long professed Physick in this Kingdom" in the Old Bailey documents of 15 October.[10] If the date of birth is correct, he was 98 in 1679 and died in 1680.

---

7 Salvator Winter, *Nothing without God* (1669). Actually this handbill presents a handwritten date – June 1664 – which contrasts with the date attributed by the *ESTC*.

8 Winter, *Directions*, p. 1.

9 "Entry Book: October 1679, 11–20", *Calendar of Treasury Books, Volume 6: 1679–1680* (1913), pp. 218–223 <http://www.british-history.ac.uk>.

10 *Old Bailey Proceedings Online* <http://www.oldbaileyonline.org>, 15 October 1679, trial of man (t16791015–13). The trial against the apprentice ended in a non-guilty verdict, whereas Mr Winter Jr was arraigned "for unlawfully breaking and entering the dwelling-house of his father" and fined accordingly. The *King's Warrant Book*, p. 121, and the *Money Book*, p. 242, record a payment due by Mr Winter Jr dated 22 October, 1679 ("Entry Book: October 1679, 11–20"). Evidently the relationship between father and son had changed and the son was also alleged to be the real thief (it is no coincidence, perhaps, that the son – in his first bill of 1665 now datable 1679, on the basis of the Old Bailey document – announces a move from St. Giles to a house "at the Sign of St. Paul upon Little Tower-Hill, near the Victualling-Office,

Historical evidence shows that Salvator Winter Sr had at least two children who died young: Govenio (a daughter; perhaps Giovanna?) was buried in the churchyard of St. Olave Hart Street, London, 10 July 1663, while an unnamed child of his was buried at St. Bene't, Paul's Wharf, London, 4 September 1657.[11]

The last extant mention of the Winters dates to May 1693, when the *Middlesex County Records. Calendar of Sessions Books 1689–1709*, Session Book 505, discharged a certain "David Goffe from his indenture of apprenticehood, it being proved that his master, Salvator Winter, of St. Giles'-in-the Fields, doctor of medicine, has gone away and made no provision for the said apprentice". Where Winter Jr went remains unknown.[12]

The Winter family, from the few data about them, had begun – at least – as mountebanks, even though they were very probably not vagrants and, judging from the various addresses printed in their handbills, had settled in London. Salvator Winter Sr calls himself "Professor" and "Excellent Master in the drawing of Teeth" (possibly his first 'specialization') in his 1647 handbill; he is silent about his titles later, while his son praises his own father by calling him "Ancient and Famous Physician" after his parent's death and, at the end of the same bill, "Dr", while calling himself "True and Only Operator". One should not forget, though, that a Salvator Winter is named "doctor of medicine" in the *Middlesex county records* for 1693 quoted above, but, unfortunately, it cannot be made clear whether the phrase refers to the father or the son (very probably it refers to the latter if the father had really died in 1680, even though nothing is known about either Winter ever taking a degree in medicine).[13] Evidently, the Winters

London", 551a32[32]). All this information and the discussion in this chapter should affect the dating of some of the Winters' works kept in the British Library.

11 The first death is attested in W. Bruce Bannerman, ed., *Parish Registers of St. Olave Hart Street* (1916), p. 197; the second in Willoughby A. Littledale, ed., *The Registers of St. Bene't and St. Peter, Paul's Wharf, London* (1912), p. 46. I am very grateful to Margaret Pelling, now involved in the "Early Modern Practitioners Project" at the University of Exeter, for sending me this information from the database Professor Jonathan Barry, Dr Peter Elmer and other researchers are working at. My special thanks to Dr Elmer for passing the information already collected to Dr Pelling (see <http://practitioners.exeter.ac.uk/> for detail about the project).

12 "Sessions Book 1693, 88–105", *Middlesex County Records. Calendar of Sessions Books 1689–1709*, Session Book 505, p. 39 <http://british-history.ac.uk>.

13 Leslie G. Matthews, without declaring his exact sources and almost certainly mistaking the father for the son, writes that "In 1688 [Winter] asked leave to be examined by the College of Physicians, intending if possible to secure a licence from the College", a licence which was refused ("Italian Charlatans in England" (1979), p. 2). In fact, this

succeeded in becoming really famous in London, and were appreciated by Charles II himself and by Sir Kenelm Digby. They disappeared from the scene, though: some years after his father's death, Winter Jr melted into thin air (or so it would appear to judge from the fact that David Goffe was released from all duties as Winter's apprentice precisely because his master had "gone away and made no provision" for him).[14]

It is worth mentioning that John Church, another "seller of medicines" who in 1682 published a booklet full of the names of patients allegedly cured by him, together with some receipts, had Salvator Winter's name printed on the title page of his own work, to testify to his profession and experience.[15]

---

piece of information derives from the Annals of the Royal College of Physicians for 1687–88: Salvator Winter [Jr] asked to be examined, but his inability to communicate in Latin saw his request turned down, i.e. he was not allowed to sit an examination. The hearing of his request took place on 23 March 1687/88. I am grateful to Peter Basham of the Heritage Centre of the Royal College of Physicians of London for confirming this detail. Previously to 1687–88, in 1679 Mr Winter Jr was licensed to practise medicine and surgery in the province of Canterbury. This latter piece of information, which I acknowledge gratefully, comes from Margaret Pelling and the "Exeter Early Modern Practitioners Project". Very probably, Salvator Winter Jr, foreseeing his famous father's death and fearing a possible loss of trust in the patients as to damage his own practice, looked for an authoratitive recognition of his activities, and it is not by chance that his first handbill can be datable to 1679, according to my recostruction of events.

14 That Salvator Winter, almost certainly the elder, was famous in Restoration London is proved by a short speech in Thomas Shadwell's comedy *The Sullen Lovers* (1668). When, towards the end of the text, Ninny (a would-be playwright, described as "a conceited poet" in the list of the *Dramatis personae*), offers Emilia, the female protagonist, the text of a new play, she answers: "And your Playes are below the Dignity of a Mountebanks stage. *Salvator Winter* wou'd have refus'd them." (Act III, p. 34). Does this imply that Winter used to perform plays when selling his medicines? Nothing is known about that. There is another literary allusion to our quack – whether senior or junior cannot be ascertained – in a satirical treatise attributed to Aphra Behn: as a cure for sore nipples Mistris Know-all, one of the characters, declares that, besides other remedies, "she hath […] never found nothing under the Sun that was more noble than Salvator Winter's Salve, for that cures immediately: And you can have nothing better" (*The Ten Pleasures of Marriage* (1922[1682]), p. 91).

15 *A Compendious Enchiridion Touching Most Distempers Incident to the Body of Man* […] *[I]n All my Travels with Salvator Winter* […] (1682).

Medical Professional Language in the Winter Family

Before proceeding to the analysis of data, I think it convenient to present, even if cursorily, the material objects containing the data themselves. What follows aims at proposing and discussing the results obtained by transcribing the five extant handbills of the Winter family, which were afterwards searched by individual lexical words (i.e. nouns, verbs, adjectives and adverbs) and some determiners. The number of word tokens in this small corpus is 3436, while the word types are 948, corresponding to 27,5 per cent of the total. Among these, the lexical items (listed in a table omitted for brevity) are 292, that is, 30,8 per cent of all types. The omitted table has been the starting point on which the tables of this chapter are based: Table 6.1 compares the results in Table 4.1 with the content of the Winters' handbills; Table 6.2 presents a list of the 56 symptoms and diseases mentioned in the Winters' handbills,[16] and Table 6.3 collects the 25 anatomical entries in the same. It is interesting to note that almost 20 per cent of the 292 lexical words refer to illnesses and 8,56 per cent to bodily parts.

General Terms

The results in Table 4.1 in Chapter 4 above show that the most largely used lexical term in the handbills corpus and 48 titles from books and/or pamphlets relating to quack medicine is ALL. The other words in that list rank differently in the two corpora, even though, when percentages are considered, such words as DISEASE, MEDICINE and PHYSICIAN (and their synonyms) also occur frequently. It sounds quite normal, given the subject matter of the analysed types of publications, that terms referring to disease, cure and healers are of such high incidence: quacks distributing their handbills at fairs and in the street aimed at an immediate and impressive appeal to their public, as if to say: 'You suffer from diverse diseases, but here I am, a physician able to cure them all'. It is not surprising, then, that the

16 Paul Slack (p. 264), writing about the vernacular medical literature in Tudor England, maintains that this type of production, especially chap-books containing 'receipts', listed symptoms rather than illnesses because of the low level of scientific knowledge of all medical practitioners (both legal and illegal), so that "agues and fevers might include anything from typhus and typhoid to malaria and influenza". Given the deeply conservative nature of this kind of literature, the quotation can well be applied to seventeenth-century popular medicine.

data emerging from those corpora are similar to those deriving from the Winters' publications (Table 6.1):[17]

Table 6.1: Lexical Words in Handbills and in the Winters' Handbills (a selection)

Word Types	**Tokens in Handbills**	**% (/198,606)**	**Tokens in the Winters' Handbills**	**% (/3436)**
All	1717	0.865	37	1.077
Any	1147	0.578	17	0.495
Many	692	0.348	11	0.320
Disease	647	0.326	13	0.378
Distemper	609	0.307	16	0.466
Medicine	538	0.271	4	0.116
Great	527	0.265	7	0.204
Most	499	0.251	9	0.262
Good	338	0.170	10	0.291
Physician	283	0.142	3	0.087
Remedy	262	0.132	9	0.262
Excellent	237	0.119	7	0.204
Doctor	228	0.115	1	0.029
Virtue	148	0.075	4	0.116
Sickness	147	0.074	1	0.029
Famous	132	0.066	6	0.175
Approved	82	0.041	2	0.058
Operator	29	0.015	2	0.058
Miraculous	18	0.009	5	0.146
Professor	12	0.006	1	0.029
Receipt	9	0.005	0	0.000

ALL, with the same positive axiological value as noted in Chapter 4, occurs 37 times in the Winters' bills, thus showing that both father and son were anxious to stress the power of their products, good for 'all' types of sickness, a real panacea, even if this noun is not used. The percentage of the word is higher than in

17 In Table 6.1 the number of word tokens from the handbills is inferior to that used in Table 4.1 (and consequently percentages differ, too), because the three Winter handbills contained in the corpus have not been taken into consideration, since they are part of the small corpus of all the Winter handbills. Both singular and plural forms of nouns are counted. Only results from the larger corpus are listed in decreasing ranking order.

the other corpora (1.07 per cent of word tokens), and so are some others (the nouns DISEASE, DISTEMPER, REMEDY, VIRTUE, OPERATOR, PROFESSOR; the modifiers GOOD, EXCELLENT, FAMOUS, APPROVED, MIRACULOUS). Two entries present in Table 4.1 are absent from this one, while some have been added for their (relative) frequency in the Winters' handbills: in the latter RECEIPT does not appear, since the Winters sold mainly their own nostrums, without offering any particular instruction for the preparation of remedies (at least in the handbills). DOCTOR occurs only as a professional title and in its abbreviated form, while there are PROFESSOR and OPERATOR, terms which better represent the Winters' language: Salvator Winter Jr names himself "operator" twice (551a32[32] and C112f9[9]), whereas his father introduced himself as "the Professor hereof Salvator Winter Moretto, a Neapolitane borne", in his 1647 bill. It is interesting to notice that in the larger handbills corpus, PROFESSOR is generally preceded by the name of the self-proclaiming person, and followed by the practitioner's specialization (for example "J. Russel, Professor of Physick", C112f9[1]). With his somewhat garbled phrase Salvator Winter seems to show his as yet imperfect knowledge of English usage, particularly of the adverbial form "hereof", which remains completely unconnected to any reference.

Another feature emerging from the general results is the more frequent employment of self-eulogistic language. In general, both Winters intersperse some effective adjectives in their handbills, from the most common ones listed in Table 6.1 to the unique SUPERCELESTIAL, certainly the most grandiloquent, together with MIRACULOUS, which occurs much more frequently in their handbills than in the whole corpus.[18]

However, what strikes one most in the series of the Winters' handbills is the frequent presence of terms related to specific diseases and to the human body, with ever-closer focus from Salvator Winter Sr's less professional bill of 1647, to his last one (when he claims to be 98 years old). When writing bills for a late Restoration public, Winter Sr seems to pay attention to the changes in medicine due to the scientific progress in the field (even though still from a clear quack-like stance, discernable, for example, when he declares that his *elixir vitæ* "is good for all sorts of Catarrhs, pains in the Head, Lethargy, any sort of Sore Eyes, for dimness of sight, hardness of Hearing, stinking Breath, Scurvy in the Mouth or any other part of the body, Tooth-ach, sore Throat, for all sorts of Coughs", 551a32[30]). Another relevant aspect of all these handbills is that Winter Jr more or less simply copied

18 SUPERCELESTIAL occurs only in Winter, *Nothing Without God* (1669).

his father's last bill, with very slight variations, thus highlighting the continuity in the family trade and sayings.

Which Diseases and What Anatomy?

The often mentioned Act approved by Henry VIII in favour of popular healers (the "Quacks' Charter") listed some diseases curable by those who had no university degree. These ailments seem indeed to be among those diseases mostly cured by Salvator Winter Sr. When reading his 1647 handbill, one soon notices that his forte at that time was certainly tooth-drawing: the word TEETH appears ten times in this bill, disappears completely in the following two and returns only once in each of Winter Jr's two documents.[19] Very probably Salvator Winter started his job simply as a tooth-drawer, selling also – like all other mountebanks – balsams and ointments. The last paragraph in *A Nevv Dispensatory* bears witness to this early specialization of his: after printing the various remedies of the title, he adds, using phrases which resemble those of his 1647 handbill: "Furthermore, I pull out all maner of Hollow Teeth, stumps, or roots, with great dexterity, and ease, without almost any pain [...] *I live at present in* Bedford-*street, next door unto the Sign of the Fox, over against the New Exchange*".[20] The sentence is repeated in the other version of the pamphlet, but no address is given.[21]

From Table 6.2 Winter Sr's medical knowledge appears limited and rather vague: he lists 20 different ailments, but he mentions PAINS, COUGHS, CORNS and WOUNDS in general together with more specific infirmities and terminology, the most 'erudite' of which being *Hernia carnosa,* not only a real medical term, but also given in Latin. His medical vocabulary seems to improve in his third broadsheet, whereas the second, so full of alchemical jargon, uses only a few familiar terms, while introducing some maladies not present in the previous handbill, such as HARE-LIPS, HERNYES (which seems to substitute the *Hernia carnosa* of the other), WENS, WOLFES, and WRYNECKS (the diseases mentioned are only 7 altogether).[22]

---

19 About quacks and tooth-drawing see M. A. Katritzky, "Gendering Tooth-drawers on the Stage", (2000) later reworked in Katritzky, *Women*, pp. 177–201.

20 Winter, *A Nevv Dispensatory*, p. 15.

21 Winter, *A Pretious Treasury*, p. 14. In 1647 Winter lived "at the Princes Armes at *Clare Street* end over against the market place [...], on the back side of *Drury Lane*" (*Nothing Without God* (1647)). At least from 1664 on he lived in "*new* Kings-Street, *at the sign of* St. Paul *between* Long-Acre, *and* St. Giles *in the fields*" (from his other bills).

22 See *OED*, s.v. WEN, 1.a: "A lump or protuberance on the body, a knot, bunch, wart"; s.v. WOLF, 7.a: "A name for certain malignant or erosive diseases in men and animals".

Table 6.2: Symptoms and Diseases in the Winters' Handbills

Disease / **Handbill**	**1647**	**1669 [1664]**	**1665 [1679]**	**Jr 1665 [1679]**	**Jr 1665? [1680]**	**Tokens**
1 ague				1	1	**2**
2 apoplexies				1	1	**2**
3 breath (stinking)			1			**1**
4 burnings	1		1			**2**
5 cankers		1				**1**
6 catarrhs			1	1	1	**3**
7 collick	1					**1**
8 consumption	1		1	1	1	**4**
9 convulsion			1	1	1	**3**
10 corns	1					**1**
11 coughs	1		1	1	1	**4**
12 dimness (of sight)			1			**1**
13 dropsy	1		1	1	1	**4**
14 epilepsies				1	1	**2**
15 fainting (fits)			1	1	1	**3**
16 falling (fits)			1	1	1	**3**
17 feavers			1	1	1	**3**
18 fits (of the mother)			1	1	1	**3**
19 fluxes				1	1	**2**
20 French (pox)	1		1			**2**
21 gangrene			1	1	1	**3**
22 gout			1	1	1	**3**
23 griping of the guts	1		1	1	1	**4**
24 hardness (of hearing)			1			**1**
25 hare-lips		1				**1**
26 hernia carnosa	1					**1**
27 hernyes		1				**1**
28 jaundice	1				1	**2**
29 lethargy			1	1	1	**3**
30 measles			1	1	1	**3**
31 noise (in the head and ears)				1	1	**2**

It is noteworthy that *hernia carnosa* (the only Latin term used by the Winters, except their *elixir vitæ*) enters English medical literature in the last quarter of the fourteenth century and is present only in surgical treatises (see Juhani Norri, *Names of Sicknesses in English* (1992), pp. 402, 420).

Disease / Handbill	1647	1669 [1664]	1665 [1679]	Jr 1665 [1679]	Jr 1665? [1680]	Tokens
32 obstruction (of the stomach, liver and spleen)			1	1	1	**3**
33 oppression (of the heart)			1			**1**
34 pain (any; in the back, in the head)	6		2	2	2	**12**
35 palsies			1	1	1	**3**
36 plague	2		1			**3**
37 pox (alone)	1					**1**
38 running of the reins			3			**3**
39 rupture	3		1			**4**
40 scalding	1		1			**2**
41 sciatica	1		1	1	1	**4**
42 scurvy	1		1		1	**3**
43 small pox			1	1	1	**3**
44 stone	1	1	1	1	1	**5**
45 stoppage of urine			1	1	1	**3**
46 throat (sore)			1			**1**
47 tooth-ach			1			**1**
48 tympany			1	1	1	**3**
49 ulcerated (sores)			1	1	1	**3**
50 venereal distempers				1	1	**2**
51 ventosities	1					**1**
52 wens		1				**1**
53 wolfes		1				**1**
54 worms			1	1	1	**3**
55 wounds	1					**1**
56 wrynecks		1				**1**
Totals	28	7	40	31	33	**139**

Winter Sr's 1665[1679] handbill (551a32[30]) enumerates a larger amount of ailments (37 word types), among which RUNNING OF THE REINS (three times),[23] to signal – perhaps – the major impact of venereal diseases on contemporary English society (FRENCH POX occurs once). Such richness may be ascribed to the progress of science and medicine (William Harvey's *De motu cordis et sanguinis*,

23 See *OED*, s.v. RUNNING, 23.a: "The flowing or discharge of fluid from the body (in later use especially from the eyes or nose); an instance of this, a discharge. Also: †a sore or wound that discharges pus (*obs.*). Also in figurative context.† running of the reins n. *Obs.* gonorrhoea; leucorrhoea; (also) discharge of semen".

1628, may be the reason behind the use of the noun CIRCULATION in this same bill). Some terms are completely new, as is evident in Table 6.2, and some have become more precise: the previously unspecified POX is here divided into SMALL POX, MEASLES and FRENCH POX; fits of various types are introduced, together with FEVERS, GOUT, and GANGRENE. What is perhaps ascribable to Mr Winter's ageing are some ailments typical of old age: DIMNESS OF SIGHT, HARDNESS OF HEARING, and LETHARGY (only the last term was kept by his son in his two handbills).

Salvator Winter Jr's own broadsheets appear as copycat reproductions of his father's last bill, as if the real operator were still the father, not the son. In his father's wake, Salvator Jr maintains the previous terminology, dismissing only a few words, some of them now perhaps old-fashioned like SCALDING or RUNNING OF THE REINS (the latter replaced by the more genteel VENEREAL DISTEMPERS), some others because strictly connected to old age. On the other hand, a few nouns are used by him for the first time in the family: APOPLEXIES and EPILEPSIES, for example (the plurals are his way to denote, possibly, strokes and seizures in general). As a total, he names 30 disease word types in his first bill, and 32 in the second.

The anatomical knowledge recognizable in all handbills by the Winters does not show any relevant progress when passing from old Winter's to his son's production (see Table 6.3).

Table 6.3: Anatomical Entries in the Winters' Handbills

	Anatomy / Handbill	**1647**	**1669 [1664]**	**1665 [1679]**	**Jr 1665 [1679]**	**Jr1665? [1680]**	**Tokens**
1	back	1		1	1	1	**4**
2	bladder		1	1	1	1	**4**
3	body	2		1	3	4	**10**
4	bone	2					**2**
5	brain	1					**1**
6	breasts	1					**1**
7	ears				1	1	**2**
8	eye			1	1	1	**3**
9	hair	1					**1**
10	head	1		1	3	3	**8**
11	hearing			1	1	1	**3**
12	heart		1	1			**2**
13	liver				1	1	**2**
14	mother			1	1	1	**3**

Anatomy / Handbill	1647	1669 [1664]	1665 [1679]	Jr 1665 [1679]	Jr1665? [1680]	Tokens
15 mouth	1		1			**2**
16 nostril	2			1	1	**4**
17 pannickle	1					**1**
18 reins			2	1	1	**4**
19 sight			3			**3**
20 sinew	2					**2**
21 spleen				1	1	**2**
22 stomack			1	1	1	**3**
23 teeth	10			1	1	**12**
24 temples				1	1	**2**
25 throat			1			**1**
Totals	25	2	16	19	20	**82**

What differs, though, is the frequency of some terms. For example, the father uses TEETH 10 times, as already seen, his son only twice; the father mentions THE HUMANE BODY 3 times in his 3 bills, the son 7 times in 2 bills; SIGHT disappears completely from Salvator Jr's broadsheets. What is noticeable is that women are taken into consideration only as sufferers from WORMS (together with men and children), from SORE BREASTS and from FITS OF THE MOTHER. This may sound strange, not least because Winter Sr devotes a whole paragraph of his *Directions* (p. 14) to "hard Labour in Women", to be treated – obviously – with his balsam and elixir.

The previous analysis shows how the medical language of the Winters did not change substantially from father to son. Times were changing, but medicine was undergoing a revolution which was still slow, especially among the lowest ranks of practitioners:[24] Salvator Winter Jr did not show any finer awareness of medical language than his father, in spite of the new entries in the professional 'family sayings'. On the contrary, Winter Sr is the one who accomplishes a more radical step from his 1647 handbill to the 1665[1679] one, where he states he is 98 years old. Of his 37 names of sicknesses, 20 are new in comparison with his

24 See Roger French and Andrew Wear, eds, *The Medical Revolution* (1989), esp. Andrew Wear's contribution in the same volume ("Medical Practice"). Quacks continued to prosper throughout the eighteenth century, attacked by the College of Physicians, but still sharing with it the traditions of old medicine: "In some ways this was still the time of the *longue durée* in medicine. Although theory changed it was still expressed in such a way that it spoke to patients and so attracted their trade" (Wear, "Medical Practice", p. 319).

previous production. Perhaps his long practice in London had made him more conscious of the necessity of appealing to readers (and/or listeners) who wanted to hear their own sufferings named, if not totally cured, at least in the most popular of vernacular medical literature, i.e. quacks' handbills, broadsheets and slim remedy books. Juhani Norri, when dealing with the way of naming illnesses in late medieval and early Tudor England, states that this sort of publication "[was] also owned by university-trained physicians", and that only the presence of prologues or dedicatory letters can reveal who the supposed addressee of this kind of literature was.[25] No such paratextual feature is present in the Winters' bills, but there is an address "To the Reader" both in Winter Sr's *A Pretious Treasury* and in his *A Nevv Dispensatory.* The text of this address, exactly the same in the two publications, reads:

> Gentle Reader,
> In my manifold Travels through *Europe, Asia, and Africa,* I have observed and learned many secrets; yea, there is scarce any thing profitable for mans body, but I have knowledge thereof. Here I do freely present you many most necessary Receipts, and very usefull in every family, whereof I have oftentimes made good proof; Accept of them thankfully, and as you shall have occasion make use thereof. So Farewell,
> Salvator Winter, Operator[26]

From the two complete titles[27] one can deduce that the booklets are targeted at house-keepers (both male and female, evidently) and are considered to be of special use for diseases occurring among family members. They are, actually, two remedy books containing various directions on how to cope with the most common symptoms, independently of the presence of a healer. The style of the address in both is that of Winter's 1647 handbill, which declared that he "having travelled through divers Countries, aswell in *Europe* as in *Asia* and *Africa*, hath by the Grace of God, learned divers secrets and arts to serve mankind therewith". The booklets were printed in 1649 and there is no sign of any great transformation having occurred in the space of two years. What is relevant, though, is that, by addressing his "Gentle Reader", Winter also tried to reach literate people,

25 Norri, p. 33. On the 'words of medicine' see also R. W. Mc Conchie, *Lexicography and Physicke* (1997). Norri and McConchie cover periods previous to the seventeenth century, but their suggestions can be useful for further research in lexicography. Especially, quacks' handbills have not been dealt with comprehensively. My study aims at being a modest contribution in this direction.

26 Winter, *A Pretious Treasury*, fol. A2^{r}, and *A Nevv Dispensatory*, fol. A2^{r-v}.

27 These are reproduced in the References.

beyond those he could speak to from his stage or who could have a brief handbill read to them by somebody able to decipher printed matter.

Near the end of his life Winter Sr, as already seen, even received a gift from King Charles II and, before that, had enlarged his practice outside London (in his *Directions* he boasts about curing people in Oxfordshire, Buckinghamshire and as far north as Newcastle upon Tyne). As for his specialty, he turned from tooth-drawer and seller of various nostrums (in 1647 Winter mentions his ointment, plaister, balsam and even an antidote, the famous "Orviatano [*sic*]"), into a quack who cured everything with just one remedy, his *elixir vitæ*. His son was, therefore, able to take over his father's practice, but it appears that he relied on the family celebrity and that he did not improve much what his elderly parent had achieved. If the date here hypothesized for Winter Sr's death is correct (1680), the son carried on the profession for thirteen more years; his vocabulary, though, and the very structure of whole sentences in his handbills remained more or less the same as his father's, thus showing the persistence and the duration of their medical 'family sayings'.

Targeting Women

As the second epigraph of this chapter highlights, women healers did not encounter the approbation of Collegiate physicians: Dr Primerose's words facing the frontispiece of his volume clearly show how lowly remedies offered by women were rated. The angel arriving at the sick person's bed sends the woman away in order to avoid a "wrack" due to the "erroneous" medicine she might administer to the sick. She is not presented as an irregular practitioner, but simply identified as a female, and as such she is denied admittance. Primerose's attitude appears in contrast to the long tradition of household health care of which women had always been in charge and also to the "Quacks' Charter" of King Henry VIII.[28] Nevertheless women, who continued to collect recipes in their home closets, besides working as nurses and midwives also for their neighbourhood, were the first to be resorted to in the event of a sick person in the house.[29] For some decades now medical and gender historians have been researching the roles played by women, belonging both to the gentry and to lower classes, in

28 About women healers practicing outside London see esp. Margaret Pelling, "Healing the Sick Poor", and "Older Women" (both 1998).

29 For manuscript collections of recipes, mainly attributable to women, see Elaine Leong and Sara Pennell, "Recipe Collections" (2007). For women's almanacs see A. S. Weber, "Women's Early Modern Medical Almanacs" (2003).

health care, and valuable studies have been produced in this field. The results open up a vast panorama of new sources and historical information that show how women worked as competent practitioners in health care (or "bodywork", the word coined by Mary E. Fissell in order to allow a whole series of female health care activities to be taken into account, well beyond the purely domestic sphere).[30] Besides being midwives, women worked in parishes for the care of the poor on the basis of the Poor Law, were searchers in plague periods, nurses in hospitals.[31] Generally speaking, women were necessary helpers in early modern heath care, even if they went unmentioned in records and were attacked by Collegiate physicians. In this chapter, though, I do not intend to deal with these social roles occupied by women, but rather with women on the one hand as irregular practitioners as they emerge from their handbills, and on the other as buyers of cosmetics, since many handbills combine the selling of medicine with the offer of beauty products.[32]

As early as 1984 Patricia Crawford drew attention to women's printed advertisements, the analysis of which "provides some information about the women practitioners and the medical care they offered".[33] Crawford, reading the handbills contained in all three British Library Collections (C112f9, 551a32, and Harley 5931), identified 66 ads "which mention women", understandably in their capacities as practitioners. One of them, Sarah Cornelius de Heusde, overtly explains that she has real medical skills, learnt from her husband and father (both doctors according to her), and denies being a deceiver. She knows very well that "there are some old Women and Midwives, who sometimes have a little Book, out of which they gather their Sciences, whereby they intend to cure all men: But it is not so

30 Mary E. Fissell thus explains her proposal of a new term: "I am not proposing that we replace the category 'medicine' with bodywork; rather, that we investigate the relationship between the work we consider medicine and the broader category of attending to the human body, and perhaps place medicine and its learned traditions within or next to the larger category of bodywork" ("Introduction: Women, Health, and Healing" (2008), p. 11).

31 For a literary case of women's role as hospital nurses, see Robert Armin, *The History of the Tvvo Maids of More-clacke* (1609), a play in which John of the Hospital, a natural fool in the play, is taken care of by his old nurse. On nurses see Margaret Pelling, "Nurses and Nurse-keepers" (1998).

32 I refer the reader to general studies on the issues only touched here, among others, Anne Laurence, *Women in England* (1994); Sara Mendelson and Patricia Crawford, *Women* (1998); Patricia Crawford, *Blood, Bodies and Families* (2004). To these the individual works quoted in these notes must also be added.

33 Crawford, "Printed Advertisements", pp. 67, 66.

with me" (C112f9[61]). Her knowledge ("these my Sciences") is based on her own practice, attested by the fact that "I have restored above a thousand Women and young Maidens". In her advertisement, which is "To be delivered in the Hands of Civil Gentlewomen and Maidens", Sarah names herself "this Famous Operatoress" (the only occurrence of the word in my corpus), and offers cures for women's diseases mainly. Another interesting detail emerges from this bill: near the end of the leaflet, she signs her paper in the following way:

> By me Sarah Cornelius de Heusde, Widdow of Dr Sasbout, and Grandmother of the Doctor that had his Stage upon Great Tower-Hill, and did so many Cures before the Fire.

That is, she offers a clear picture of a family business involving not only two generations as in the case of the Winters, but three, since one of her grandchildren is said to have a stage from which he works as a doctor himself. Since she practices "from Eight in the Morning, till Eight in the Evening" "at the Sign of the Red Lyon by the Postern Gate, in George Yard, between Great and Little Tower-Hill", i.e. at her house like all other women who published information about their abodes, by contrasting this detail with what we learn of her grandchild, the reader can deduce that women rarely, if ever, worked on stages, while men did (at least some). Actually the extant images of mountebanks' stages hardly ever show women as protagonists, but only in the role of helpers or, on the Continent mainly, of entertainers and instrumentalists useful to gather an audience around a stage.[34]

In my handbills corpus the word WOMAN occurs 99 times, while the plural WOMEN is present much more often: 347 times (together they are equal to 0.22 per cent of all tokens). The bills contain 26 occurrences of the cluster 'man or woman', which testifies to no specific interest on the writer's part in stressing sexual differences; the cluster 'woman with child' is present in 5 cases to which the variant 'if a woman be with child' must be added (three times) and 'women with child' in 11 occurrences, i.e. thus signalling prospective mothers. Three times the term is used in the compound WOMAN-KIND by two women healers (twice by the already mentioned Ann Laverenst – C112f9[26] and 551a32[31] – and once by Elizabeth Maris, 551a32[49], who also coins WOMEN KIND). This usage is particularly revealing, since – being used instead of MANKIND – it seems to show a relevant gender awareness, especially if one considers Laverenst's first handbill addressed to "TO LADIES AND All Others OF THE FEMALE SEX". In one case only we have the cluster 'Woman Physician', used by Agnodice, who

---

34 See Chapter 1, and the plates reproduced in Katritzky, *Women*.

describes herself with this title (551a32[199]).[35] The more complex cluster 'If any Woman be unwilling' occurs 4 times: this phrase is mentioned in male practitioners' handbills to inform the public that the practitioner's wife will receive girls and women who do not want to be seen by a man.

Generally women's diseases are linked to the sexual apparatus, as causing both physical illness and mental distress (the often mentioned "fits of the Mother" is the most widely studied female ailment because of its psychological interpretation as hysteria).[36] The cures offered by irregular practitioners also included the treatment of barrenness (a term with 63 occurrences when adjective and its derivative noun are taken together), and the prevention of miscarriage (MISCARR* has also a relatively high frequency: the lemma occurs 56 times). The often dubious activities of practitioners, though, do not allow a clear-cut separation between the administration of abortifacients and of substances really favouring female fertility, above all considering the spread of venereal diseases and the influence of poverty and prostitution in the lower social classes.[37] An interesting cluster connected to female fertility is 'capable of conception' (11 cases), whereas male fertility is hinted at only once when a certain pill is praised for making "both Sexes capable of Generation" (C112f9[144]). The major concern touched, evidently, the female body, given the belief that procreation depended on it in many of its aspects (for example, infertility and the sex of children).

GENTLEWOMAN occurs in 34 cases. The term is used simply to designate a patient, especially in the many lists of testimonials, or – more frequently – to introduce a female healer. The plural form occurs 6 times. LADIES and MAIDS have 12 and 59 occurrences, respectively, to which the forms LADY and MAIDENS

35 Nothing is known about this modern 'Agnodice': the name might also be a pseudonym taken by a man profiting from the legend connected to this ancient Greek midwife. The London Agnodice is quoted, with no further detail, also in Edith Snook, *Women, Beauty and Power* (2011), p. 36.

36 In the corpus this cluster occurs 29 times. A fairly recent study on the female body is Mary E. Fissell, *Vernacular Bodies* (2004). On the theatrical performance of medicine, see Stephanie Moss and Kaara L. Peterson, eds, *Disease, Diagnosis, and Cure* (2004), and, for the interpretation of hysteria in early modern times and its representation in Shakespeare, Kaara L. Peterson, *Popular Medicine* (2010).

37 In the discussion of women's almanacs, Weber, p. 389, observes that "Jinner's [one of the writers of medical almanacs] 'Pills to expel a dead Child' in her almanac, containing pennyroyal (*Mentha pulegium L.*), would [...] have been equally effective in aborting a live fetus, but she again does not mention this property of the drug".

must be added, severally present 6 and 9 times.[38] If all the occurrences of words signalling members of the female gender are summed, the amount is equal to 572, i.e. 0.29 per cent of all tokens. In the word list it would rank in 46th position, that is, very high, considering that only the lemma CURE appears in the first 45 positions (the first lexical word), the higher ranking terms being only functional words. If the high frequency of CURE can be easily explained given the topic and purpose of the handbills, the numerous female indicators (even if derived from a sum of various word types) seem to require some interpretation, especially since by summing up all terms denoting members of the male gender the total number reaches only 404 cases (0.20 per cent of the tokens). The great difference between gender-identifiable people can be attributed to the fact that women were considered either the ideal addressees of the leaflets (notwithstanding the latter's distribution in coffeehouses, typically frequented by men) because of their role as health carers, or the sex more affected by diseases. In his study of Richard Napier's medical practice Michael MacDonald, supported by his research into Napier's papers, asserted that seventeenth-century English women suffered from mental illnesses more than men and, speaking more generally, that "Women sought medical treatment more often than men because they were more often ill. In addition to the affections men bore, women also suffered from diseases that tormented only their sex", a phenomenon not difficult to envisage if one thinks of the many and serious cases in which female health was in danger (childbirth, difficult deliveries, gynaecological ailments, malnutrition).[39] Therefore both explanations tentatively given above turn out to be true: women were the special target of irregular practitioners' handbills because they were expected to take charge of their family's health, and because they were more often sick than men. And so nearly every single bill mentions women's diseases, and some of them directly address "Ladies and all others of the Female Sex" (C112f9[26]) or entitle a bill "Advice to Ladies, Gentlewomen, And Others" (551a32[187]).

Among the bills which try to involve women in a very direct way, there are those, though, which advertise few medical cures, while listing cosmetics and beauty treatments. To these the following paragraph is devoted.

---

38 LADY actually occurs 22 times, but in 16 cases the word is used as a title in a person's name.

39 Michael Mac Donald, *Mystical Bedlam* (1981), p. 38.

"Ladies, Beauty is a Blessing of God" (C112f9[125])

Not all women practitioners sold cosmetics: especially those who declared they were of German origin, including Elizabeth Maris (551a32[49]), and Ann Laverenst (C112f9[26] and 551a32[31]), presented themselves as healers only, whereas Sarah Cornelius de Heusde briefly states that she makes "a Beautifying for the Body" and other cosmetics (C112f9[61]). Mrs Mary Green was another who practised solely medicine, while a lady (possibly English, even if no nationality is mentioned) proffers astrological services in particular, even though – at the end of her short bill – she indirectly allows one to understand that her profession consists of 'mixed' expertise (astrology, medicine, and cosmesis):

> She Calculates Nativities, according to the exactest Rules yet known.
>
> Lastly, She hath all sorts of excellent Medicines, ready prepared, fitted for the cure of all Diseases (that are curable) in the bodies of Men, Women or Children; she Resolveth what the Disease is, and whether it will end in life or death; If incurable, she taketh it not in hand: she also hath a proper Specifick that cureth Barreness in Women; and a rare Water which beautifies the Face. (551a32[86])

There were men, nevertheless, that sold toiletries together with other services. The author of the phrase used as the title of this paragraph, who introduces himself as "Stephen Draper, the approved Physician and Man-Midwife […] M.D.", addresses women directly from the *incipit* of his bill: "Most dear and highly esteemed Women". Later in the text women are called "Beloved", "Good", "Adored", then "Ladies" in a crescendo up to the final part of the advertisement where Draper exhibits his poetical skill in a twenty-two-line doggerel made of eleven rhyming couplets (with uncouth lines of various length). His bill is graphically well arranged, though crammed with letters like many others: after the initial vocative, the recto lists all the cures he can bestow, while the verso shows a decorated frame at the top, circling the doctor's image, some wording and a date (MDCLXXXVI), followed by his "praise of women's beauty". The poem comes at the bottom, in two columns. This part of the handbill is, in spite of its elegance, the more commercial of the two pages: the first never mentions the cost of the cures Dr Draper can make, the second shows a true price list of all the cosmetics he sells. There is no article not followed by its price. Before starting his catalogue, Draper adds that, since "Beauty is a Blessing of God",

> every one ought to preserve it, in fine, they do as much offend that neglect it, as they do that Paint their Faces. I heretofore commend unto you the Virtue of the Water of Pearl with several other Cosmeticks for the Face, faithfully prepared without Mercury. (C112f9[125])

His products, therefore, are guaranteed not to contain dangerous ingredients on the one hand, and on the other to be such as to preserve nature, contrary to the fashion of making up one's face, condemned very strongly in English culture as early as Thomas Tuke's *A Treatise against Painting and Tincturing of Women* (1616), albeit there is no trace in Draper of Tuke's anti-Catholic zeal and of his strenuous attack on women.

Dr Draper's beauty products include:

The Water of Pearl[40]	10s. each bottle
A teeth Powder	2s. 6d. each tin box
Fore-head pieces	1s.
An unguent for lips	1s. each box
An anti-wrinkle pomatum	1s. each box
[Cleansing] water	2.s 6d. each bottle
A hand powder	2s. 6d. each paper
A hand ointment	3s. each glass

When compared with medicine prices seen in Chapter 2 of this volume, these prices appear objectively higher (even if nothing is known about the exact contents of boxes, tin boxes, bottles etc.). Evidently cosmetics and their costs were not targeted at the general public of ladies, but at a more gentrified (and better off) one. The previous list, together with other entries, can be considered to form a catalogue of interesting key words to be looked up in the handbills corpus, in order to find out which beauty products were on the market. In order to attain reliable results, I have built up a smaller sub-corpus made of only those handbills which deal, at least partially, with cosmetics.

"A most delicate Oyntment to anoint the Face" (551a32[24])

The smaller sub-corpus just mentioned consists in 14,639 word tokens (i.e. 7.29 per cent of the total amount of tokens in my corpus), included in 24 handbills chosen on the basis of their being 'dedicated' to promoting cosmetics, of which 18 are published by women. A first search has been carried out in order to find which body parts the bills privilege as the target of their advertising: the results show that FACE, HAIR, SKIN, HAND and TOOTH are the terms with the highest frequency (Table 6.4). They denote the same body parts as those to which twenty-first-century advertising is mostly addressed, while the female body as such is not specified because of early modern cultural constraints (and also

40 The terminology has been drawn from Dr Draper's handbill. Additions are between square brackets.

because it was nearly 'invisible' under cumbrous clothing: the term BREAST occurs only twice, very probably in its meaning of *décolleté*, it being linked with NECK, 551a32[150]). Apart from MOTHER that still refers to the womb since some handbills also deal with health care and not only with cosmesis, all the other entries in the table name parts of the face, evidently those which were considered to be the fittest to receive cosmetic treatment. In his bill Dr Draper, while condemning the use of paint, stresses that "Nature without Art is frail", therefore in need of his "Cosmeticks" (C112f9[125]); and all the other sellers, as the table evidences, agreed on that.

Table 6.4: Lexical Words for Body Parts

	Tokens	% /14,639	All Tokens	% /200,583
Face	78	0.533	164	0.082
Hair	45	0.307	59	0.029
Skin	31	0.212	56	0.028
Hand	27	0.184	191	0.095
Tooth	27	0.184	202	0.101
Forehead	22	0.150	26	0.013
Lips	16	0.109	40	0.020
Mother	14	0.096	77	0.038
Gum	10	0.068	61	0.030
Eyebrow	9	0.061	10	0.005

The skin of the face had to be cleansed with "waters" and "washes" which also helped in curing spots and other skin ailments, and beautified by the products on sale (see Table 6.5). Waters also served to colour hair: when red – a colour not very fashionable, evidently – it could be turned into "a lovely Brown, which never decays", as promised by the gentlewoman who lived "In Surry-street, in the Strand, at the Corner-House with a White-Balcony and Blue-Flower-Pots" (551a32[95]). Eyebrows were shaped "taking off the uneven Hair, with little or no pain" (551a32[123]), and freed of superfluous hair that might also disfigure "Forehead [...] Lips, Chin, or any other part, in a quarter of an Hour, so dexterously that it shall never come again" (551a32[171]). Among the products, powders, sold generally in packets or "papers", were the most widely offered remedies, sometimes extolled with high-sounding names (e.g. the already mentioned "Princesses Powder", C112f9[19], advertised as capable of preserving Madam de Montespan's beauty "that she does not appear above eighteen or twenty years of Age, though she be above fifty five"). Powders were also used to whiten the teeth: the "rare Powder" sold by Dr Draper "makes Black and Yellow Teeth as white as Ivory".

Table 6.5: Beauty Products

Word Types	Word Tokens	% /14,639	All Tokens	% /200,583
Water	62	0.424	280	0.140
Powder	42	0.287	118	0.059
Wash	30	0.205	35	0.017
Pomatum	18	0.123	27	0.013
Ointment	17	0.116	19	0.009
Paste	10	0.068	10	0.005
Cosmetics	8	0.055	8	0.004
Plaister	5	0.034	11	0.005
Salve	5	0.034	5	0.002
Mask	4	0.027	5	0.002

Ointments and "pomatums" were equally used for lips, hands and the face (to repair wrinkles, for example), while "salves" only helped repair chapped lips, or coloured them if the salve was red. The term PASTE only referred to a product "to smooth and whiten the Hands" (551a32[96] and 551a32[123]), but – if it is "Super-super-excellent" – it also serves "for the shaking and trembling of the Hands after hard drinking, or otherwise" (551a32[171]).

Two words deserve special attention, although they seldom occur: PLAISTER and MASK. The former – present in a gentlewoman's handbill to relieve "the back, or to strengthen any ach, or pain in the limbs and prevents miscariages in women with Child" (C112f9[67]), that is, with a similar medical function to those offered by "the ever famous Physician Gilbert Anderson" to cure "all pains in the Body, gotten by Falls, Strains, Bruises, or Colds, but especially in the Back and Sides" (C112f9[30])[41] – is sold "to take of Hair from any part of the Body" (551a32[24], 551a32[96], 551a32[123], 551a32[207]). This means that hair removal with depilatory wax or similar procedures was carried out then as it is now. Masks, on the other hand, were used to 'eliminate' wrinkles: evidently they were worn at night, for they are either called "Night-Masks" (551a32[95]), or are said "To be worn at Night" (551a32[119]). Nothing, unfortunately, is revealed as to the ingredients which gave these masks a "Vizard"'s power (551a32[119]). As beauty masks, women were also invited to buy "Forehead pieces" (551a32[95]) or "Forehead cloths, which take out all Spots, Pits or Scars caused by the Small-Pox; and so also all Wrinckles" (551a32[230]).

41 This handbill is not included in the sub-corpus of handbills dealing with toiletries.

The word list in Table 6.6 collects the lexical words connected to toiletries (with the exclusion of those already inserted in the previous two tables), in their ranking order: they are nouns of skin problems, general terms such as beauty (and its derivatives, including the verb 'to beautify'), and mainly modifiers. A brief consideration of these last is proper here: as might be expected, the highest ranking modifiers have a clear positive meaning, this being always part of effective marketing and advertising procedures.

Table 6.6: Lexical Words in the Cosmetic Field

Word Types	Word Tokens	% /14,639	All Tokens	% /200,583
Woman	76	0.519	446	0,222
Excellent	63	0.430	237	0,118
White*	49	0.335	219	0,109
Beaut*	45	0.307	62	0,031
Red*	43	0.294	146	0,073
Smooth*	37	0.253	40	0,020
Colour*	26	0.178	45	0,022
Delicate	25	0,171	28	0.014
Gentlewoman	22	0.150	40	0.020
Maid*	21	0.143	71	0.035
Soft*	19	0.130	19	0.009
Fair	17	0.116	29	0.014
Freckle	16	0.109	21	0.010
Young	16	0.109	72	0.036
Complexion	14	0.096	36	0.018
Old	14	0.096	197	0.098
Morphew	13	0.089	23	0.011
Pimples	13	0.089	32	0.016
Lady	11	0.075	34	0.017
Plump	11	0.075	47	0.023
Spot	9	0.061	9	0.004
Wrinckle	9	0.061	11	0.005
Brown	6	0.041	7	0.003
Bright	5	0.034	5	0.002

In the two collections of handbills included in my corpus there are some selling "that most Famous and well approved Water of Talk, and Pearl, the clearest and brightest of all Waters" (551a32[119]), otherwise simply called "The Water of Talk" (C112f9[146]) in an eye-catching handbill the structure of which resembles

Professor Russel's leaflet (Fig. 7). The text is placed inside a frame made of alchemic symbols, such as two shining suns at the bottom (at the two corners of the sheet of paper), alembics and heated furnaces. The advertised product, which is still sold nowadays especially for children's skin care, has a long history that goes back at least to the Italian Renaissance. Actually the recipe "A fare acqua De Talcho" [for the preparation of the water of talc] can be found in Caterina Sforza's book of experiments, datable at the latest to the very beginning of the sixteenth century.[42] Caterina, illegitimate daughter of Galeazzo Maria Sforza, Duke of Milan, and mother of Giovanni dalle Bande Nere, was born in Milan in 1463 and throughout her life practised alchemy, cosmesis and herbal medicine. In her collection of recipes she jotted down the following instructions:

> Piglia el talcho calcinato [...] de sopra et ponilo alambicho inquesto modo farai um fornello dauento e mectiui un catinecto de ramo che sia copoluto in fondo e sempre se uada alargando in cima [...] poi li darai focho lemtamente de carbone continuando sinche uederai uenir lacqua agocia agocia [...] et tiella cara che e una cosa miracolosa e diuina et adopera come sai.[43]

> [take calcined talc [...] and put it into an alembic. Prepare a wind furnace on which to lay a small copper basin concave at the base and wider towards the top [...] then burn coal in it slowly, until you see the water fall drop by drop [...] and keep it very dearly for it is a miraculous and divine thing, and use it as you know.]

To these she added a note referring to the efficacy of the water: "per fare le donne belle e leuarsi omni segno e machia del uiso de sorte che se una donna fuse de sesanta annj la fara parere de uinti" [to make women beautiful and eliminate all signs and marks from the face, so that a sixty-year-old woman will look twenty years of age].[44] The beauty-prolonging effect of Caterina's water of talc is very similar to that described in the "Princesses Powder" handbill (mentioned above, C112f9[19]) which, however, does not reveal any ingredient: very probably talc was also at the basis of the extraordinary powder advertised in this bill.

The C112f9 Collection also includes three similar four-page pamphlets completely dedicated to cosmetics, in particular to selling a "Beautifying Cream": C112f9[168], C112f9[169] and C112f9[169bis]. They differ mainly in the engraving on the title page: C112f9[168] shows a woman sitting alone at a dressing table with mirror; C112f9[169] presents only the bust of a fine lady; the image in

42 See my "L'Acqua di talco'" (2010).

43 Caterina Sforza, *Experimenti de la ex.ma s.ra Caterina da Furlj* (2009), Chapter 3, p. 21.

44 Sforza, Chapter 1, pp. 19–20.

C112f9[169bis] resembles the one in C112f9[169], but the figure of a young page boy is added, handing a letter (presumably). The first and the third are dated 1716, while the worn out frontispiece of the second allows the reader to glimpse only a partial date: 17… The fourth page of each is occupied by a separate advertisement of Dr Paul Chamberlain's necklaces for easing the cutting of teeth in children. Therefore the text of the beauty advertisement consists, in effect, of two pages only. The three documents clearly have the same origin (in all of them the name of the author appears as that of "a Gentlewoman Up One pair of Stairs at the Sugar Loaf, a Confectioners Shop, over against Old Round Court, near the New Exchange in the Strand"). The wording is more or less the same in the three pamphlets. What is interesting is that the same product is sold not only to women, in spite of the images on the first pages, this being "The only Delicate Beautifying Cream, For Gentlemen and Ladies. For the Face, Neck & Hands" (C112f9[168]): clearly men started to be the target of cosmetic advertising at least as early as the first decades of the eighteenth century.[45]

From the last three tables it becomes clear that some word types are used nearly exclusively in the handbills printed by (mainly) women practitioners for female customers. The 'bodywork' connected to beauty and cosmetic products had started to become a special and gendered language in the more and more complex medical marketplace. Many manuscript and printed recipe books contain information about beautifying products which could be prepared within the household as part of the general 'bodywork' and health care practices of a family. Handbills, however, show the progressive commodification undergone by beauty practices in early modern London: products are now sold and have a market, advertisements are printed to publish waters, powders, and ointments. The ideals of traditional beauty remain the same in time: white face and hands, soft skin, plump and rosy lips, pearly teeth; but now eye-brows can also be shaped and excessive hair removed; hair growth can be favoured or stopped; the colour of

45 From the purely lexicographic point of view, it is also interesting to see that CREAM is used here instead of the then evidently obsolete POMATUM and OINTMENT (the 'new' word is totally absent from the handbills corpus). The *OED* gives 1765 as the date of first use of the term for cosmesis (s.v. cream, n.2, 2.d.: "A cream-like preparation used cosmetically"). The occurence in the pamphlets could therefore be a case of antedating, even if – under COLD CREAM – the earliest *OED* quotation is dated 1709. I thank Simon Jarvis for reminding me of Alexander Pope's *Epistle to Dr Arbuthnot*, which, at l. 310, satirizes John Hervey by calling him "This painted Child of Dirt that stinks and stings", thus pointing to the man's use of rouge and (unpleasant) perfumes (1734 [1735]).

hair can be changed. The long period of the Restoration, while cancelling the puritanical anathema against paint, retained the stress on the use of natural substances (or, at least, so it appears from the handbills) and women practitioners – more than men – offered their cosmetics to deal with beauty problems, which, furthermore, often originated from various diseases. Therefore the cosmetic art can rightly be included within the larger field of health care, with all its possible social effects and issues.[46] As Margaret Pelling writes, the appearance of the skin was of paramount importance in checking one's health: "As well as local infections, several major diseases of the time [...] manifested themselves strikingly on visible parts of the body such as the face, neck, and hands".[47] Products to repair the disfiguring effects of some ailments started to be sold, then, in the same way as medicines to cure the illnesses which had caused them. Not by chance, then, women practitioners often advertised cosmetics together with their remedies.

In the preface "To all truly vertuous Ladies" introducing Johann Jacob Wecker's posthumously printed booklet entitled *Cosmeticks or, the Beautifying Part of Physick*, the author – who signs himself only as L. D. – invites ladies to buy "these few Receipts", alluding to the content of the booklet itself, i.e. a series of recipes for home-made products.[48] The volume can be considered the cosmetic counterpart of recipe books such as Salvator Winter's *Pretious Treasury*, and shows how 'bodywork' continued to be in the hands of the house women also when it was a question of beauty. Nevertheless, as already mentioned, beauty products, alongside medicines, began being produced outside the customer's home, and sold well wrapped in parcels, boxes and glasses: they, too, became marketplace commodities.

The Bendo Affair

Nearly halfway through *The Libertine*, the 2004 film with Johnny Depp in the title role, John Wilmot 2nd Earl of Rochester is shown practising on a trestle stage in a street, accompanied by a Merry Andrew wearing a Harlequin costume.[49] The immediately following sequence displays him inside a gloomy room with some alembics and books, examining a naked young woman. The next shot,

46 See Snook for an in-depth analysis of how beauty culture also characterised and influenced gender, racial, moral and social parameters in early modern England.

47 Margaret Pelling, "Occupational Diversity" (1998), p. 204.

48 Johann Jacob Wecker, *Cosmeticks* (1660), fol. A4^{v}.

49 *The Libertine*, Dir. Laurence (2004). The film is the cinematic adaptation of Stephen Jeffrey's 1994 play with the same title.

again outside, focuses on a printed piece of paper held by one of the onlookers: on it the words 'Alexander Bendo' are clearly visible. Apart from the filmic invention of King Charles II arriving at the mountebank's hovel to call Rochester back to court, the rest of the sequence faithfully reproduces what is known about Rochester's life during some months' exile from the royal entourage.

In 1676, due to one of his notorious extravagant frolics, Rochester was banned and decided to turn mountebank. A lover of the theatre (and of actresses: Elizabeth Barry was his lover for a certain time), he put on the 'costume' of an irregular practitioner, practised on a stage, and produced printed matter advertising his activities. But it was not simply a handbill: what is extant is a page-numbered pamphlet which can be found in the British Library Collection shelfmarked C112f9. It consists of eight pages and is numbered in pencil '41' (C112f9[41]). It was included as early as the end of the seventeenth century in various editions of Rochester's poems.[50] It is also part of D. G.'s *Harangues*, where it occupies pp. 23–35. In 1687 Thomas Alcock, a servant of Rochester's, dedicated a manuscript transcription of the pamphlet to Ann Baynton, Rochester's eldest daughter, accompanying it with an epistle dedicatory. Now, under the title of "Alexander Bendo's Brochure", it is collected in Rochester's *Works*.[51]

The episode of Rochester's adventure as a quack, also recorded by his deathbed biographer Gilbert Burnet, as the third epigraph to this chapter witnesses, was apparently successful: that is, Dr Bendo/Rochester managed to gather a clientele without being detected.[52]

Scholars of Rochester's production recognise the pamphlet as one of the author's very few prose works (apart from the letters) and have studied it in its complexity as a sharp satire on Charles II's court and on the king himself. Given the scope of the present study, it will mainly be considered as a quack's work, of course in the knowledge of what it also aimed at, and thus of its multiple design.[53]

---

50 See Pinto, pp. 11–13.

51 The texts of both the letter and the pamphlet are in Alcock. For a more recent edition of the pamphlet, see John Wilmot, Earl of Rochester, *The Works of John Wilmot* (1999), pp. 112–17. My quotations will be drawn from the original pamphlet, and Alcock's letter from Pinto's edition.

52 Gilbert Burnet, *Some Passages of the Life and Death* (1680). On Burnet's debated reliability as a biographer (esp. about Rochester's pious conversion on the point of death), see Susanna Zinato, "Burnet's Heterobiography of John Wilton" (2008).

53 For an analysis of Dr Bendo's pamphlet and of its satirical and parodical charge, see Bourne, and Kirk Combe, *A Martyr of Sin* (1998).

"To ALL *Gentlemen*, *Ladies*, and *others*"

The pamphlet consists of 2275 word tokens, with 873 word types. Astonishingly – this work being written by a declared atheist – the highest ranking word type is GOD with 8 occurrences, followed by SAY and CURE (6 cases), and by COME and GREAT (5 occurrences each). Other terms connected to the semantic area of illness and health care are also present: DISTEMPER (5), DISEASE and PHYSICIAN (4), SICKNESS and DOCTOR (2). A word which has never been seen so far in any other document is POLITICIAN, which has 5 occurrences. Dr Bendo also deals with BEAUTY (2), and declares that his medical knowledge consists in SECRETS (3) gathered during his TRAVELS (2). He talks of MAN (7) and WOMAN (5), but never mentions 'children' (a word so often present in many bills). Parts of the body are also mentioned such as FACE (4), TEETH (2), LIVER, STOMACH, SPLEEN, JOYNTS, LEGS, KIDNEYS, BLADDER, REINS, WOMB (all once). To these the writer adds his polemics – like many other irregular practitioners – against MOUNTEBANKS (4), CHEATS (3), COUNTERFEITS (2), and QUACKS (2), accusing them of sending out fraudulent BILLS (4). Besides the scurvy other ailments or general body affections can be found in the pamphlet: freckles, pimples, the small pox, the green sickness, barrenness, inflammations and obstructions, gouts, dropsies, consumptions (each once only). It may be no accident that the alleged disease he would die of four years later, i.e. that 'French pox' the cure of which so many handbills advertised, is not named in Bendo's pamphlet. Actually, when promising secrecy and privacy to his prospective patients, Bendo only uses the modifier VENEREAL referring to the previously introduced "diseases", but with no more addition, as if to say that he knows of the existence of that malady, and that is enough. Moreover, when declaring that he will not present a long list of diseases, he at once adds: "it behoves a Physician I am sure to understand them all" (C112f9[41], p. 5). From just one modifier, then, his readers will know that he knows.

As for the high frequency of GOD in the pamphlet, it must be said that the word is not used to invoke any blessing on the practitioner or to thank the divinity for special gifts, but on very circumstantial occasions, in themselves revelatory of a different use (and meaning) of the word by the writer. On the first of these occasions – "thanks to my God" – GOD is preceded by the possessive MY, thus inviting those in the know to decode the hidden sense of the phrase as void, as just an addition to propitiate the reader (C112f9[41], p. 1). The second occurrence of the word is to be found after the 'digressive' paragraphs of political satire: "First, I will (by the leave of God) perfectly cure […]" (C112f9[41], p. 4), that is, when the pamphlet imitates a quack's bill at its best, thus stressing the parodic effect exactly when the cluster simply reads as a quack's wording. In fact the phrase "by the leave of God" never occurs in the handbills corpus. Naming the divinity, also in the other textual cases, is only a tool to play up to the pious and religious addressee. It often sounds so in many handbills, but here the high frequency of the term (and the knowledge about its writer) results in the creation of a deceptive mask, linguistically equivalent to the whole hoax.[54]

Already from the list of the principal lexical words, one can deduce that the content and the language of this pamphlet are quite different from, and at the same time paradoxically similar to the quacks' literature seen up till now. Apart from the stylistic quality of the text (by far above the best written handbills) and the interspersed Latin phrases used *ad hoc* and correctly, it is the ranking of the various words which signals the difference. The presence of such a term as POLITICIAN reveals that the pamphlet allows (invites, rather) a multiple-levelled reading.[55] The equation between politicians and quacks starts on p. 3, occupying most of it, and ends on p. 4 (half page), where – as if after a digression – the author writes: "But that I may not prove too tedious, I will proceed faithfully to inform you, what are the things in which I pretend chiefly at this time to serve my Country" (C112f9[41], p. 4). The satire against politicians has just ended before these words with an epigrammatic sentence: "So you see the Politician is, and must be a Mountebank in State Affairs; and the Mountebank (no doubt if he thrives) is an errant Politician in Physick." (p. 4). The parallel between the two activities is well highlighted and all the satirical weight of Bendo's words is thus enhanced.

In spite of all this, though, Dr Bendo's pamphlet retains the structure and the (at least partial) content of an irregular medical practitioner's advertisement. Let me recall the list of items identified as constituting a model for London handbills discussed in Chapter 2, although one has to keep in mind that Bendo's is not a letter-crammed single sheet, but an eight-page booklet, well studied and articulated. It starts with a 'title' (the address to "all Gentlemen and Ladies" has this function), and ends with the doctor's practice hours plus address. It attacks possible rivals, states credentials (if in a very general way), lists diseases (albeit while denying it: "I will not here make a Catalogue of Diseases and Distempers", p. 5), names God's blessing. It also offers his cures and services, especially to women, not without sexual innuendoes when he declares he has resolved many problems of barrenness in women:

---

54 See the paragraph "How to appear pious and charitable" in Chapter 4 above.
55 These are the issues well discussed by Bourne and Combe.

> Cures of this kind I have done signal and many, for the which I doubt not but I have the good wishes and hearty Prayers of many Families, who had else pin'd out their days under the deplorable and reproachful misfortunes of Barren Wombs. (C112f9[41], p. 6)[56]

It is clear, then, that it is also a satire and a parody of irregular practitioners' advertising, since it imitates and ridicules their printed materials while promoting Dr Bendo's own practice, though fake.

Thomas Alcock's letter dedicatory adds some more details to Dr Bendo's pamphlet and practice. Rochester's servant shows he has understood the far-reaching mode of his master's activities when he writes that "[Rochester] esposes that Ignorant sort of People, the Mock Astrologers, Mountebanks, Quack Salvers, Empiricks, and their insensible admirers" (Alcock, p. 25). He also specifies that Rochester acted

> under the disguise of an Italian Mountebank, […] deluding his Ignorant and Malicious Enimies; who thought they had exil'd him into France; when he was selling to them, their Wives, and Children, Washes, Paint, Powders, Oyntments […] diureticks, Tinctures, Chimicall Preparations of all Sorts, with Specificks and Nostrums innumerable. (p. 26)

He explains as well that, in case a woman was shy about being seen by a man-doctor, "she was to leave a token with the Doctor and appoint an hour when his Wife was to bring it, as a Credential that she came on that Errand": like many other male practitioners, Dr Bendo also offered the services of a female healer. But actually there was no Dr Bendo's wife, and "this part of the comedy" (as Alcock calls it) consisted in a true theatrical performance:

> [w]e divested the Noble Doctor of his Magisterial Robes, and by the assistance of a Tyre Woman putt him into the habit of a grave Matron; so away she trudged with the return of the expectant Lady's Token, by which Ticket, she soon found the admittance agreed on between the Lady and the Doctor, and did her business Effectually. (p. 27)

What Alcock may have meant by the final adverb remains once again in the shade of sexual innuendoes, especially if connected to Rochester's words in his pamphlet about solving barrenness in women.

From Alcock we also get to know that Dr Bendo performed on a stage, helped "by his Merry Andrew", that he was an efficient self-advertiser (by "publishing & dispensing his Bills"), and that "he hourly received good Gold and Silver, which was Chearfully paid him, by his credulous Patients, with thanks to boot" (p. 27).

---

56 One is reminded of Chaucer's lines devoted to the Friar in the "General Prologue" of *The Canterbury Tales*, when the friar is ambiguously said to have made "ful many a marriage | Of younge women at his owene cost" (ll. 212–13).

He sold 'medicines' produced by concocting the most improbable ingredients such as "Ashes, Soote, Lime, Chalk, Clay, old Wall, Soap [...] with the assistance of a little blue Verditor, red Russet, white Lead, Yellow Oaker, Umber [...] to discoulour, tinge, and fix Medicaments into the proper view, and Shape", so that – also because of the "reasonable rate for the Simples, with which he compounded their Specifick remedies" – "all the Apothicaries and Drugsters in the Neighbourhood, were cursing him" (p. 28). From Alcock's testimony, even if perhaps a little exaggerated, Dr Bendo's persona emerges not only as that of a most infamous quack, but also as a remarkable and successful actor.

As an actor, in fact, Rochester performed his double quack role: in a woman's clothes he played his wife, under disguise, *en travesti*, helped in this by a "Tyre woman", i.e. by somebody expert in theatre life and goings on; as a man, he camouflaged himself by wearing a stage costume, as it were. The "noble Doctor Alexander Bendo", surrounded by his helpers ("all of them dress'd like the old Witches in Macbeth"), was clad with

> an old overgrown Green Gown which he religiously wore in memory of Rabelais his Master put on at the reception of his Doctor's Degree at Montpellier, lined through with exotic furs of diverse colours, an antique Cap, a great Reverend Beard, and a Magnificent false Medal sett around with glittering Pearl, rubies, and Diamonds of the same Cognation, hung about his Neck in a Massy Gold like Chaine of Princes mettle. (p. 29)

From these particular items describing Bendo's attire we can understand that not much had changed since John Rastell's 1566 book: more than a century had passed, but a mountebank's garments – a theatrical mountebank's, rather – had not undergone any transformation. According to Rastell's quotation reproduced in Chapter 1, mountebanks were conspicuous because of their "silkes and veluettes", their "braslettes & bowed peeces of golde", and were "chained about the neck with a great thing (of copper and gylt, as many iudge, but) of pure and fine gold" (Rastell, fol. Aiii^{v}). In 1602 John Oberndorff had also dwelt on irregular practitioners' attire:

> he [a mountebank] is like an Ape clad in Purple, with a whole table of Toyes and Trinkets that by Garish, Outlandish, and uncouth Apparell, his great Golden chaine, and glittering Rings upon every Finger, he may draw the Concourse, and Admiration of the People. (Oberndorff, p. 14)

Dr Bendo's gown is not purple, or made of silk and velvet, but the choice of green is explained in that revealing phrase "in memory of Rabelais his Master", which links Bendo to a long tradition of irreverent, saucy, and ironic literature. Evidently, the role required showy apparel and 'trinkets', although made of base metals. Real mountebanks' jewels, then, are fake, their clothes ostentatious. But so are theatrical costumes and stage necklaces and rings, and Bendo – as a counterfeiting quack – really performed a 'comedy' of quacks, on a trestle stage, on Tower Hill instead of at the Theatre Royal. His performance might even be labelled metatheatrical, since it mirrors and parodies quacks' everyday shows. On top of all this, the picture gets its 'sound track' made up of orders and directions "which neither he [Rochester], nor they [his helpers] understood one word of" (Alcock, p. 30). Alcock's savoury narrative goes on piling up grotesque details to portray to Rochester's daughter the picture, or rather the scene, of Dr Bendo's theatrical performance: customers, definitely called "spectators", were admitted inside the "laboratory" so that they could see crucibles, alembics, pestles and mortars, all in all a real stage scenery full of props.

Dr Bendo's pamphlet, as stated above, is also included in the various editions of D. G.'s *Harangues*. The structural features it presents make it rather a written piece than a spoken text, even if there are forms of direct address to 'listeners' (or readers) and the sender uses the first person to speak to his addressees. Its textual complexity testifies, if necessary, to the fact that that collection is seldom a transcription or the 'language really spoken by quacks', but mostly a series of literary inventions. And certainly nobody more that John Wilmot, 2nd Earl of Rochester, the courtier, the libertine, the poet, was able to create such a hoax as his double- or triple-edged printed pamphlet.

When Rochester was allowed to return to court, some months after his debut as a mountebank, he, his acolytes and his practice dissolved into thin air (according to Alcock, "It was some time rumour'd that they were an Inchanted Crew, raised and laid by Necromancie"), the stage was abandoned so that "[t]he poor Carpentars that sett up the Stage were glad to take it for their Pains", and the laboratory deserted for the joy of the goldsmith who "had the utensils left in the Labratory for the Rent of his House" (Alcock, p. 30). The performance mounted on the street stage was over, its main actor back to his milieu. The two extant documents about this enterprise, Bendo/Rochester's pamphlet and the additional information offered by Alcock, make a very impressive quack of John Wilmot, able, though intent on targeting a plural audience and satirising those in power, to write, imitate, and surpass the literature of less aristocratic and favoured – but certainly more authentic – irregular practitioners.

Conclusion

Il nome di Ciarlatano per ordinario è preso per mala parte.
[The name of charlatan has customarily a strongly negative bias]
(Giovanni Domenico Ottonelli, *L'ammonitioni a' recitanti*)

The handbills written by London healers in the second half of the seventeenth century are complex texts: they are narratives, since they often tell stories (of the writer's therapeutic success and of the people cured); they may contain the writer's biographical details; they offer, in their totality, a lot of information for the composition of a particularised map of London commercial activities; they are the first advertising means British culture produced, availing itself of the advantages deriving from print;[1] they are documents attesting the state of medicine at the time; they are mirrors of late seventeenth-century non-literary prose, thus helping us to inquire into the state of popular English. They are cultural products often forgotten (or dismissed soon after acknowledging them) on the basis of the prejudice and condemnation voiced against their writers by Collegiate physicians. They are certainly marginal cultural products; nevertheless they deserve attention and fuller consideration.

The historical linguists of the EMEMT research group have recently published some studies resulting from the analysis of the various text types collected in the EMEMT corpus, besides the already quoted volume itself including the CD with the texts (2010). Among these studies, some have approached the "Materia medica" section of that corpus, mentioned here in Chapter 3: that is, the medical texts that are more similar to what has been the focus of this book.[2] In particular, these researchers have scrutinized recipe books, examining the interpersonal rhetorical strategies authors adopted in order to convince readers of the efficacy of the medicines described in their collections.[3] The practice of marketing nostrums through whole pamphlets has also been canvassed in order to study the linguistic features that mostly denote (and connote) the special relationship between seller and customer. These articles stress the fact that – in Ratia and Suhr's words –

1 Other printed ephemera existed, of course, such as play bills, but they did not advertise commodities.

2 See Taavitsainen and Pahta, eds, *Medical Writing* (2011).

3 See Ville Marttila, "New Arguments for New Audiences" (2011), and Martti Mäkinen, "Efficacy Phrases" (2011).

> [m]edical pamphlet advertisements have to a large extent been ignored by historical linguists studying advertising as they have focused their analyses on newspaper advertising during the eighteenth century [...] However, in light of their popularity in the latter half of the seventeenth century, it is clear that these early forms of advertising merit closer study.[4]

Working independently from the EMEMT research group, I have dealt with handbills, i.e. with even more ephemeral and cheap print than pamphlets (although I studied some of them which are included in the two British Library Collections of advertisements). They also deserve deeper attention since they are capable of supplying information valuable both for the history of advertising and for the role they played in medical history. In the end they have emerged as really amounting to a specific text type, given the formulaic features their analysis has shown (see Chapter 3 above in particular), and the fact that they came to be the object of parody (see Chapters 5 and 6). Actually, part of *The Character of a Quack-Doctor* (1676) and the whole of Alexander Bendo's pamphlet are parodies of what, at the time, were well known and recognizable printed products and they use the basic model, style and content of their 'sources' in order to camouflage their own satiric intent. The former, as part of a deliberate attack on quacks, creates a fake handbill to expose medical practitioners' deceitful tactics. The latter uses the same textual strategies to mask its own social and political satire. This shows that medical handbills were socially identifiable; they had become text types in which one could detect common and shared features, and from which one could expect certain uses of language, certain details and also repeated discursive units. D. G.'s *Harangues* may also belong to this parodic wave, but it contains attempts at reproducing real speeches, too, for the mere sake of imitating a popular sub-genre of public oral communication.

The handbills corpus I built has allowed not only a quantitative analysis, shedding light onto some of the linguistic and rhetorical features of leaflets marketing medical services and proprietary medicines, but also a qualitative and intertextual investigation which I think can help us understand better the social phenomenon of medical advertising by irregular medical practitioners.

One of the problems also dealt with by the EMEMT researchers is the extent of the readership of their objects of investigation. I tried to give answers to this question at the end of Chapter 1, but I think that some of the issues resulting from the analysis of the texts included in the EMEMT "Materia medica" section might be applied to my work, so as both to contrast and validate it. The problem

4 Maura Ratia and Carla Suhr, "Medical Pamphlets" (2011), p. 184.

of ascertaining the extent of literacy in early modern England and in London in particular, as already mentioned, has been debated by many scholars who take into consideration the different skills necessary to sign a document, write something, read handwritten or printed material.[5] In the case of handbills, apart from the fact that they could be read aloud on many occasions and thus understood by the illiterate as well as the literate, a minimum of functional medical literacy among the lowest social ranks can be assumed.[6] Handbills, therefore, can be considered as having the widest circulation and readership, they being easily accessible printed material dealing with medical problems, and – moreover – freely available since, unlike pamphlets and recipe books which were actually sold (however cheaply), they were distributed gratis.

As discussed in Chapters 4 and 5, most handbills appear to reproduce the tactics and the phases typical of the oral performances of stage mountebanks (first the introduction of the healer by a 'helper' through the use of third person singular pronouns, then the writer-practitioner taking centre stage with the proclamation of his/her individuality by first person singular pronouns). Practitioners, in spite of being resident in London and practising at the addresses always accompanying any single handbill, actually 'performed' even when writing bills, and if the few documented real mountebanks can be considered as actors performing on street stages, all writers of printed medical bills can be interpreted as "actors who mount the stage of medical practice", so much so that, according to William Kerwin, "[t]he full-time physicians, as part of their attempts to establish a 'profession', attack their largely part-time rivals as dangerously theatrical pretenders". Kerwin's analysis of the attacks of the College of Physicians against irregular practitioners highlights the former's relationship with the antitheatrical prejudice and polemics and interprets irregular medical practice as parallel to actors' activities, since "[p]hysicians have always performed".[7] This stance recalls Giovanni Domenico Ottonelli's *Della christiana moderatione del theatro libro, detto L'ammonitioni a' recitanti* (1652) in which the Italian author (discussed

5 See Slack; Cressy (*Literacy*, and *Society and Culture*); Ong (*Orality*); Barry; Fox; Furdell (*Publishing and Medicine*), and Fissell ("The Marketplace of Print").

6 "The reading of medical texts in English would seem most obviously to belong to the category of functional literacy, since the acquisition of medical information was of direct help to those trying to maintain or restore the health of members of any household, rich or poor." (Peter Murray Jones, "Medical Literacies" (2011), p. 32).

7 William Kerwin, *Beyond the Body* (2005), pp. 133, 137. For the extended discussion of this point (and in particular of the point of view expressed by Oberndorff), see Kerwin, pp. 137–44.

in Chapter 1) combines his complaints against Commedia dell'Arte players with those of charlatans selling their remedies from raised stages, two social types guilty of making money out of performing what he considers promiscuous, obscene and licentious 'actions'.

That medicine could be practised by laypeople of various social and mercantile extractions, that is, by a promiscuous human congeries which deeply disturbed the College of Physicians of London, is a point strongly stressed by Pelling and Webster (1979), and by Pelling: "[b]oth formally and informally, a great many medical practitioners either practised medicine part-time, or combined it with a range of associated activities".[8] Pelling also resumes this topic in her monograph when she writes: "Ironically, medicine, an apparently vocational pursuit, provides some of the most instructive examples of occupational diversity".[9] But that absolutely does not mean that all male and female unlicensed practitioners were ignorant and unskilful (or dangerous) as the College of Physicians described them. In London, at least, i.e. in an "early modern metropolitan culture", information spread via "informal mechanisms":

> These informal mechanisms, which included observation, private reading, kinship and household links, and formative experiences, were as important among the educated élites as among the commonalty, and had a status in medicine in particular which even the College could hardly reduce.[10]

From whatever trade they came, seventeenth-century unlicensed practitioners resorted to publicity to make their 'specialization' known, and sell their remedies. Before the expansion of newspaper advertising, handbills were the preferred means of communication, and all irregular healers availed themselves of them, apparently not trusting specialised publications which the "Office of Public Advice of London and Westminster" offered. As early as 1657 this office sent out a broadside announcing its intention to collect different and sundry advertisements into a booklet to be published every Tuesday morning, upon the payment of fees varying from 1 penny per ton (for publicity of ships above 100 tons) to the highest fee of 10 shillings, a price reserved for the advertisements of such professions as a) "Professors of Sciences, Teachers of *Hebrew*, *Greek*, *Latin*, *English*, *French*, *Italian*, *Dutch*, or any other Languages [...]", and b) "Physitians and others, that have any rare and approved Receipt or Medicine for any Pain or Disease", but also the

8 Margaret Pelling, "Trade or Profession?" (1998), p. 242.

9 Pelling, *Medical Conflicts*, p. 149. On the medical activities of lay people also see, by the same author, "Occupational Diversity".

10 Pelling, "Knowledge Common and Acquired", p. 269.

advertisements "Of such as having such Pains, look for any one to help them".[11] What emerges from this is that both categories of professionals were thought of as charging more than others for their activities, i.e. they would get large amounts of money from the encounter of supply and demand in a well-ordered market, and therefore their publicity was charged more. Very probably quacks in particular did not take special advantage of this commercial offer, since their surviving handbills certainly testify to their preference for the single leaflet. Evidence of this preference is the issue of an anonymous bill "printed by Andrew Clark" in 1675, which reiterates the offer of the Office of Public Advice, not limiting it, though, to advertisements being printed in a collection. This "Advertisement" is addressed to those who "are at great expence in printing, publishing and dispersing of Bills of Advertisement", and to whom the new enterprise offers its services as a sort of agency for the printing, delivery and distribution of the material entrusted to it "in every house where the Bills of Mortality are received".[12] "Physitians and others" are not mentioned in this second document, perhaps for two reasons: on the one hand, regular practitioners disdained this type of publicity, considering it too lowly for their status, as already mentioned; on the other, irregular practitioners preferred what they had always done, i.e. publicity through direct contact and face-to-face interaction with their addressees, occurring when either they 'performed' on a mountebank's stage, or handed out bills to prospective customers.

After completing a book I think it normal to look back not only at what one has done, but – especially – at what one has omitted or overlooked. It may prove a hazardous procedure, since it might reveal extensive omissions. My final appraisal is that I would like to have been able to draw a fresh and detailed map of London on the basis of all the topographical indications to be found in the handbills; that I would also like to have transcribed the third collection of handbills held in the British Library (Harley 5931); and that, above all, I would like to have worked at my corpus more 'scientifically' (for example after parsing it and – why not – after publishing it and making it available to others). But all this appears to me now as belonging to another, future research phase which – if the first proves coherent – may grow out of it.

Nevertheless, I think that this book – with all its limits – has delved into a cultural territory which had been neglected till now. My approach to the language

11 Anon., *The Office of Publick Advice* (1657). Elliott (p. 38) writes that the first number of *The Publick Adviser* collecting various advertisements in book form was dated 19–26 May 1657.

12 Anon., *Advertisement* (1675).

of irregular practitioners has tried to make themselves speak well beyond any biased label attached on them by their ferocious critics. The novelty of this has allowed an interdisciplinary analysis that in the end returns a many-sided picture of a relevant social phenomenon in early modern London. For the first time London unlicensed practitioners – empirics / quacks / irregulars – are centre-stage, speaking to us once again, not only as an object of satire, derision and disapproval, but also as the self-aware agents of an entrepreneurship for which words – written and/or orally exhibited – were certainly more important than even the medicaments for sale. Those words cured: they were (palliative) healing words.

Appendixes

Appendix A

Transcription of C112f9[77]

With Liberty of the Colledge of Physitians of the Royal Head City of LONDON in ENGLAND

This High-German Doctor, cured the Emperor of the *Turk's* Brother, who was Blind 13 Years.

Be it made known by this, to all high and lower Persons, that here lately is Arrived, an Experienc'd, most Famous, *German, Turkish,* and *Imperial* Physitian, whose like has not been in this Kingdom, who hath Learned such a curious and strange Art, which no other Doctor doth understand, and can Cure alla sorts of Patients which are left off by other Doctors. He can show his Testimonies from 3 Emperors and 9 Kings, as also from 7 Dukes and Electorat Princes, as the *Romish, Turkish,* and *Japanish* Emperors; he can show his Testimonies in 36 Languages, which no other Doctor can show: He hath Cured the Brother of the Turkish Emperor, which was blind 13 years, and hath obtained his Natural Sight again. This *German* Physitian has Travelled through 3 parts of the World.

1. He lets understand, that he is Famous, that the like of him is not to be found, an Occulist, Stone, and Rupture-Cutter, *Medicinæ Chymicus Pratticus,* if any such Patients do meet, which are troubled with blindness of the Eyes, though they were Born Blind from the very Womb, he knows to Cure those Patients, with the help of God, for their Life time, as there are Cataracts, Obstructions, Suffusion, all so[rts] of Blindness, Darkness of the Eyes, that Men must Write and Read by Spectacles, those he Cures by the help of God, that they may Write and Read without them. He also Cureth Redness, Hotness, or running of the Eyes, or any other Distemper of the Eyes which are not mentioned here, by the help of God he cures in a very short time.
2. He helps also all Bursten or broken Bellies, either in Men, Women or Children, whether the Rupture be in the Groin or Navel, and if the Rupture be as bigg as a Mans Head, then trust to God, and his Art, you shall have your Cures, that you may go about in a short time without a Truss, if they have been Bursten for 20 or 30 years together. He maketh also Artificially all sorts of Trusses, which no other Doctor doth understand, the Patients may go in the same, Ride, Dance, and Spring, and do what they will without any danger, which healeth Artificially under the same. Of these Ruptures are found seven

sorts, as *Hernia Intestinalis, Ventosa, Aquosa, Carnosa, Humoralis, Zis[?]ttis, Hernie;* all these this Famous Doctor con help in a short time, either by Cutting, or without Cutting, according as he finds the Patients.

[verso] [illegible] any one be troubled with Hair-Lips, and Born with the same, either Children, or older Person [illegible] to make a fair Mouth in 6 days time. He cureth also great Wens, Cancers, Fistulas, either [illegible] eggs, Eyes, *etc.* which no other Doctor can Cure, he cureth Artificially in a short time.

4. This Doctor beyond other Doctors, is able to Cure the Venereal Disease, called the *French Pox*, [illegible] all their Appendences, he cureth them going and standing in a short time; if he is a Man, he cureth him that his Wife shall not perceive it, and so the contrary.
5. This High German Doctor has a curious art to help and give counsel to such kind of Women that are unfruitful and bare no Children, which is the defect of Nature, or the effect of Witchcraft; and hath such secret Medicines, which (by the help of God) in a little time will make them fruitful and bare Children.
6. He cureth all sorts of deafness, noise in the Ears, in a short time; the Head-ach, Giddiness, and other distempers of the Head, which are not here related.
7. This Doctor hath a curious way, which no other Doctor hath, for the curing of the Falling Sickness, either in Men, Women, or Children, if they have been troubled with the same 10 or 20 years, so that they shall not be troubled with it again for their life time.
8. If any person is troubled with the Stone, either in the Kidney or Bladder, he cureth the same either by cutting, or most commonly without cutting, by breaking the Stone artificially in the Bladder, by Medicines according to the Consitution and Habit of the Patients body, by Gods assistance in few days.
9. He cureth artificially all distempers in Men and Women, as Dropsies, Yellow Jaundice, Scurvy, cold and Phlegmatick Stomachs, windy and tedious Coughs, spitting of Bloud, Phtisick, stoppage of the Liver, hardness of the Spleen, over-running of the Gall, Agues, Fevers, Pleurisie, *Passionem Cholicam*, Diarrhæas, Piles in the Fundament.
10. He likewise cureth Women and Maids of many Infirmities, as the rising of the Mother, or the stoppage of the same, causing them to think that they are poisoned. Also such Women as labour under any secret distempers, or in difficulty of Child-bearing. Likewise such women as have received any detriment in Child-bed, these he cures in half an hour, and they shall remain so their life time: but if they are unwilling to impart their distempers unto me, his Wife shall receive the Information, and return them such Medicines that (by Gods help) will recover them.

This Physitian is a great Artist, whose like is not in this Kingdom, he draws teeth most artificially, whole Teeth, little Teeth, the Roots of Teeth, if they were so fast in the Gums that they cannot be seen he knowth to draw them with great dexterity, without trouble or pain to the Patient. He puts in artificially Teeth of Ivory, Silver, or Gold, as if they were natural [illegible] ment, which taketh a mans heart away to see it; he maketh loose Teeth fast, tho the Gums are consumed, takes away a stinking Breath, Scurvey, and Foulness of the Mouth; he has brought with him a precious Medicine for the Tooth-ach, which performeth the effect in a quarter of an hour; he hath likewise brought with him all sorts of smelling and well-tasting Teeth-powder to clear the Teeth, and to make them white; as also a sweet-smelling Mouth. If any one hath occasion for these his Rarities, let them come to his Lodging, and to Persons of Quality that sends for him he will wait on them. This Famous Physitian knoweth to cure all other distempers which are not mentioned here.

This German Physitian doth cast all sorts of Humane Urine, none like him in that Art; gives judgment in all distempers, to know by this accordingly, if the disease hath been of twenty years standing, whether it be curable or not. He tells you to prevent Charges, if no necessity, or else will use Moderation according to their Qualities. Let the Patients water be brought to him which was made after midnight.

He hath within few days cured several Patients which were left off by other Doctors, as well in distempers of the Body, as Blindness of the Eyes; the first he cured was blind 9 years, the second 15, the third 18, and the fourth 23 years, which for Credits sake would not be named, as also in the *French Pox*, and other distempers more.

This said Imperial Physitian has brought his Apothecaries Shop along with him, and carries it wherever he goes, for the good of his Patients.

This is to give notice to all Gentry and others, that this High-German Doctor, hath in his House in *Moorfields*, made (by his Art) a most excellent sweating and Bathing house, after the High German Manner, in which he uses for his Baths, the best smelling and odoriferous Herbs, through which (by the help of God) many diseases are cured thereby; those that have occasion to make use of this Bath, may repair to my House, where they shall be entertain'd according to their Ability, at reasonable Rates.

Whoever hath occasion for this Imperial Physitian, may come to his Lodging, or else send for him, and he will wait upon them according to their Qualities.

This Imperial Operator and Doctor is at present in LONDON, **and now liveth at a New House the corner of** White-Cross-Alley in Moorfields, **next door to the** Star **Musick-House, where you may see the** High-German **Spread Eagle hang over the Door.**

Transcription of 551a32[112]

In Bruges-Street *in* Covent-Garden, *over-against the* Kings-Play-House *or* Rose Tavern, *where you will see* the Kings-Arms *Hang over the* Balconey, *Dwelleth*, Cornelius à Tilbourn, the *Famous* German *Physitian and* Operator, *Sworn Chyrurgeon to the late King* Charles *the* II, *And now Priviledg'd by Our Gracious Soveraign King* William, *who*

By His great Diligence and Study, hath lately found out some admirable Remedies, which was never yet made Publick in any of his former Bills: These are therefore to Advertise all Persons concern'd, that have either Weak or Dimm Sight, occasion'd by Age or otherwise, and are oblig'd to wear *Spectacles,* He undertakes to bring them to see well without them in a Weeks time, altho' they have used them 20 Years before: He Infallibly Cures all sorts of Sore Eyes whatsoever, otherwise demands no Money for his Pains. He takes off all Pearls, Pins, Webbs, Cataracts, both White and Black, and Skins of all kinds, growing upon, or settled in the Eye, and gives immediate Sight to those that are termed Stone-Blind, where [verso] the Visive faculty is not quite lost, and all by an outward Application: And to the end, that none may refrain coming to him, for fear of an unnecessary Expence, they are all hereby Invited to come and accept a Tryal for nothing; and if in a quarter of an hour they do not find great benefit, it's left to their Discretion to preceed or not.

If any Person, by Accident or Misfortune, looseth one of their Eyes, He can Artificially put in another, not to be discern'd by any one, without being informed of it before hand.

He hath likewise an admirable Remedy to prevent Miscarriage in Women, although they have Miscarried for five or six times before.

He likewise Cures all Vapours, Giddiness, or Swimming in the Head, or any Fainting Fits, and takes away all Pains and Aches in the Limbs, or any part of the Body; and immediately Cures the Griping in the Guts, although it be in the greatest extremity, only by an outward Application. And as this is the first time, that he has made use of this way of Advertisement for these particular Remedies, so he gives you to understand, that after these are disposed of, you must expect no more: Therefore, you are desired to keep these Bills, to the End you may know where to apply yourselves in your Extremity.

If any Person that is Sick, send but their Urine to me, I will give them my Advice faithfully; and if desire, prescribe them such Remedies, as shall be suitable to their Distemper.

I Cure the *French Pox,* with all its Accidents, as the *Running of the Reins, Shankers, Buboes,* or swelling in the *Groin*, after a new Method, and in a short time, without Baths or Stoves, and without *Mercury*, which many times proves destructive to the Patient. And for the satisfaction of all those that have been Sporting in the Garden of *Venus*, and in seeking of Pleasure, have met with a *Clap* or *Gonorrhœa*, I promise to Cure them in six or seven days time, or desire nothing for my Pains; which is as much as to say, *No Cure, No Money.*

Transcription of C112f9[117]

At the Golden-Ball *in* Princes-street, *near* Stocks Market, *you may have*

A Certain, Safe and *Private Cure* for any *Venereal* **Pox** or **Clap**, by a *Physician* that design'd not to make this further Publication after Fifteen Years Successful Practice, only to oppose the late *Upstart Pretenders*, and prevent the Ruin of such as labour under this Disaster. I shall not use many *Invitations*, rather leave you to make *Experience*, which is beyond all Arguments. In a Word, let *Your* Condition be never so bad, *Distrust not*, although you have been under the Hands of several *Doctors*, and by the Use of their Medicines grown rather worse than better, and tho' *Fluxed* several Times to no Purpose; nay, if you have Languished under it several Years, and are **Pored** to that Degree that you are broke out in an Hundred Places, I promise faithfully (under God) to make a **Perfect Cure** in a reasonable Time, or desire Nothing for my Pains.

But for those who have been lately Sporting, and by Chance have got a **Clap**, or **Running of the Reins**, I promise to cure them in a few Days, without Loss of Time, or Hindrance of any Business.

Advice of Proper Medicines in any Distemper.

Note, The *Golden-Ball* in *Princes-street* is a Corner House, about the middle of the Street, (where you will see a Back-door) turning down to *Lothbury,* near the *Royal Exchange.*

Transcription of 551a32[139]

IN

Frogmorton-Street[1]

At the *Golden Ball* over against *Draper's* Hall, between *Batholomew* Lane and *Broad. street,* near the *Royal Exchange,* May be had of *T. C.* an approved Physician of long Practice, A pleasant Drink which purges by Urine, at two shillings

1 The name of the street in the title position is actually Throgmorton, but the printer used a single capital 'F', instead of 'Th'.

six pence the Bottle, with my Anti-Venerial Pills, which purge by Stool, at three shillings the Box. They will be delivered to any Messenger with Directions sealed up how to take them. Secrets so excellent in operation, and so friendly to Nature, that in my constant practice, and great experience for Twenty Years, in this City of *London*, is well known to be the most successful, both for preventing, and curing, perfectly and speedily the *Venereal POX*; A Disease destructive to the body of Man, if not timely and carefully prevented; It proceeds from a virulent, venomous Matter suckt into the body by a strong attractive Faculty in time of Copulating with an unclean Woman, which excoriates the whole passage of Urine, and causes a foul stinking Issue, or Running; this Ulceration is the cause of scalding heat of Urine, pricking, and painful standing of the Yard, and if neglected, and not carefully cured causes swellings in the Cod, Buboes, or swellings in the Groin, and infects the body in general with the *POX*, as by an Ulcer upon the outside of the Yard, called a Shanker, ragged Warts in the privy Parts, pains and Scabs in the Face, Head, or Neck, and sometimes over the whole body; Inflammations and Ulcers in the Mouth and Throat. To prevent these dangerous Evils, be so kind to your selves, to be constantly provided with my Anti-Venerial Medicines; that Infallibly eradicate all poysonous Matter and Steems that are contracted in the body, in as short a time as can [verso] be expected. Therefore do not hazard your bodies with unskilful Pretenders, nor neglect your selves, to let it fix upon the bones, for then you must be confined; if you expect a Cure, which may be prevented by my never-failing Medicines, wherewith any new contracted *POX*, Runnings, or Clap of what kind soever, are all cured with that great Success, by the use of these excellent Cleansers, which operate so moderately by Stool and Urine, that all the heat of Urine is immediately abated, the poisonous Cause throughly cleansed, and the great danger of the *POX* assuredly prevented, and all Persons at what distance soever, either by Land or Sea, without giving cause of Suspicion to their nearest Relations, may with ease, speed, and privacy, free from Relapse, help themselves, Directions observed, without hazard either of Body, Purse, or Reputation, as hath been throughly proved, to the great Satisfaction of hundreds of Persons.

[pointing hand] If you have been concerned, and fear you have got any hurt, some few Dozes do certainly prevent it. Many are bashful, and loath to come to me, let such send the Particulars of their present Condition, and they may have Medicines sent them for a perfect Cure.

[pointing hand] This excellent Drink, and Incomparable Pills, which I here recommend, Reader, to your use, whether in health, or Sickness, in respect of their preparation, and operation, are not only effectual for the abovesaid Distemper, but are a sure Antidote against the Scurvy and Dropsies, and will prove as great an advantage to you, as any as yet you have met with, if timely used, and duely observed, according to Directions.

He may be spoken with from Seven in the Morning till Twelve, and from Three till Ten at Night.

Keep this Bill, and bring it with you.

Appendix B

Topography of the Coffeehouses Mentioned in the Handbills

Since neither in Ogilby and Morgan's London map nor in Morgan's is it possible to trace the location of coffeehouses (while both cartographers give information about churches, main buildings, taverns and inns), what follows is an attempt at situating the coffeehouses mentioned in the handbills, and – through Figure 14 – at visualising those active in the area of the Royal Exchange. The information in the following list is based on a recent edition of Morgan's survey of the town (Morgan 2013).[1]

Coffeehouses Positioned in William Morgan's Map

Name*	BL Shelfmark	Morgan**	Additional information***
Amsterdam Coffee-House in Bartholomew-lane	551a32[27]	23-A2	1. Throgmorton Street to Threadneedle Street
Arabian Coffee-House [in Haughton street near Clare-market]	C112f9[105]	20-A2/A3	2.
Ben's Coffee-House opposite St. Christopher's Church in Threadneedle street	551a32[4]	23-B2	3.
Bennet's Coffee-House under Moor-gate	C112f9[17]	12-D2	4.
Blacket's Coffee-House at the end of Smock-Alley in Spittle-fields	C112f9[17]	13-C2	5.
Bloomsberry Coffee-House in Silver-street, Bloomsberry	C112f9[17]	9-C1	6.
Brown's Coffee-House at Wapping Old-stairs	C112f9[17]	37-C3	7.
Buckeridge's Coffee-House near Aldersgate	C112f9[17]	11-D2	8.
Chandlers Coffee-House in Barbican	C112f9[17]	11-B2/B3	9.
Christian Coffee-House at West-smithfields-Barrs	C112f9[17]	11-C1	10.

1 To avoid repetitions, the list does not take into account the various occurrences of the same coffeehouse name as they appear in the handbills.

Name*	BL Shelfmark	Morgan**	Additional information***
Coffee-House [at the Hospital Gate in Smithfield]	551a32[193]	11-C1	11.
Coffee-House near St. Magnus Church London-Bridge	551a32[46]	23-D2	12.
Cripple-gate Coffee-House at Cripple-gate	C112f9[17]	11-C3	13.
Essex's Coffee-House at White-Chappel, by the Barrs	C112f9[17]	24-A2/A3	14.
Freeman's Coffee-House in Cheapside near Bow Church	C112f9[17]	22-B3 (L. 475) [?]	15. Bow Lane, west side
Great Coffee-House in Freemans Yard near the Royal Exchange	C112f9[151]	23-B2 (L.708)	16. Cornhill, north side
Grecian Coffee-House, at Katherine-street-End, near the Strand	C112f9[17]	20-B2	17. The Strand, north side
Gregory's Coffee-House, at Barnaby street End	C112f9[17]	35-B3/C3, 36-C1	18. Southwark
Gurney's Coffee-House on Garlick-hill	C112f9[17]	22-B3/C3	19. Thames Street, north side
Hamett's Coffee-House, on London-Bridge, near the Draw-Bridge	C112f9[17]	23-D2	20.
Hill's Coffee-House in Holbourn, over against Hatton-Garden	C112f9[17]	10-C2/D2/D3	21.
Hindmarsh's Coffee-House, in Bull-Inn[?] Court in the Strand	C112f9[17]	20-C1 (W.275)	22. The Strand to Maiden Lane
Hunlin's Coffee-House in Swithings-Alley [Sweetings, Swythings]	551a32[127]	23-A2/B2	23. Cornhill to Threadneedle Street
Jamaica Coffee-House in St. Michaels Alley	551a32[152]	23-B2/B3 (L. 660)	24. Cornhill
Joe's Coffee-House over against Chancery Lane in Holb[orn]	C112f9[17]	9-C2 to 21-A1	25. Holborn to Fleet Street
Joe's Coffee-House, called the Blue-coat Coffee-House, in Sweetings-Alley, near the Royal Exchange	C112f9[75]	23-A2/B2	26.
John's Coffee-House in Fuller's Rents in Holbourn	C112f9[17]	9-C3 (W.364)	27. High Holborn to Grays Inn
John's Coffee-House in the Rules, over against the Kings Bench	C112f9[17]	35-C1	28. Southwark

Name*	BL Shelfmark	Morgan**	Additional information***
John's Coffee-House, above the Royal Exchange in Cornhil	C112f9[33]	23-B2	29.
John's Coffee-House, in the Great Old-Baily	551a32[204]	22-A1	30.
Linty's Coffee-House near Charing Cross	C112f9[17]	19-D2/D3	31.
Lloyd's Coffee-House in Lombard Street	C112f9[31]	23-B2	32.
Lloyd's Coffee-House in Tower street	C112f9[17]	23-C3, 24-C2/D2	33.
M. Lord's Coffee-House in St. Martins le Grand	C112f9[18]	11-D2, 22-A2	34.
Man's Coffee-House at Charing-Cross	C112f9[17]	19-D2/D3	35.
Marine Coffee-House in Birchin-lane	C112f9[17]	23-B2	36. Lombard Street to Cornhill
Mr. Bisby's Coffee-House in Tower-street, near Mincing-lane	C112f9[75]	24-C1	37.
Mr. Bridge's Coffee-House in Popes-Head-Alley in Cornhil	551a32[218]	23-B2	38. Cornhill to Lombard Street
Mr. Clark at his Coffee-House in the Half-Moon Tavern-yard in Cheap-side	C112f9[58]	22-B3 (L. 475)	39. Bow Lane, west side
Mr. Cradocks Coffee-House at the Crown in Birchen [Birching]-Lane	C112f9[89]	23-B2	40.
Mr. Gander, at the Tower Royal Coffee-House against St. Antholine's Church	C112f9[1]	23-B1	41.
[Mr. Man's] Coffee-House in Abchurch-Lane	C112f9[33]	23-B2/C2	42. Lombard Street to Cannon Street
Mr. Nest at Westminster-hall door his Coffee-House	C112f9[137]	31-D3 (W.264)	43.
Mr. Richard's Coffee-House in Fleet-street	551a32[116]	21-A1/A2/A3	44.
Mr. Sacketrell, at Drury lane Coffee-House, near the Maypole	C112f9[102]	20-B2	45.

Name*	BL Shelfmark	Morgan**	Additional information***
Mr. Shuttleworth's Coffee-House at Charing-Cross	C112f9[55]	19-D2/D3	46.
Mr. Th. Oliver at his Coffee-House at Westminster-hall-gate	C112f9[16]	31-D3 (W.264)	47.
Mr. Towne's Coffee-House at Billingsgate	C112f9[75]	23-D3	48.
Mr. Yardley at the Black-boy Coffee-House in Ave-mary lane	C112f9[16]	22-A1	49. Ludgate Street, north side
Mrs. Lansdale in Sweething-Alley near the Exchange Coffee-House	C112f9[8]	23-A2/B2	50.
Mrs. Oliver, at the Coffee-House, New Palace Yard, Westminster	C112f9[102]	31-D3	51.
Mrs. Ward, at her Coffee-House in Snow-hill	C112f9[1]	10-D3, 11-D1	52. Hart Street to Holborn Bridge
Neds Coffee house in the Old Jury [Jewry]	C112f9[71a]	23-A1	53.
North's Coffee-House in Kings-street near Guild Hall	C112f9[17]	23-A1	54.
Norwich Coffee-House in Deans Court in St. Martins Le Grand near Aldersgate	551a32[27]	11-D2 (L.410)	55. St. Martin le Grand to Foster Lane
Old-Amsterdam Coffee-House [at the End of Swithing's-Rents]	C112f9[178]	23-A2/B2	56.
Peter's Coffee-House in Charles-street, Covent Garden	C112f9[17]	20-B1	57.
Post-Office Coffee-House in Pope's-head Alley [Mr. Bridge at the]	551a32[152]	23-B2	58.
Rainbow Coffee-House in West-smithfield	C112f9[17]	11-C1	59.
Rainbow Coffee House [b]y Fleet Bridge	551a32[64]	21-A3	60.
Richard's Coffee-House at Temple-Bar	C112f9[17]	21-A1	61.
Sam's Coffee-House in Ludgate-street	551a32[228]	22-A1	62.
Smither's Coffee-House in Thames-street near the Custom-House	C112f9[17]	24-D1	63.
Star Coffee-House [in the Piazza in the Royal Exchange]	551a32[213]	23-B2	64.

Name*	BL Shelfmark	Morgan**	Additional information***
Symonds-Inn Coffee-House in Chancery Lane	C112f9[17]	9-C2 to 21-A1	65. Holborn to Fleet Street
Tom's Coffee-House, in Half-Moon Court between the Old Baily and Ludgate on Ludgate Hill	551a32[227]	22-A1	66.
Turpin's Coffee-House just at Billingsgate	C112f9[17]	23-D3	67.
Union Coffee-House at Charing-Cross	C112f9[171]	19-D2/D3	68.
Victualling Office Coffee-House on Little-Tower Hill	C112f9[17]	24-C3/D3	69.
Vigure's Coffee-House near Parliament-House	C112f9[17]	31-D3	70.
Vintner's[?] Coffee-House in Redriff near Kings stairs	C112f9[17]	38-D1	71.
West's Coffee-House at the Postern in Aldermanbury	C112f9[17]	11-D3	72.
Whitehall Coffee-House in Buckingham Court near Whitehall	551a32[124]	31-B3[?]	73.
White Lion in Russel-street over against the Coffee-House in Covent-Garden	C112f9[58]	20-A2/B1/B2	74.
Wilkins's Coffee-House near Bishops-Gate	C112f9[17]	23-D1	75.
Will's coffee-House in Bow-street, Covent Garden	C112f9[17]	20-B1	76.
Yate's Coffee-House in Leaden-Hall-Market	C112f9[17]	23-B3	77. Leadenhall Street, south side

* The names of the various coffeehouses are spelt according to the original handbills in which they occur (mentioned in the BL shelfmark column). In square brackets are to be found both spelling variants and details taken from the handbills, whose linguistic structure, though, has been changed for correctness sake.

**The topographical information is drawn from the Index compiled by Robert Thompson in Morgan 2013 and refers to the fifty plans into which Morgan's map has been divided for this edition. Bracketed references are to Morgan's lists and numbers, where L and W identify "City and Liberties of London" and "Westminster, etc.", respectively (Morgan 2013, 119).

*** The additional information also derives from the same source, and aims at avoiding confusion in case of homonyms.

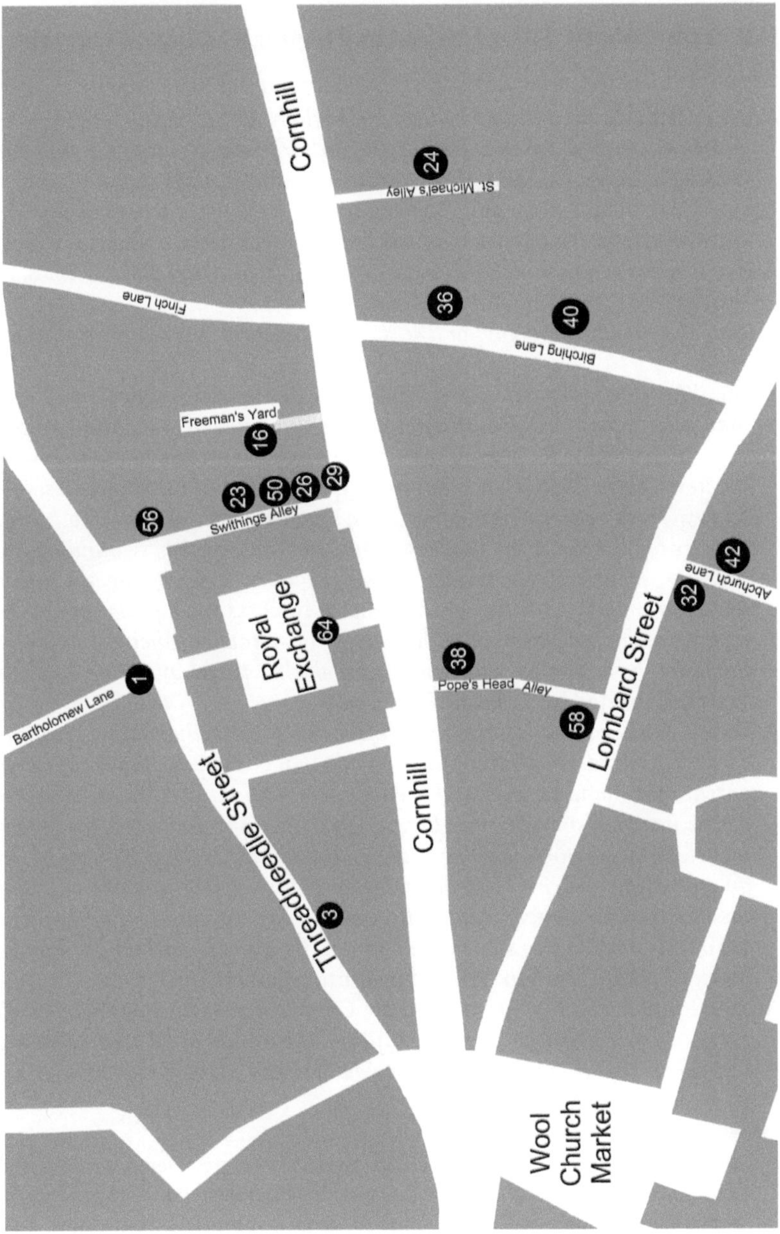

Figure 14: Map of the Royal Exchange area showing the tentative positions of some coffeehouses (by Alessandro Zanarini, after Morgan's map; numbers as in the list)

Appendix C

List of the Volume Titles Utilized in Chapter 4 (Adapted from the *ESTC*)[1]

Amyas, Richard, *An antidote against melancholy. Or, A treasury of 53. rare secrets & arts discovered, by an expert artist, Richard Amyas. Licensed, and entred according to order*, London: Printed for the authour, 1659.

Anon., *The Character of a quack doctor, or, The Abusive practices of impudent illiterate pretenders to physick exposed*, London: Printed for Thomas Jones, 1676.

Anon., *The French mountebank, or An operator fit for these present times*, London: Printed for R. Austin, and A. Coe, 1643.

Anon., *The quacks academy; or The dunce's directory*, London: Printed for A. B., 1678.

Anon., *The sick-mans rare jewel wherein is discovered a speedy way how every man may recover lost health, and prolong life, how he may know what disease he hath, and how he himself may apply proper remedies to every disease, with the description, definition, signs and syptoms [sic] of those diseases. (Viz.) The scurvy, leues venerea, gonorrhea, dropsies, catarrhs, chollick, gouts, madness, frensies of all sorts, fever, jaundise, consumptions, ptisick, swoundings, histerick passions, pleurisies, cachexia's, worms, vapours, hypochondriack melancholly, stone, strangury, with the whole troop of diseases most afflicting the bodies of men, women and children; with a supply of suitable medicines; ... a piece profitable for every person and family, and all that travel by sea or land. By B. A.*, London: Printed by T. R. and N. T., 1674.

Anthony, Francis, *The apologie, or defence of a verity heretofore published concerning a medicine called aurum potabile that is, the pure substance of gold, prepared, and made potable and medicinable without corrosiues, helpfully giuen for the health of man in most diseases, but especially auaileable for the strenghning [sic] and comforting of the heart and vitall spirits the perfomers of health: as an vniversall medicine. Together with the plaine, and true reasons ... confirming the vniversalitie thereof. And lastly, the manner and order of administration or vse of this medicine in sundrie infirmities. By Francis Anthonie of London, doctor in physicke*, London: Printed by Iohn Legatt, 1616.

Archer, John, *Every man his own doctor. Compleated with an herbal: Shewing how every onemay know his own constitution, the nature of all food, what is good or hurtful to any: shews how to know whether any place is scituated in a good or*

1 Bibliographical details of early modern publications are given according to the conventions of the *ESTC*. What follows is not a bibliography, but it simply lists the documents of which the small corpus used in Chapter 4 is made. Some titles, if quoted in the text, are also included in the final Bibliography.

bad air: of the passions of the minde, exercise, venery, tobacco, a new hot bath, with other observable things; the knowledg, danger, and cure of the pox, running of the reins, consumptions, gout dropsie, scurvy, melancholy, with the most speedy cure. The herball treats of all herbs growing in this kingdom, and shews what planet governs each herb, and how to gather them in their planetary hour: This book hath proved so useful to the publike benefit, that the booksellers have printed some thousands, and sent them to all parts abroad. ... By J. A. one of hs Majesties physicians, London: s.n., 1671–1680.

Barrough, Philip, *The methode of phisicke conteyning the causes, signes, and cures of invvard diseases in mans body from the head to the foote. VVhereunto is added, the forme and rule of making remedies and medicines, which our phisitians commonly vse at this day, with the proportion, quantitie, & names of ech [sic] medicine*, London: Imprinted By Thomas Vautroullier, 1583.

Browne, Thomas, Sir, *Pseudodoxia epidemica: or, Enquiries into very many received tenents, and commonly presumed truths. By Thomas Brovvne Dr of Physick*, London: Printed for Tho. Harper for Edvvard Dod, 1646.

Bruele, Gualtherus, *Praxis medicinae, or, the physicians practice vvherein are contained inward diseases from the head to the foote: explayning the nature of each disease, with the part affected; and also the signes, causes, and prognostiques, and likewise what temperature of the ayre is most requisite for the patients abode, with direction for the diet he ought to obserue, together with experimentall cures for euery disease. ... Written by that famous and worthy physician, VValter Bruel*, London: Printed by Iohn Norton, for William Sheares, 1632.

Bullein, William, *A briefe and short discourse of the vertue and operation of balsame with an instruction for those that haue their health to preserue the same. VVhereunto is added Doctor Bullins diet for health*, London: Imprinted for Iohn Perin, 1585.

–, *A newe booke entituled the gouernement of healthe wherein is vttered manye notable rules for mannes preseruacion, with sondry symples and other matters, no lesse fruiteful then profitable: colect out of many approued authours. Reduced into the forme of a dialogue, for the better vnderstanding of thunlearned. Wherunto is added a sufferain regiment against the pestilence. By VVilliam Bulleyn*, Londo[n]: Imprinted By Iohn Day, 1558.

–, *Bulleins bulwarke of defe[n]ce againste all sicknes, sornes, and woundes, that dooe daily assaulte mankinde, whiche bulwarke is kepte with Hillarius the gardiner, Health the phisician, with their chyrurgian, to helpe the wounded soldiors. Gathered and practised fro[m] the moste worthie learned bothe old and newe: to the greate comforte of mankinde: doen by Williyam Bulleyn, and ended this Marche. anno salutis. 1562*, London: Imprinted By Ihon Kyngston, 1562.

Caius, John, *A boke, or counseill against the disease commonly called the sweate, or sweatyng sicknesse. Made by Ihon Caius doctour in phisicke. Very necessary for euerye personne, and muche requisite to be had in the handes of al sortes, for their better instruction, preparacion and defence, against the soubdein comyng, and fearful assaultying of the same disease*, London: Imprinted By Richard Grafton printer to the kynges maiestie, 1552.

Church, John, *A compendious enchiridion touching most distempers incident to the body of man, with the best and easiest cures thereof Wherein the author desires the reader seriously to consider the particulars before censure be passed. [I]n all my travels with Salvator Winter, and many years after with that famous phisitian and chirurgeon John Ponteus; I never exacted on, or denied the poor my skill and medicines gratis, but still my house to them was as free as an hospital; the like never hath been performed but by your friend and neighbor John Church. [Ge]ntlemen take notice, that besides the old tract I gave you; I have now added for the good and benefit of my countrymen, a true way of making some cheap and necessary medicines; as balsomes, plaisters. Oyntments, diascordium and mithridate. [Wi]th the number of all the bones, veins, muscles and arteries in the body of man*, London: Printed for the author, 1682.

Clowes, William, *A short and profitable treatise touching the cure of the disease called (Morbus Gallicus) by unctions, set forth by William Clowes, of London, chirurgion*, London: Printed by Iohn Daye, 1579.

–, *A prooued practise for all young chirurgians, concerning burnings with gunpowder, and woundes made with gunshot, sword, halbard, pyke, launce, or such other Wherein, is deliuered with all faithfulnesse, not onely the true receipts of such medicines as shall make them bolde, but also sundry familiar examples, such, as may leade them as it were by the hand, to the doyng of the lyke. Heereto is adioyned a treatise of the French or Spanish pockes, written by Iohn Almenar, a Spanish physition. Also, a commodious collection of aphorismes both English and Latin, taken out of an old written coppy. Published for the benefyte of his countrey, by Wylliam Clowes, mayster in chirurgery. Seene, and allowed, according to the order appoynted*, London: Printed by Thomas Orwyn, for Thomas Cadman, 1588.

Cotta, John, *A short discouerie of the vnobserued dangers of seuerall sorts of ignorant and vnconsiderate practisers of physicke in England profitable not onely for the deceiued multitude, and easie for their meane capacities, but raising reformed and more aduised thoughts in the best vnderstandings: with direction for the safest election of a physition in necessitie: by Iohn Cotta of Northampton Doctor in Physicke*, London: Imprinted for William Iones, and Richard Boyle dwelling in the Blacke-Friers, 1612.

–, *Cotta contra Antonium: or An Ant-Antony: or An Ant-apology manifesting Doctor Antony his apologie for aurum potabile, in true and equall ballance of right reason, to be false and counterfait. By Iohn Cotta Doctor in Physicke*, Oxford: Printed by Iohn Lichfield & Iames Short for Henry Cripps, 1623.

Culpeper, Nicholas, *Mr Culpepper's Treatise of aurum potabile being a description of the three-fold world, viz., elimentary, celestiall, intellectuall: containing the knowledge necessary to the study of hermetick philosophy: to which is added, Mr Culpepper's Ghost, giving advice to all the lovers of his writings*, London: Printed for G. Eversden, 1656.

–, *The English-physicians dayly practise. Or, Culpeper's faithful physitian. Teaching every man and woman to be their own doctor In this book is set forth near 40 most choice, excellent, and approved receipts in physick and chyrurgery, for the rooting out, and curing most diseases; with easie directions for making divers salves. oyntments. sear-cloths, and plaisters, for divers maladies, being a salve for every sore: and that at an easy rate. To which is added, Mr Culpepper's new, excellent, and very useful herbal; being the rare vertues of XI. herbs and plants, growing in most gardens in England; on which herbs is framed near one hundred medicines, for curing most diseases in men, women and children; a great many of them but at a penny or two pence charge; being good tidings to the sick and lame, and all others that would preserve their bodies in health, by Dr Nich. Culpepper, and Dr Ponteus. The like not hitherto printed. Licensed and entred according to order. A table of some principal things in this little book. 1. For the rheum in the eyes, 2. For the stone.... 26. For a consumption. 27. For the green-sickness*, London: Printed for J. Conyers, 1680.

Du Laurens, André, *A discourse of the preseruation of the sight: of melancholike diseases; of rheumes, and of old age. Composed by M. Andreas Laurentius, ordinarie phisition to the King, and publike professor of phisicke in the Vniuersitie of Mompelier. Translated out of French into English, according to the last edition, by Richard Surphlet, practitioner in phisick*, London: Imprinted by Felix Kingston, for Ralph Iacson, 1599.

Elyot, Thomas, Sir, *The castel of helth gathered and made by Syr Thomas Elyot knyghte, out of the chiefe authors of physyke, wherby euery manne may knowe the state of his owne body, the preseruatio[n] of helthe, and how to instructe welle his physytion in syckenes that he be not deceyued.* [Londini: In aedibus Thomae Bertheleti typis impress. 1534 [i.e. Anno. M.D.XXXIX [1539]].

Fletcher, R., *Good tydings to the sick and lame: or, The sick-man's library. Teaching both high and low, rich and poor, next under God, how to prescribe to, or procure ease for the pained, strength for the weak, health for the sick, and cure for sores. Being a true and candid relation of the vertue and uses of four excellent medicines, viz. Arcanum vegetabilium, Pilulae vegetantes, Balsamum vitae, Unguentum refrigerans, whereunto is added, a few of the many testimonies and cures performed by the same ... published for the good of all who labour under pain and misery*. By Rich. Fletcher, Nath. Merry Professors of chymical physick in London, London: Printed for the author, 1674.

–., *The vertues of that well-known and often experienced medicine Fletcher's Powder*, London: Printed by Tho. James for the author, 1679.

Gesner, Konrad, *The treasure of Euonymus conteyninge the vvonderfull hid secretes of nature, touchinge the most apte formes to prepare and destyl medicines, for the conseruation of helth: as quintesse[n]ce, aurum potabile, hippocras, aromatical wynes, balmes, oyles perfumes, garnishyng waters, and other manifold excellent confections. Wherunto are ioyned the formes of sondry apt fornaces, and vessels,required in this art. Translated (with great diligence, et laboure) out of Latin, by Peter Morvvying felow of Magdaline Colleadge in Oxford.* Imprinted at London: By Iohn Daie, dvvelling ouer Aldersgate, beneath Saint Martines. Cum priuilegio ad imprimendum solum, 1559.

Guardano, Joannes Baptista Lodovico puncto, *The skilfull mountebanke. Or, Come, and I'le cure you*, London: Printed by I. O. for Thomas Lambert, 1638.

Jones, of Hatton-Garden, *Jones of Hatton-Garden, two doors from the sign of the New-Hole in the Wall, his book of cures*, London: s.n., 1674?

Lanfranco, of Milan, *A most excellent and learned vvoorke of chirurgerie, called Chirurgia parua Lanfranci Lanfranke of Mylayne his briefe: reduced from dyuers translations to our vulgar or vsuall frase, and now first published in the Englyshe prynte by Iohn Halle chirurgien. Who hath thervnto necessarily annexed. A table, as wel of the names of diseases and simples with their vertues, as also of all other termes of the arte opened. ... And in the ende a compendious worke of anatomie ... An historiall expostulation also against the beastly abusers, both of chyrurgerie and phisicke in our tyme: with a goodly doctrine, and instruction, necessary to be marked and folowed of all true chirurgie[n]s. All these faithfully gathered, and diligently set forth, by the sayde Iohn Halle*, London: Imprinted by Thomas Marshe, 1565.

Le Medde, *Theod. Elixyrlogia, or, A compendious discourse wherein the eminent and effectual virtues and properties of the universal elixyr are set forth not only for the particular use of them that would prevent the contagion of the plague ... but for the general cure, remedying, and certain prevention of most acute diseases incident to mankind ...: with the manner of taking it ... and a rational accompt how it may certainly conduce to the prolonging of life if medically administred in a little quantity every morning to an empty stomach / by Theod. Le Medde, M.D.*, London: Printed for Henry Eversden, 1665.

Lomax, Nathaniel, *Delaun reviv'd, vix. A plain and short discourse of that famous doctor's pills, their use and virtues VVith choice receipts for the cure of the scurvy, dropsy, jaundies, venereal and other diseases. Before I speak to this famous medicine, I will declare who Delaun was; then, the price of his pill and how to take it, and of its several virtues in order, in such plain words, as to the weakest capacity may understand: and I intreat those who hope for help hereby, would throughly read this short book, and observe my directions for their own good and the authors's credit*, London: s.n., 1680?

–, *Launaeus redivivus: or, A true narrative of the admirable effects of Delaun's pill that ancient & excellant Galenick medicine, approved of, and sold for above fifty years, in Black-Fryers, now newly reviv'd, and exposed to sale, at the signe of Delaun's Head there, for the good of all, by especially the poor, whose purses reach not *to whole boxes or bottles of physick. For, the patient is not now obliged to expend above six pence to prove the operation of this peerless pill; one being a sufficient dose for most constitutions: yet is above twice as costly, and but half the purchase of any other. With some reflexions on the danger of mercurial medicines, practis'd and invented by ignorant and impudent empericks. As also, a short discourse and description of the scurvy, dropsie, venereal, and other distempers. By Nathaniel Lomax, student in physick*, London: Printed by J. C. for the author, 1675.

Marriott, John, *The English mountebank: or, a physical dispensatory, wherein is prescribed, many strange and excellent receits of Mr Marriot*, London: Printed for George Horton, 1652.

Maynwaringe, Everard, *Medicus absolutus adespotos the compleat physitian, qualified and dignified: the rise and progress of physick, historically, chronologically,and philosophically illustrated: physitians of different sects and judgements, charactered and distinguished: the abuse of medicines, imposture of empericks, and illegal practisers detected: cautioning the diseased in the use of medicines, and informing them in the choice of a good physitian / by Everard Maynwaring …*, London: Printed for the booksellers, 1668.

Merret, Christopher, *The accomplisht physician, the honest apothecary, and the skilful chyrurgeon detecting their necessary connexion and dependence on each other: withall a discovery of the frauds of the quacking empirick, the praescribing surgeon, and the practicing apothecary*, London: s.n.,1670.

Ponteus, John, *The true every man & woman their own doctor: or, a salve for every sore Being a book full of rare receipts for the most dangerous distempers incident to the bodies of men, women and children; and is very fit to be in all families against any time of sickness, gathered out of the library of that famous traveller Dr Ponteus and now publish'd for the good and benefit of the kingdom; and being nothing but what is experienced by many thousands of people in city and country, doing good to many. Don't read only but practice also, then speak as you find; and give God the praise in all things. With six most excellent receipts for all sorts of cattle whatsoever. Licensed according to order*, London: Printed by F. L. for Matthias Drew, 1676.

Primerose, James, *Popular errours. Or the errours of the people in physick, first written in Latine by the learned physitian James Primrose Doctor in Physick. Divided into foure bookes. viz. 1. The first treating concerning physicians. 2. The second of the errours about some diseases, and the knowledge of them. 3. The third of the errours about the diet; as well of the sound as of the sick. 4. The fourth of the errours of the people about the use of remedies. Profitable and necessary to be read of all. To which is added by the same authour his verdict concerning the antimoniall cuppe. Translated into English by Robert Wittie*, London: Printed by W. Wilson for Nicholas Bourne, 1651.

Rogers, Timothy, *A discourse concerning trouble of mind and the disease of melancholly in three parts: written for the use of such as are, or have been exercised by the same by Timothy Rogers ...; to which are annexed, some letters from several divines, relating to the same subject*, London: Printed for Thomas Parkhurst, and Thomas Cockerill, 1691.

Smart, quack doctor, *Smart's aurum purgans*, s.l., s.n., 1665?

Sydenham, Thomas, *Dr Sydenham's compleat method of curing almost all diseases, and description of their symptoms to which are now added five discourses of the same author concerning the pleurisy, gout, hysterical passion, dropsy, and rheumatism/ abridg'd and faithfully translated out of the original Latin; with short and useful notes on the former part, written by a late learned physician, and never before printed*, London: Printed for H. Newman and Rich. Parker, 1695.

–, *The compleat method of curing almost all diseases to which is added an exact description of their several symptoms written in Latin by Dr Thomas Sydenham; and now faithfully Englished*, London, Printed and are to be sold by Randal Taylor, 1694.

Trigg, William, practicioner of physick, *Dr Trigg's secrets, arcana's & panacea's approved by his long admired experience and practice, whereby he wrought such wonderfull cures. With his most experienced secrets particularly appropriated to womens distempers. Now after his death to fulfill his request published as a legacy to his patients. By Eugenius Philanthropos*, London: Printed by R. D. for Dixy Page, 1665.

Willis, Thomas, *An essay of the pathology of the brain and nervous stock in which convulsive diseases are treated of being the work of Thomas Willis ...; translated out of Latine into English, by S. P.*, London: Printed by J. B. for T. Dring, 1681.

–, *Two discourses concerning the soul of brutes which is that of the vital and sensitive of man. The first is physiological, shewing the nature, parts, powers, and affections of the same. The other is pathological, which unfolds the diseases which affect it and its primary seat; to wit, the brain and nervous stock, and treats of their cures: with copper cuts. By Thomas Willis doctor in physick, professor of natural philosophy in Oxford, and also one of the Royal Society, and of the renowned college of physicians in London. Englished by S. Pordage, student in physick*. London: Printed for Thomas Dring [...] Ch. Harper [...], and John Leigh, 1683.

Winter, Salvator, *A nevv dispensatory of fourty physicall receipts. Most necessary and profitable for all house-keepers in their families. Besides three other pleasant arts fit for young gentlemen*, Published by Salvatore Winter of Naples, an expert operator, London: s.n., 1649.

–, *A pretious treasury: or a new dispensatory. Contayning 70. approved physicall rare receits. Most necessary and needfull for all sorts of people to have in their families. Collected out of the most approved authors, both in physick and chyrurgery: by Salvator Winter, and Signieur Francisco Dickinson, expert operators. In two bookes*, London: Printed by Tho. Harper for Richard Harper, 1649.

–, *Directions for the use of my elixir my philosophical petza or plaister, my balsom, and also my purging drink / by Salvator VVinter, an Italian of the city of Naples*, London: s.n., 1664.

Woodall, John, *The cure of the plague by an antidote called aurum vitae. Being well approved to be an easie safe, and perfect cure thereof; as also of contagious agues, or feavers beginning either hot or cold. The description, order and use whereof, together with the said antidote, and are to be sold at the shop of Nicholas Bourne, stationer, at the south entrance of the royal exchange. Invented and produced by John Woodall, master in surgery*, Published by authority, London: Printed by E. P. for Nicholas Bourne, 1640.

Appendix D

"The Harangue, or Quack Speech of T. Jones at York" (D. G., *Harangues*, pp. 19–22)

Gentlemen and Ladies,
YOU that have a mind to preserve your own and your Families Health, may here, at the Expence of a Two-Penny Piece, furnish yourselves with a Packet, which contains several Things of great Use, and wonderful Operation in human Bodies, against all Distempers whatsoever.

Gentlemen, Because I present my self among you, I would not have you think, I am any Upstart Glister-Pipe, Bum-Peeping Apothecary: No, *Gentlemen*, I am no such Person, I am a regular Physician; and have travell'd most Kingdoms in the World, purely to do my Country good. I am not a Person that takes delight, as a great many do, to fill your Ears with hard Words, in telling you the Nature of *Turpet Mineral, Mercuri Dulcis, Balsamum Capiviet, Astringents, Laxations, Hardboundations, Circulations, Vibrations, Salivations, Excoriations, Scaldations, Urinations*. These Quacks, may fitly be called, *Solimites*, because they prescribe only one sort of Physick for all Distempers, that is, a Vomit.

If a Man has bruis'd his Elbow; *Take a Vomit*, says the Doctor. If you have any *Corns*; *Take a Vomit*. If he has torn his Coat, *Take a Vomit*. For the *Jaundice, Fevers, Flux, Gripe, Gout, Stone, Pox*, nay, even the Distempers that only my Friend, the famous Doctor *Tuff*, whom you all know, as the *Hocognicles, Marthambles*, the *Moon-Paul*, and the *Strong-Fives*; *A Vomit*; *Tantum. Gentlemen*, These Impostors value killing a Man, no more, than I value drawing an old Stump of a Toothe, which has long troubled any of you; so that, I say, They are a pack of *Tag-Rag, Assifetida, Glister-Pipe Doctors.*

Now, *Gentlemen*, having given you a short Account of this Spurious Race, I shall present you with my Cordial Pills, being the Tincture of the Sun, having Dominion from the same Light, giving Relief and Comfort to all Mankind: They cause all complexions to Laugh or Smile, in the very taking them, they presently cure all Dizziness, Swimmings, Dulness in the Head, and Scurvy.

In the next Place, I recommend to you my incomparable Balsam, which heals all Sores, Cuts, Ulcers, new and old.

'Tis good for Burns, Scalds, Swellings, Bruises, Strains, Aches, Weakness in the Joints and Limbs, &c. it cures the King's Evil, sore Breasts, and scald Heads; and it is taken inwardly for a Cough, Consumption, short Breath, Weakness of the Back, or any inward Hurt.

The next unparallel'd Medicine, contain'd in this my Packet, is an admirable Electuary, celebrated throughout all *England, Scotland, France*, and *Ireland*,

Dominion of *Wales*, and Town of *Berwick* upon *Tweed*. It cures all curable Diseases, by very easy and gentle purging; it causes an Appetite, helps all Distempers in the Eyes, Face, swelled Lips; and opens the Stoppage of the Liver and Spleen, &c.

The next I present you with, is my Specifick, which certainly cures all Agues in a Minuet.

The next is my Red Plaister, which radically cures the most inveterate Rheumatism and Gout in a few Day's Time.

The last, and most useful Medicine prepared throughout the whole World, is this my *Pulvis Catharticus*: Its Virtues are such, it will, equally with the Unicorn's Horn, expel the rankest Poison; 'tis a perfect, safe, and speedy Cure, for all venereal Maladies, of what Degree soever, and fortifies the Heart against all Fainting.

I do assure you, Country Folk, these Medicines are as good as any Physician can make, or Patient take; their Virtues are too well known, to say any more; so I shall leave you to experience them. And so I wish you Health, and Happiness.

You may come to my Lodgings, at the Barber's Pole Stone-Gate: *At home from Seven to Eleven.*

Appendix E

"Pharmacopola Circumforaneus or The Horse Doctor's Harangue to the Credulous Mob" (from D. G. *Harangues*, pp. 13–19), and its 'Analogue' in *The Character of a Quack-Doctor* (1676)[1]

1. Gentlemen, I Waltho van Claturbank, High German Doctor, Chymist, and Dentifricator, **Native of Arabia Deserta**, Citizen and Burgomaster of the City of Brandipolis, Seventh Son of a Seventh Son, Unborn Doctor of above 60 Years Experience, having studied over Galen, Hypocrates, Albumazar, and Paracelsus, am now become the Æsculapius **of this Age**. Having been educated at twelve Universities, and travelled through Fifty two Kingdoms, and been Counsellor to the Counsellors of several Monarchs, **Natural Son of the Wonder-working Chymical Doctor** Signior Hanesio, lately arrived from the farthest Parts of Utopia, **Famous throughout Asia, Africa, Europe and America, from the** Sun's **Oriental Exaltation to his Occidental Declination:** Out of dear **Pitty** to my **own dear Self, and languishing Mortals**, have **by the earnest Prayers and Intreaties of several Lords, Earls, Dukes, and Honourable Personages, been** at last **prevail'd upon to oblige the World with this Notice.**
2. **That all Persons, Young and Old, Blind or Lame, Deaf or Dumb, Curable or Incurable, may know where to repair for Cure, in all Cephalalgia's, Paralytick Paroxysms, Palpitations of the Pericardium, Empyemas, Syncopes, and Nasieties, arising either from a Plethory or a Cacochymy,** Vertiginous Vapours, Hydiocephalus Dissenteries, Odontalgick, or Podagrical Inflammations, <u>Iliack Passions, Icterical Effusions</u>, **Exanthemata, the Hen pox, the Hog Pox, the Whores Pox, and the Small Pox, the Ascites, Tympanites, Anasarca**, and the entire Legion of Lethiferous Distempers.
3. Imprimis, Gentlemen, I have a **never-failing Styptick, corroborating, odoriferous, anodinous,** balsamic **Balsam of Balsams, made of dead Mens**

---

1 The text is copied from G. D., *Harangues* (original italics are not reproduced) and checked with the 'Waltho' broadsides (which respect both the wording and the paragraphs' structure of the original). Paragraph numbers are mine. The following typefaces are used to highlight the parts also to be found in *The Character of a Quack-Doctor*: boldface shows repetitions of exactly the same wording in the same position; italics are used for similar-*cum* changes wording; underlining signals the occurrence of identical portions of text, which are placed in a different position in the 'analogue' (spelling variations are not taken into consideration, while some variants occurring in *The Character* are added between square brackets).

Fat, Rosin, and Goose Grease, which infallibly restores lost Maidenheads, raises demoish'd Noses, and by its abstersive, cosmetick Quality, preserves *superannuated* **Bawds from Wrinkles.**

4. Item. I have the **True** *Carthramophra* of the Triple Kingdom, my never-failing Heliogenes, being the Tincture of the Sun, deriving Vigour, Influence, and Dominion from the same Light; it causes all Complexions to Laugh or Smile, at the very Time of taking it; **is seven Years in preparing, and being compleated, secundum Artem // by Fermentation**, Cohobation, Calcination, Sublimation, Fixation, Philtration, Circulation and **Quidlibitification, in Balneo Mariæ, Crucible and Fixatory, the Athanor, Cucurbita and Reverberatory,** is the only Sovereign Medicine in the World.
5. **This is Natures Palladium, Health's Magazine;** it works seven manner of Ways, in order as Nature herself requires, for it scorns to be confin'd to any particular way of Operation; so that it effecteth the Cure, either Hypnotically, Hydrotically, Cathartically, Poppismatically, Hydrogogically, Pneumatically, or Synechdochically; it mundifies the Hypogastrium, wipes off abstersively those tenacious conglomerated sedimental Sordes that adhere to the Oesophagus and Viscera; extinguishes all supernatural Fermentations and Ebulitions, and, in fine, annihilates all Nosotrophical Morbifick Ideas of the whole Corporeal Compages.
6. **A Drachm of it is worth a Bushel of March Dust; for, if a Man chance to have his Brains beat out, or his Head chop'd off, 2 Drops, I say, 2 Drops Gentlemen, seasonably apply'd, will recall the fleeting Spirits, re-inthrone the deposed Archeus, cement the Discontinuity of the Parts, and in six Minutes restore the lifeless Trunk to all its pristine Functions, Vital, Natural, and Animal;** so that this, believe me, Gentlemen, is the only Sovereign Remedy in the World.
7. I have the chiefest **Antepudenda Gragran Specifick in Venus Regalia, which infallibly cures the French Pox, with all its Train of Gonorrheas, Bubo's and Shankers**, Carnosities, Phymosis, Paraphymosis, Christalline Priapismus, Caudalomata and Ragades, without Baths and Stoves, and that **with as much Pleasure as the same** *was* **contracted; so that** *'tis worth any Person's while* **to get the Distemper once a Fortnight, if it be to be had for Love or Money, to enjoy the** Benefit **of so diverting a Remedy**.
8. I have the *Panchymagogon* of **Hermes Trismegistus, an incomparable Spagyric Tincture of the Moons Horns**, which is the only infallible Antidote **against the Contagion of** *Cuckoldom*.
9. Besides, my Vermifugus Pulvis, or Antivermatical Worm-conquering Powder, so famous for destroying all the Sorts of 'em, incident to human

Bodies, breaking their complicated Knots in the Duodenum, and dissolving the Phlegmatick Crudities that produce these Anthropohagous Vermine: It hath brought away Worms by Urine, as long as the May-Pole in the Strand, when it flouresh'd in its Primative Prolixity, tho' I confess not altogether so thick.

10. Look ye Gentlemen, I have it **under the Hands and Seals of all the Greatest** *Sultans* [Caliphs], Sophys, Bashas, Viziers, Chams, Serasquiers, *and Mufties*, &c. **in Christendom, to verificate** the Truth **of my Operations**, that I have actually performed such Cures as are really beyond human Abilities.
11. **I cur'd *Prestor John's* Godmother, to the great Admiration of all the Court, of a stupendious Dolour about the Os Sacrum, so that the good** old **Lady really feared the Perdition of her Huckle-Bone; I did it by fomenting her Posteriors, with a Mummy of Nature, *alias,* called Pilgrim's Salve, mix'd up with the Spirit of Mugwort**, *tartaragraphated thorough* **an Alembick of Christalline Transfluency.**
12. Thence was I sent for to Sultan Gilgon, Despote of Bosnia, who was violently afflicted with the Spasmus: He came to meet me 300 Leagues in a Go Cart: But I gave him so speedy an Acquittance of his Dolour, that the next Night I caused him to dance a Saraband, with Flipflaps and Somersets.
13. I restor'd Virility, and the Comforts of Generation, to above 150 Eunuchs in the Grand Senior's Seraglio, and by a Pair of Prolifick Pills, lately caused a Vintner's Widow, who had been barren *all her Days, to conceive of a Man Child* [all her life time, to bring forth a lusty boy] in the twelfth Lustre of her Age, without the Help of her Husband.
14. I cured likewise the **Dutchess** of *Boromolpho* [Promolpho] **of a Cramp in her Tongue**, and **the Count de Rodomontado Corrept with an Illiack Passion, contracted by eating butter'd Parsnips**.
15. I also cured **an Alderman of Grand Cairo, who had been sick seven Years of the Plague, in 46 Minutes: And by the like Empirical Remedies I lately cured Duke** *Philorix*, ***of*** **a Dropsy, of which he died.**
16. **Venienti occurite morbo. Down with your Dust.** Principiis obsta. No Cure, no Money [No mony, no Cure]. **Quarenda Pecunia primum. Be not sick too late**.
17. You that are willing **to render yourselves Immortal**, buy this Packet, or else repair to the Sign of the Prancers in Vico vulgo dicto Rattlecliffero, something South-East of the *Teplum Danicum*, in the Square of Profound-Close, not far from Titter-Tatter Fair, and you may see, hear, and return Reinfecta.

Bibliography

Primary Sources[1]

A Collection of 185 Advertisements, Chiefly Relating to Quack Medicines. The Greater Part English, the Rest French, German and Italian [1660–1716] (BL C112f9).

A Collection of 231 Advertisements, etc. *The Greater Part English and Chiefly Relating to Quack Medicines, the Rest German Descriptions of Commemorative Coins and Medals [1675–1715]* (BL 551a32).

A Collection of Titlepages, Fragments of Printed Books and Other Material Assembled by John Bagford. [1528–1715] (BL Harley 5931).

A., B. *The Sick-mans Rare Jewel*, London: Printed by T. R. and N. T., 1674.

Addison, Joseph, *The Tatler* n. 224, 12–14 September 1710, in *The Tatler*, ed. by G. A. Aitken, 4 vols, IV, London: Duckworth, 1898.

Alcock, Thomas and John Wilmot, *The Famous Pathologist, or the Noble Mountebank*, ed. by Vivian De Sola Pinto, Nottingham: Sisson and Parker for The University of Nottingham, 1961.

Ancrene Riwle, The English Text of the "Ancrene Riwle" Edited from B.M. Cotton Ms. Cleopatra C vi, ed. by Eric J. Dobson, EETS O.S. 267, Oxford: Oxford University Press, 1972.

Anon., *A Bold Challenge to the whole Colledge of Physicians*, London: Printed for J. Roberts, 1740?

Anon., *Advertisement. Whereas Divers People are at Great Expence in Printing*, London: Printed by Andrew Clark, 1675.

Anon., *An Approved Antidote or Cordiall Medicine*, London: s.n., 1650?

Anon., *The Character of a Quack-Doctor, or, The Abusive Practices of Impudent Illiterate Pretenders to Physick Exposed*, London: Printed for Thomas Jones, 1676.

Anon., *The French Mountebank, or An Operator Fit for these Present Times*, London: Printed for R. Austin, and A. Coe, 1643.

Anon., *The Grete Herball*, London: Printed by Peter Treveris, 1526.

1 This list reproduces only the initial words of long titles as they appear in the *ESTC*.

Anon., *The Harangues, or Speeches, of Several Celebrated Quack-doctors,* London: Printed for J. Thomson, 1762. (BL General Reference Collection 11770.b.1(4)).

Anon., *The High German Doctor's Speech*, London: Printed for T. Kitchin, 1730–40?

Anon., *The Infallible Mountebank, or Quack Doctor*, London: Printed by H. Hills, 1707.

Anon.,*The Modern Quack,* London: Printed for J. Roberts, 1718.

Anon., *The Modern Quacks Detected,* London: Printed for M. Cooper, 1752.

Anon., *The Office of Publick Advice, Newly Set up in Several Places in and about London and Westminster*, London: Printed by Tho. Newcomb, 1657.

Anon., *The Quack Doctor's Speech to the Credulous Mob. Supposed to be Spoke by the Famous Lord Rochester*, London: s.n., 1800[?].

Anon., *The Quacks Academy*, London: Printed for A. B., 1678.

Archer, John, *Compleated with an Herbal*, London: Printed for the author, 1673.

Armin, Robert, *The History of the Tvvo Maids of More-clacke*, London: Printed by N. O. for Thomas Archer, 1609.

Bacon, Francis, *THE Tvvoo Bookes of FRANCIS BACON. Of the Proficience and Aduancement of Learning*, London: Printed for Henrie Tomes, 1605.

Bacon, Roger, *This Boke doth Treate all of the beste Waters Artyfycialles*, London: Printed by Rober Wyer, 1550.

Bate, George, *Pharmacopoeia Bateana* […] *The Second Edition, With Emendations, and Enlarged with Several Extraordinary Preparations* […] *By William Salmon, M.D.*, London: Printed for S. Smith and B. Walford, 1700.

Behn, Aphra, *The Second Part of The Rover*, London: Printed for Jacob Tonson, 1681.

–, *The Ten Pleasures of Marriage and the Confession of the New Married Couple*, London: Privately printed for the Navarre Society, 1922 (1682).

Bright, Timothy, *A Treatise of Melancholy*, London: Printed by John Windet, 1586.

–, *A Treatise: wherein is declared the sufficiencie of English medicines, for cure of all diseases, cured with medicine*, London: Printed by Henrie Middleton for Thomas Man, 1580.

British Museum Collection on Line, "Satirical Print" <http://www.britishmuseum.org/research/collection_online/collection_object_details.aspx?objectId=3059769&partId=1&searchText=quack&images=true&page=2> [accessed 2 January 2014].

Brown, Thomas, *Letters from the Dead to the Living*, London: s.n., 1702.

–, *Letters from the Dead to the Living*, London: Printed, and sold by B. Bragg, 1707.

–, *The Works of Mr Thomas Brown*, London: Printed for Sam. Briscoe, 1715 [-20].

Brugis, Thomas, *Marrow of Physicke*, London: Printed by Richard Hearne, 1640.

Brunschwig, Hieronymus, *A Most Excellent and Perfecte Homish Apothecarye*, Imprinted at Collen, by Arnold Birckman, 1561.

–, *The Vertuose Boke of Distyllacyon*, London: Imprynted by me Laurens Andrewe, 1527.

Bullein, William, *Bulleins Bulwarke of Defe[n]ce againste all Sicknes*, London: Printed by Ihon Kyngston, 1562.

Burnet, Gilbert, *Some Passages of the Life and Death of the Right Honourable John Earl of Rochester*, London: Printed for Richard Chiswel, 1680.

Burton, Robert, *The Anatomy of Melancholy*, Oxford: Printed for Henry Cripps, 1621.

Calendar of State Papers, Domestic Series, of the Reign of Charles II: 1682, ed. by M. A. E. Green, London: Longman and Co, 1860.

Carroll, Lewis, *Alice's Adventures in Wonderland*, in *The Annotated Alice*, ed. by Martin Gardner, London: Penguin, 2001 (1865).

Chambers, Robert, *The Book of Days*, 2 vols, Edinburgh: W. & R. Chambers, 1864.

Chaucer, Geoffrey, *The Canterbury Tales*, in *The Riverside Chaucer*, ed. by. Larry Benson, Robert Pratt, F. N. Robinson, Boston: Houghton Mifflin (3rd edition), 1986.

Cheyne, George, *The English Malady: or, a Treatise of Nervous Diseases of All Kinds*, London: Printed for G. Strahan, 1733 <http://archive.org/stream/englishmaladyort00cheyuoft#page/274/mode/2up/search/hypochondriacal> [accessed 8 October 2013).

Church, John, *A Compendious Enchiridion*, London: Printed for the author, 1682.

Cicero, *M. Tulli Ciceronis: Pro A. Cluentio Oratio*, ed. by W. Peterson, London: Macmillan and Co., Ltd, 1920.

Claturbank, Waltho, van, *Pharmacopola Circumforaneus, or the Horse Doctor's Harangue to the Credulous Mob*, Dublin: s.n., 1737[?].

–, *Quack doctor's speech*, London[?]: s.n. 1760[?].

Coryate, Thomas, *Coryats Crudities*, London: Printed by VV. S. for the author, 1611.

Cotta, John, *A Short Discouerie of the Vnobserued Dangers of Seuerall Sorts of Ignorant and Vnconsiderate Practisers of Physicke in England*, London: Imprinted for William Iones, and Richard Boyle, 1612.

–, *A True Discouery of the Empericke with the Fugitiue, Physition and Quacksaluer*, London: Imprinted by William Iones, 1617.

Coxe, Thomas, *A Discourse, wherein the Interest of the Patient in Reference to Physick and Physicians is Soberly Debated*, London: Printed for Richard Chiswel, 1669.

Cruys, Francis, *Art Nova Natandi*, Bristol: Printed by Will. Bonny, 1698.

Culpeper, Nicholas, *The English Physitian*, London: Printed by Peter Cole, 1652.

–, *Galen's Art of Physick*, London: Printed by Peter Cole, 1652.

–, *A Physical Directory*, London: Printed by Peter Cole, 1649.

–, *These are to Give Notice to all His Majesties Subjects*, London: s.n., 1668[?].

D. G., *The Harangues or Speeches of Several Famous Mountebanks in Town and Country*, London: Printed for T. Warner, 1700[?] (BL General Reference Collection 1038.g.46).

–, *The Harangue or Speeches of Several Famous Mountebanks in Town and Country*, London: Printed for T. Warner, 1725[?] (BL General Reference Collection 12330.k.121)

Defoe, Daniel, *A Journal of the Plague Year*, London: Printed for E. Nutt; J. Roberts; A. Dodd; and J. Graves, 1722.

Dickinson, Francisco, *A Precious Treasury of Twenty Rare Secrets*, London: Printed for the author, 1649.

Digby, Sir Kenelm, *Choice and Experimented Receipts in Physick and Chirurgery*, London: Printed for the author, 1668.

Donizetti, Gaetano, *L'elisir d'amore. Melodramma in due atti di Felice Romani*, Milan: G. Ricordi & C., 1832.

Donne, John, "Fourth Satire", in *Poems*, Menston: Scolar Press, 1969 (1633).

"Entry Book: October 1679, 11–20", *Calendar of Treasury Books, Volume 6: 1679–1680* (1913), pp. 218–23 <http://www.british-history.ac.uk/report.aspx?compid=83507> [accessed 22 November 2013].

Gale, Thomas, *Certaine VVorkes of Chirurgerie*, London: By Rouland Hall [for Thomas Gale], 1563.

Galt, John, *The Lives of the Players*. 2 vols, London: Henry Colburn and Richard Bentley, 1831.

Garzoni, Tomaso, *La piazza universale di tutte le professioni del mondo, e nobili et ignobili*, Venice: Appresso Gio. Battista Somascho, 1585.

Giustinian, Sebastiano, "Letter to Desiderius Erasmus", in *Letters and Papers, Foreign and Domestic, of the Reign of Henry VIII*, ed. by J. S. Brewer, Vol. 2: *Part II: 1517–18*, n. 3414, London: Longman, Green, Longman & Roberts, 1864.

Goodall, Charles, *The Royal College of Physicians of London*, London: Printed by M. Fletcher, for Walter Kettilby, 1684.

Grand Opera Librettos, Boston: Oliver Ditson 1885 <https://archive.org/stream/cu31924098674538#page/n5/mode/2up> [accessed 18 July 2013].

Grey, Elizabeth, *A Choice Manual of Rare and Select Secrets in Physic and Chyrurgery*, London: Printed for R. Norton, 1653.

Guardano, Joannes Baptista Lodovico puncto, *The Skilfull Mountebanke*, London: Printed by I.O. for Thomas Lambert, 1638.

Harvey, Gideon, *Morbus Anglicus: or, The Anatomy of Consumptions*, London: Printed for Nathaniel Brook, 1666.

Harvey, William, *Exercitatio Anatomica de Motu Cordis et Sanguinis in Animalibus*, Francofurti: Sumptibus Guilielmi Fitzeri, 1628.

Head, Richard [?], *Proteus Redivivus*, London: Printed by W. D., 1675.

Heresbach, Conrad, *Foure Bookes of Husbandry*, Trans. by Barnabe Googe, London: Printed by Richard Watkins, 1577.

Heywood, John, *The Plays of John Heywood*, ed. by Richard Axton and Peter Happé, Cambridge: Brewer, 1991.

Holy Bible, The, King James Version, Imprinted at London by Robert Barker, 1611.

Jeffrey, Stephen, *The Libertine*, London: Nick Hern Books, 1994.

Johnson, Samuel, *A Dictionary of the English Language: A Digital Edition of the 1755 Classic by Samuel Johnson* (1755) <http://johnsonsdictionaryonline.com/? p=1762> [accessed 12 August 2013].

Jonson, Ben, *Volpone*, in *Three Comedies*, ed. by Michael Jamieson, Harmondsworth: Penguin, 1966.

–, *Workes of Benjamin Jonson*, London: Imprinted by Will Stansby, 1616.

Joubert, Laurent, *Erreurs populaires au fait de la médecine et regime de santé*, Paris: V. de Mehubert, 1578.

Killigrew, Thomas, *Thomaso. In Two Parts* (1663), in *Comedies and Tragedies*, London: Printed for Henry Herringman, 1664, pp. 313–464.

Lanfranco, of Milan, *A Most Excellent and Learned VVoorke of Chirurgerie, Called Chirurgia Parua* […], London: Imprinted by Thomas Marshe, 1565.

Langham, William, *The Garden of Health*, London: s.n., 1597.

Langland, William, *Piers the Plowman*, B-text, ed. by W. W. Skeat in four parts, Oxford: Clarendon Press, 1867–85.

Letters and Papers, Foreign and Domestic, of the Reign of Henry VIII, 21 vols, ed. by James Gairdner and others (London: 1864–1920), II, ed. by J. S. Brewer, London: Longman, Green, Longman & Roberts, 1864.

The Libertine, Dir. Laurence Dunmore, Perf. Johnny Deppe, John Malkovich, Samantha Morton, The Weinstein Company, 2004.

Littledale, Willoughby A., *The Registers of St. Bene't and St. Peter, Paul's Wharf, London. Vol. IV Burials. St. Bene't, 1619–1837*, London: Harleian Society, 1912.

Lomax, Nathaniel, *Delaun Reviv'd*, London: s.n., 1680?

Marriott, John, *The English Mountebank*, London: Printed for George Horton, 1652.

Maximinus, Jacobus, *Whereas the Professor hereof, Iacobus Maximinus, Borne in Italy* […], London: s.n., 1622.

Maynwaringe, Everard, *Medicus Absolutus*, London: Printed for the booksellers, 1668.

Mercurii [Mercuri], Scipione, *De gli Errori popolari d'Italia. Libri sette*, In Venetia: Appresso Gio. Battista Ciotti Senese, 1603.

Merret, Christopher [?], *The Accomplisht Physician*, London: s.n., 1670.

Merret, Christopher, *A Collection of Acts of Parliament*, London: s.n., 1660.

Molière, *Monsieur de Pourceaugnac*, English translation, <http://www.monologuearchive.com/m/moliere_018.html> [accessed 7 May 2012].

–, *Monsieur de Pourceaugnac*, in Molière, *Les Furberies de Scapin*, Paris: Gallimard. 1978 (1670), pp. 139–212.

Monardes, Nicolás, *Ioyfull Newes out of the Newfound World*, London: Imprinted by [Thomas Dawson for] William Norton, 1580.

Morgan, William, *London &c. Actually Survey'd by Wm Morgan*,1681/2.

Motteux, Peter Anthony, *Farewel Folly: or, the Younger the Wiser*, London: Printed for James Round, 1707.

Oberndorff, John, *The Anatomyes of the True Physition, and Counterfeit Mountebanke*, London: Printed for Arthur Johnson, 1602.

Old Bailey Proceedings Online <http://www.oldbaileyonline.org>, version 7.0, October 1679, trial of man (t16791015–13) [accessed 13 January 2014].

Ottonelli, Giovanni Domenico, *Della christiana moderatione del teatro*, 5 vols, In Fiorenza: Luca Franceschini & Alessandro Logi, 1646–52.

–, *Della christiana moderatione del theatro libro, detto L'ammonitioni a' recitanti*, In Fiorenza: Gio. Antonio Bonardi, 1652. [fourth volume [?] of the previous entry, by a different printer]

Paracelsus, *Paracelsus his Aurora*, London: Printed for Giles Calvert, 1659.

Pechey, John, *The Compleat Herbal of Physical Plants*, London: Printed for Henry Bonwicke, 1694.

Pepys, Samuel, *The Diary of Samuel Pepys: A New and Complete Transcription*, 11 vols., ed. by Robert Latham and William Matthews, Berkeley and Los Angeles: University of California Press, 1970–83.

Pharmacopoeia Londinensis, London, Printed [by E. Griffin] for Iohn Marriot, 1618.

Ponteus, John, *The True Every Man & Woman their Own Doctor*, London: Printed by F. L. for Matthias Drew, 1676.

Pope, Alexander, *An Epistle from Mr Pope, to Dr Arbuthnot*, London: Printed by J. Wright, for Lawton Gilliver, 1734 [1735].

Porta, Giambattista della. *Natural Magick by John Baptista Porta, a Neapolitane*, London: Printed for Thomas Young and Samuel Speed, 1658.

Primerose, James, *Popular Errours*, London: Printed by W. Wilson, 1651.

Proceedings of the Old Bailey. Ref: t16791015–13, relating to 15th October 1679. <http://www.oldbaileyonline.org/browse.jsp?ref=t16791015–13> [accessed 22 November 2013).

Rands, Thomas, *Pax in Crumena: or, The Trooper Turn'd Poet*, London: Printed for the author, 1713.

Rastell, John, *The Third Booke*, Antwerp: Ex officina Ioannis Fouleri, 1566.

Romani, Felice, *L'elisir d'amore*, libretto, 1832 <http://www.librettidopera.it/eldam/a_01.html#s_03> [accessed 25 July 2013].

Rondelet, Guillaume, *The Countrey-man's Apothecary*, London: Printed for Th. Andrews, 1649.

Rowe, Nicholas (ed.), *The Works of Mr William Shakespeare*, 6 vols, London: Printed for Jacob Tonson, 1709.

Russell, John, *J. Russel, Physician and Ocultist* [Oculist], *at the two Blew-Posts against Grays-Inn in Holbourn*, London: s.n., 1680[?].

Rutebeuf, *Oeuvres Complètes de Rutebeuf*, 2 vols, recueillies et mises au jour par la première fois par Achille Jubinal, Paris: Edouard Pannier, 1839.

Salmon, William, *Pharmacopoeia Bateana: or Bate's Dispensatory. Translated from the Last Edition of the Latin Copy* [...] *By William Salmon, M.D.*, London: Printed for S. Smith, and B. Walford, 1700.

–, *Phylaxa Medicinæ*, London: Printed by I. Dawks, 1700.

Securis, John, *A Detection and Querimonie of the Daily Enormities and Abuses Committed in Physick*, Londini: In aedibus Thomae Marshi, 1566.

"Sessions Book: 1693", *Middlesex County Records. Calendar of Sessions Books 1689–1709* (1905), pp. 88–105. <http://www.british-history.ac.uk/report.aspx?compid =66110> [Accessed 22 November 2013].

Sforza, Caterina, *Experimenti de la ex.ma s.ra Caterina da Furlj*, Imola: bim 2009 (reprint of the edition ed. by Pier Desiderio Pasolini, Imola: Galeati, 1894).

Shadwell, Thomas, *The Sullen Lovers: or The Impertinents*, London: Printed for Henry Herringman, 1668.

Shakespeare, William, *The Complete Plays*, Electronic Edition, ed. by Stanley Wells and Gary Taylor, Oxford: Oxford University Press, 1989.

–, *King Edward III*, The Project Gutenberg <http://www.gutenberg.org/cache/epub/1770/pg1770.html> [accessed 26 September 2013].

Slater, T., *Pharmacopola Circumforaneus, or the Horse Doctor's Harangue to the Credulous Mob*, London: J. Harrison, 1700–1750[?].

Smart, Quack Doctor, *Smart's Aurum Purgans*, London?: s.n., 1665[?]

Sonnet de Courval, Thomas, *Satyre contre les Charlatans et Pseudomedecins Empyriques.*, Paris: J. Milot, 1610.

Steele, Richard, *The Tatler. Complete in One Volume*, Philadelphia: Woodward, 1831 <http://books.google.it/books?id=x_dDAAAAYAAJ&printsec=frontcover&hl=it&source=gbs_atb#v=onepage&q&f=false> [accessed 13 August 2013].

Tuke, Thomas, *A Treatise against Painting and Tincturing of Women*, London: Printed by Tho. Creed, and Barn. Allsope, 1616.

W., M., *The Queens Closet Opened*, London: Printed for Obadiah Blagrave, 1679.

Ward, Edward (Ned), *The London Spy Compleat in Eighteen Parts*, London: Printed by J. How, 1703.

Wecker, Johann Jacob, *Cosmeticks or, the Beautifying Part of Physick*, London: Printed by Tho. Johnson, 1660.

Whetstone, George, *An Heptameron of Civill Discourses*. London: Printed for Richard Jones, 1582.

Whitlock, Richard, *Zwotomia*, London: Printed by Tho. Roycroft, 1654.

Wilmot, John, Second Earl of Rochester, *The Works of John Wilmot, Earl of Rochester*, ed. by Harold Love, Oxford: Oxford University Press, 1999.

Winter, Salvator, *Directions for the Use of my Elixir my Philosophical Petza or Plaister, my Balsom, and also my Purging Drink, by Salvator VVinter, an Italian of the city of Naples*, London: s.n., 1664.

–, *A Nevv Dispensatory of fourty Physicall Receipts. Most necessary and profitable for all House-keepers in their Families. Besides three other pleasant Arts fit for young Gentlemen*, London: s.n., 1649.

–, *Nothing without God*, London: s.n., 1647.

–, *Nothing without God*, London: s.n., 1669 [1664].

Winter, Salvator, and Francisco Dickinson, *A Pretious Treasury: Or a New Dispensatory. Contayning 70. approved Physicall Rare Receits. Most necessary and needfull for all Sorts of People to have in their Families. Collected out of the most approved Authors, both in Physick and Chirurgery, by Salvator Winter, and Signieur Francisco Dickinson, expert Operators. In two Bookes*, London: Printed by Tho. Harper for Richard Harper, 1649.

Woolley, Hannah, *The Gentlewomans Companion*, London: Printed by A. Maxwell for Dorman Newman, 1673.

Wycherley, William, *The Country-Wife*, London: Printed for Thomas Dring, 1675.

Secondary Sources

Anselment, Raymond A., *The Realms of Apollo: Literature and Healing in Seventeenth-Century England*, Newark: University of Delaware Press, 1995.

Anthony, Laurence, *AntConc 3.2.1w* (software), 2009, <http://www.antlab.sci.waseda.ac.jp/software.html> [downloaded 21 March 2009].

Babb, Lawrence, *The Elizabethan Malady: A Study of Melancholy in English Literature from 1580 to 1642*, East Lansing, Mich.: Michigan State College Press, 1951.

Bannerman, W. Bruce, ed., *Parish Registers of St. Olave Hart Street, London, 1563–1700*, London: Harleian Society, 1916.

Barry, Jonathan, "Literacy and Literature in Popular Culture: Reading and Writing in Historical Perspective", in *Popular Culture in England, c. 1500–1850*, ed. by Tim Harris. New York: St. Martin's Press, 1995, pp. 69–94.

Beecher, Donald, and Massimo Ciavolella, eds, *Eros & Anteros: The Medical Traditions of Love in the Renaissance*, Ottawa: Dovehouse Editions, 1992.

Benveniste, Émile, *Problèmes de linguistique générale*, Paris: Gallimard, 1966.

–, *Problems in General Linguistics*, Transl. by Mary Elizabeth Meek, Coral Gables, Florida: University of Miami Press, 1971.

Biber, Douglas, *Variations Across Speech and Writing*, Cambridge: Cambridge University Press, 1988.

Biber, Douglas, Edward Finegan, Stig Johansson, and Susan Conrad, *Longman Grammar of Spoken and Written English*, Harlow: Longman Pearson Education, 1999.

Bourne, Don, "'If I appear to any one like a counterfeit': Liminality in Rochester's *Alexander Bendo's Brochure*", *Restoration*, 32.1 (2008), pp. 3–17.

bpi1700 (British Printed Images to 1700) <http://www.bpi1700.org.uk/research/printOf TheMonth/september2008.html> [accessed 28 October 2013].

Brown, Penelope, and Stephen Levinson, "Universals in Language Usage: Politeness Phenomena", in *Questions and Politeness: Strategies in Social Interaction*, ed. by E. N. Goody, Cambridge: Cambridge University Press, 1978, pp. 56–311.

Brownlee, Alexander, *William Shakespeare and Robert Burton*, n.p.: R. L. Cook, 1960.

Brownlees, Nicholas, "Spoken Discourse in Early English Newspapers", *Media History*, 11 (2005), pp. 69–85.

Burnby, Juanita, "Pharmaceutical Advertisement in the 17th and 18th Centuries", *European Journal of Marketing*, 22.4 (1988), pp. 24–40.

Camporesi, Piero, ed., *Il libro dei vagabondi*, Turin: Einaudi, 1973.

Catalogue of Prints and Drawings in the British Museum Division I: Political and Personal Satires, 4 vols, Prepared by Frederic George Stephens (1870–83), II, June 1689 to 1733, No. 1236 to No. 2015, London: Printed by order of the Trustees, 1873.

Chambers, Robert, *The Book of Days*, 2 vols, Edinburgh: W. & R. Chambers, 1864.

Clark, Carol, "'The onely-languag'd men of all the world': Rabelais and the Art of the Mountebank", *Modern Language Review*, 74.3 (1979), pp. 538–52.

Combe, Kirk, *A Martyr of Sin: Rochester's Critique of Polity, Sexuality, and Society*, Newark: University of Delaware Press, 1998.

Cook, Guy, *The Discourse of Advertising*, London: Routledge, 1992.

Cook, Harold J., *The Decline of the Old Medical Regime in Stuart London*, Ithaca: Cornell University Press, 1986.

Cosmacini, Giorgio, *Ciarlataneria e medicina: Cure, maschere, ciarle*, Milan: Raffaello Cortina Editore, 1998.

Crawford, Patricia, *Blood, Bodies and Families in Early Modern England*, Harlow: Pearson Education, 2004.

–, "Printed Advertisements for Women Medical Practitioners in London, 1670–1710", *The Society for the Social History of Medicine Bulletin*, 35 (December 1984), pp. 66–70.

Cressy, David, *Literacy and the Social Order: Reading and Writing in Tudor and Stuart England*, Cambridge: Cambridge University Press, 1980.

–, *Society and Culture in Early Modern England*, Aldershot: Ashgate, 2003.

Curth, Louise Hill, "Medical Advertising in the Popular Press: Almanacs and the Growth of Proprietary Medicines", in *From Physick to Pharmacology: Five Hundred Years of British Drug Retailing*, ed. by Louise Hill Curth, Aldershot: Ashgate, 2006, pp. 29–47.

–, "The Medical Content of English Almancs, 1640–1700", *Journal of the History of Medicine and Allied Sciences*, 60.3 (2005), pp. 255–82.

Dawson, Lesel, *Lovesickness and Gender in Early Modern English Literature*, Oxford: Oxford University Press, 2008.

Early Modern Practitioners <http://practitioners.exeter.ac.uk/> [accessed 9 August 2013].

Elliott, Blanche, *A History of English Advertising*, London: Business Publications Limited, 1962.

English Short Title Catalogue, British Library <http://estc.bl.uk/F/?func=file&file_name=login-bl-estc> [accessed 5 September 2014].

Feinberg, Anat, "Quacks and Mountebanks in Stuart and Caroline Drama", *Ludica*, 5–6 (2000), pp. 116–26.

Ferguson, John, *Bibliographical Notes on Histories of Inventions and Books of Secrets*, Glasgow: At the University Press, 1896.

Fissell, Mary E., "Introduction: Women, Health, and Healing in Early Modern Europe", *Bulletin of the History of Medicine*, 82.1 (2008), pp. 1–17.

–, "The Marketplace of Print", in *Medicine and the Market in England and its Colonies, c. 1450-c. 1850*, ed. by Mark S. R. Jenner and Patrick Wallis, 2007, pp. 108–32.

–, *Vernacular Bodies: The Politics of Reproduction in Early Modern England*, Oxford: Oxford University Press, 2004.

Forbes, Edward Robinson, *The Early History of Coffee Houses in England*, London: Kegan Paul, Trench and Trübner & Co, 1893.

Fox, Adam, *Oral and Literate Culture in England, 1500–1700*, Oxford: Oxford University Press, 2000.

French, Roger, and Andrew Wear, eds, *The Medical Revolution of the Seventeenth Century*, Cambridge: Cambridge University Press, 1989.

Furdell, Elizabeth Lane, *Publishing and Medicine in Early Modern London*, Rochester, N.Y.: University of Rochester Press, 2002.

–, *The Royal Doctors, 1485–1714: Medical Personnel at the Tudor and Stuart Courts*, Rochester, N.Y.: University of Rochester Press, 2001.

Gambaccini, Piero, *I mercanti della salute*, Florence: Le Lettere, 2000.

Genette, Gérard, *Seuils*, Paris: Éditions du Seuil, 1987.

Gentilcore, David, "'Charlatans, mountebanks and other similar people': The Regulation and Role of Itinerant Practitioners in Early Modern Italy", *Social History*, 20.3 (1995), pp. 297–314.

–, *Healers and Healing in Early Modern Italy*, Manchester: Manchester University Press, 1998.

–, *Medical Charlatanism in Early Modern Italy*, Oxford: Oxford University Press, 2006.

–, "Was there a 'Popular Medicine' in Early Modern Europe?", *Folklore*, 115 (2004), pp. 151–66.

Gotti, Maurizio, "Advertising Discourse in 18th-Century English Newspapers", in *Opening Windows on Texts and Discourse of the Past*, ed. by Janne Skaffari, Matti Peikola, Ruth Carroll, Risto Hiltunen and Brita Wårvik, Amsterdam: Benjamins, 2005, pp. 23–38.

–, "The English of Eighteenth Century Advertising", *Merope*, 6.13 (1994), pp. 97–117.

–, "Linguistic and Stylistic Features of 18th-Century English Advertisements", in *Thou sittest at another book... English Studies in Honour of Domenico Pezzini,* ed. by Giovanni Iamartino, Maria Luisa Maggioni, and Roberta Facchinetti, Monza: Polimetrica, 2008, pp. 369–85.

Gowland, Angus, *The Worlds of Renaissance Melancholy: Robert Burton in Context*, Cambridge: Cambridge University Press, 2006.

–, "The Problem of Early Modern Melancholy", *Past & Present*, 191 (May 2006), pp. 77–120.

Halliday, M. A. K., *Spoken and Written Language*, Oxford: Oxford University Press, 1989.

Heffernan, Carol Falvo, *The Melancholy Muse: Chaucer, Shakespeare and Early Medicine*, Pittsburgh, PA: Duquesne University Press, 1995.

Helfand, William H., *Quack, Quack, Quack: The Sellers of Nostrums in Prints, Posters, Ephemera & Books*, A Winterhouse Edition, New York: The Grolier Club, 2002.

Hughes, Rebecca, *English in Speech and Writing*, London: Routledge, 1996.

Jahandarie, Khosrow, *Spoken and Written Discourse*, Stamford, Conn.: Ablex, 1999.

Jenner, Mark S. R, and Patrick Wallis, "The Medical Marketplace", in *Medicine and the Market in England and its Colonies, c. 1450-c. 1850*, ed. by Mark S. R. Jenner and Patrick Wallis, 2007, pp. 1–23.

–, eds, *Medicine and the Market in England and its Colonies, c. 1450-c. 1850*, Basingstoke: Palgrave-MacMillan, 2007.

Jones, Peter Murray, "Medical Literacies and Medical Culture in Early Modern England", in *Medical Writing in Early Modern English*, ed. by Irma Taavitsainen and Päivi Pahta, Cambridge: Cambridge University Press, 2011, pp. 30–43.

Katritzky, M. A., "Gendering Tooth-drawers on the Stage", *Ludica*, 5–6 (2000), 144–81.

–, *Healing, Performance and Ceremony in the Writings of Three Early Modern Physicians*, Aldershot: Ashgate, 2012.

–, "Marketing Medicine: The Image of the Early Modern Mountebank", *Renaissance Studies* 15 (2001), pp. 121–53.

–, *Women, Medicine and Theatre, 1550–1750: Literary Mountebanks and Performing Quacks*, Ashgate: Aldershot, 2007.

Kerbrat-Orecchioni, Catherine, *L'énonciation de la subjectivité dans le langage*, Paris: Colin, 1980.

Kermas, Susan, "From Herbal to Advert", in *News Discourse in Early Modern Britain*, ed. by Nicholas Brownlees, Bern: Peter Lang, 2006, pp. 175–97.

Kerwin, William, *Beyond the Body: The Boundaries of Medicine and English Renaissance Drama*, Amherst and Boston: University of Massachusetts Press, 2005.

King, Helen, *The Disease of Virgins: Green Sickness, Chlorosis and the Problems of Puberty*, London: Routledge, 2004.

Laurence, Anne, *Women in England 1500–1760: A Social History*, London: Weidenfeld & Nicholson, 1994.

Leech, Geoffrey N., *A Linguistic Study of Advertising in Great Britain*, London: Longmans, 1966.

Leong, Elaine, and Sara Pennell, "Recipe Collections and the Currency of Medical Knowledge in the Early Modern 'Medical Marketplace'", in *Medicine and the Market in England and its Colonies, c. 1450-c. 1850*, ed. by Mark S. R. Jenner and Patrick Wallis, 2007, pp. 133–52.

Lund, Mary Ann, *Melancholy, Medicine and Religion in Early Modern England: Reading "The Anatomy of Melancholy"*, Cambridge: Cambridge University Press, 2010.

MacDonald, Michael, *Mystical Bedlam: Madness, Anxiety, and Healing in Seventeenth-Century England*, Cambridge: Cambridge University Press, 1981.

Mäkinen, Martti, "Efficacy Phrases in Early Modern English Medical Recipes", in *Medical Writing in Early Modern English*, ed. by Irma Taavitsainen and Päivi Pahta, 2011, pp. 158–79.

Maple, Eric, *Magic, Medicine and Quackery*, London: Hale, 1968.

Marland, Hilary, and Margaret Pelling, eds, *The Task of Healing: Medicine, Religion and Gender in England and the Netherlands, 1450–1800*, Rotterdam: Erasmus, 1996.

Marttila, Ville, "New Arguments for New Audiences: A Corpus-based Analysis of Interpersonal Strategies in Early Modern English Medical Recipes", in *Medical Writing in Early Modern English*, ed. by Irma Taavitsainen and Päivi Pahta, 2011, pp. 135–57.

Matthews, Leslie G., "Italian Charlatans in England", *Pharmaceutical Historian*, 9 (1979), pp. 2–4.

–, "Licensed Mountebanks in Britain", *Journal of the History of Medicine and Allied Sciences*, 19.1 (1964), pp. 30–45.

Mazella, David, "Diogenes the Critic in the *Dialogues of the Dead* of Thomas Brown, Lord Lyttleton, and William Blake", *Texas Studies in Literature and Language*, 48.2 (2006), pp. 102–22.

McConchie, R. W., *Lexicography and Physicke: The Record of Sixteenth-Century English Medical Terminology*, Oxford: Clarendon Press, 1997.

McDowell, John M., "Some Pictorial Aspects of Early Mountebank Stages", *PMLA*, 61.1 (1946), pp. 84–96.

Mendelson, Sara, and Patricia Crawford, *Women in Early Modern England*, Oxford: Oxford University Press, 1998.

Mirabella, Bella, "'Quacking Delilahs': Female Mountebanks in Early Modern England and Italy", in *Women Players in England, 1500–1660*, ed. by P. A. Brown and P. Parolin, Aldershot: Ashgate, 2005, pp. 89–105.

Morgan, William, *The A to Z of Charles II's London 1682*, ed. by Ann Saunders, Introduction by Peter Barber and Ralph Hyde, Index by Robert Thompson, London: London Topographical Society, 2013.

Moss, Stephanie, and Kaara L. Peterson, eds, *Disease, Diagnosis, and Cure on the Early Modern Stage*, Aldershot: Ashgate, 2004.

Mullini, Roberta, "L''Acqua di talco' da Caterina Sforza ai ciarlatani londinesi del Seicento", *Università aperta. Terza pagina*, 20.4 (2010), pp. 6–7.

–, "The First Medical Practitioners in English Drama: Medical Knowledge and Quackery in *The Play of the Sacrament* and in John Heywood's *The Foure PP*", *Linguæ &*, 1 (2011), pp. 43–60.

–, *Mad merry Heywood: la drammaturgia di John Heywood tra testi e riflessioni critiche*, Bologna: CLUEB, 1997.

–, *La scena della memoria: intertestualità nel teatro Tudor*, Bologna: CLUEB, 1988.

–, "Shakespeare and the Words of Early Modern Physic: Between Academic and Popular Medicine. A Lexicographical Approach to the Plays", *Journal of Early Modern Studies*, 2 (2013), pp. 63–89.

Nagy, Doreen G., *Popular Medicine in Seventeenth-Century England*, Bowling Green: Bowling Green State University Popular Press, 1988.

Nevett, T. R., *Advertising in Britain. A History*, London: Heinemann, 1982.

Norri, Juhani, *Names of Sicknesses in English, 1400–1550: An Exploration of the Lexical Field*, Helsinki: Suomalainen Tiedeakatemia, 1992.

Ogilby, John and William Morgan, *A to Z of Restoration London: City of London, 1676*, Introduction by Ralph Hyde, Lympne: Harry Margary, 1992.

Ong, Walter, *Orality and Literacy*, London: Methuen, 1982.

–, "Oral Residue in Tudor Prose Style", *PMLA*, 80.3 (1965), pp. 145–54.

Oxford Dictionary of National Biography <http://www.oxforddnb.com/> [accessed 20 October 2013].

Oxford English Dictionary, Third edition, March 2011, Online version <http://www. oed.com/> [last accessed 23 December 2014].

Pahta, Päivi, "*Ful Holsum and Profetable for the Bodi*: A Corpus Study of Amplifiers in Medieval English Medical Texts", in *Diachronic Perspectives on Domain-Specific English*, ed. by Marina Dossena and Irma Taavitsainen, Bern: Peter Lang, 2006, pp. 207–28.

Pahta, Päivi, and Irma Taavitsainen, "Introducing *Modern English Medical Texts*", in *Early Modern English Medical Texts*, ed. by Irma Taavitsainen and Päivi Pahta, 2010, pp. 1–7.

Pelling, Margaret, *The Common Lot: Sickness, Medical Occupations and the Urban Poor in Early Modern England*, London: Longman, 1998.

–, "Compromised by Gender: The Role of the Male Medical Practitioner in Early Modern England", in *The Task of Healing: Medicine, Religion and Gender in England and the Netherlands, 1450–1800*, ed. by. Hilary Marland and Margaret Pelling, 1996, pp. 101–33.

–, "Healing the Sick Poor: Social Policy and Disability in Norwich, 1550–1640", in Pelling, *The Common Lot* (1998), pp. 79–102.

–, "Knowledge Common and Acquired: The Education of Unlicensed Medical Practitioners in Early Modern London", in *The History of Medical Education in Britain*, ed. by Vivian Nutton and Roy Porter, Amsterdam: Rodopi, 1995, pp. 250–79.

–, *Medical Conflicts in Early Modern London: Patronage, Physicians and Irregular Practitioners 1550–1640*, Oxford: Clarendon Press, 2003.

–, "Medicine and the Environment in Shakespeare's England", in Pelling, *The Common Lot* (1998), pp. 19–37.

–, "Nurses and Nurse-keepers: Problems of Identification in the Early Modern Period", in Pelling, *The Common Lot* (1998), pp. 179–202.

–, "Occupational Diversity: Barber-Surgeons and Other Trades, 1550–1640", in Pelling, *The Common Lot* (1998), pp. 203–29.

–, "Older Women: Household, Caring and Other Occupations in the Late Sixteenth-Century Town", in Pelling, *The Common Lot* (1998), pp. 155–75.

–, "Thoroughly Resented? Older Women in the Medical Role in Early Modern London", in *Women, Science and Medicine 1500–1700,* ed. by Lynette Hunter and Sarah Hutton, Phoenix Mill: Sutton Publishing, 1997, pp. 63–88.

–, "Trade or Profession? Medical Practice in Early Modern England", in Pelling, *The Common Lot* (1998), pp. 230–58.

Pelling, Margaret, and Charles Webster, "Medical Practitioners", in *Health, Medicine and Mortality in the Sixteenth Century*, ed. by Charles Webster, Cambridge: Cambridge University Press, 1979, pp. 165–235.

Pelling, Margaret, and Frances White, *Physicians and Irregular Medical Practitioners in London 1550–1640: Database*, 2004 <http://www.british-history.ac.uk/report.aspx?compid=17785> [accessed 9 September 2013].

Peterson, Kaara L., *Popular Medicine, Hysterical Disease, and Social Controversy in Shakespeare's England*, Aldershot: Ashgate, 2010.

Pinto, Vivian de Sola, "Introduction", in Thomas Alcock and John Wilmot, Earl of Rochester, *The Famous Pathologist or the Noble Mountebank*, ed. by Vivian De Sola Pinto, Nottingham: Sisson and Parker for the University of Nottingham, 1961, pp. 7–21.

Pollard, Tanya, "'No Faith in Physic': Masquerades of Medicine Onstage and Off", in *Disease, Diagnosis, and Cure on the Early Modern Stage*, ed. by Stephanie Moss and Kaara L. Peterson, Aldershot: Ashgate, 2004, pp. 29–41.

Pomata, Gianna, *Contracting a Cure: Patients, Healers, and the Law in Early Modern Bologna*, Baltimore: The Johns Hopkins University Press, 1998.

Porter, Roy, "Before the Fringe: Quackery and the Eighteenth-Century Medical Market", in *Studies in the History of Alternative Medicine*, ed. by R. Cooter, Basinstoke: Macmillan, 1988, pp. 1–27.

–, *Bodies Politic: Disease, Death and Doctors in Britain 1650–1900*, Ithaca-New York: Cornell University Press, 2001.

–, *Health for Sale: Quackery in England 1650–1850*, Manchester: Manchester University Press, 1989.

–, "The Language of Quackery in England", in *The Social History of Language*, ed. by Peter Burke and Roy Porter, Cambridge: Cambridge University Press, 1987, pp. 73–103.

–, *Mind-Forg'd Manacles: A History of Madness in England from the Restoration to the Regency*, London: The Athlone Press, 1987.

–, *Quacks: Fakers and Charlatans in Medicine*, Illustrated edition, Stroud: Tempus, 2000.

–, *Quacks: Fakers and Charlatans in Medicine*, Illustrated paperback edition, Stroud: Tempus, 2003.

Pugliatti, Paola, *Beggary and Theatre in Early Modern England*, Aldershot: Ashgate, 2003.

–, "The Hidden Face of Elizabethan-Jacobean Theatre", *Revue Internationale de Philosophie*, 2 (2010), pp. 177–98.

Ratia, Maura, and Carla Suhr, "Medical Pamphlets: Controversy and Advertising", in *Medical Writing in Early Modern English*, ed. by Irma Taavitsainen and Päivi Pahta, 2011, pp. 180–203.

Rawcliffe, Carole, *Medicine & Society in Later Medieval England*, Stroud: Sutton, 1997.

Raymond, Joad, *The Invention of the Newspaper: English Newsbooks 1641–1649*, Oxford: Clarendon Press, 2008.

–, *Pamphlets and Pamphleteering in Early Modern Britain*, Cambridge: Cambridge University Press, 2003.

Righetti, Angelo, "Pox in Restoration Comedy and What It Tells Us", in *Distraction Individualized: Figures of Insanity in Early Modern England*, ed. by Silvia Bigliazzi, Verona: Cierre Grafica, 2012, pp. 233–58.

Rollins, H. E., "The Black-Letter Broadside Ballad", *PMLA*, 34.2 (1919), pp. 258–339.

Schmidt, Jeremy, *Melancholy and the Care of the Soul: Religion, Moral Philosophy and Madness in Early Modern England*, Aldershot: Ashgate, 2007.

Shuttleton, David E., *Smallpox and the Literary Imagination 1660–1820*, Cambridge: Cambridge University Press, 2007.

Siena, Kevin P., "'The 'Foul Disease' and Privacy: The Effects of Venereal Disease and Patient Demand on the Medical Marketplace in Early Modern London", *Bulletin of the History of Medicine*, 75 (2001), pp. 199–224.

–, *Venereal Diseases, Hospitals and the Urban Poor: London's "Foul Wards", 1600–1800*, Woodbridge: University of Rochester Press, 2004.

Silvette, Herbert, *The Doctor on the Stage: Medicine and Medical Men in Seventeenth-Century England*, Knoxville: The University of Tennessee Press, 1967.

Slack, Paul, "Mirrors of Health and Treasures of Poor Men: The Use of the Vernacular Medical Literature of Tudor England", in *Health, Medicine and Mortality in the Sixteenth Century*, ed. by Charles Webster, Cambridge: Cambridge University Press, 1979, pp. 237–73.

Snook, Edith, *Women, Beauty and Power in Early Modern England: A Feminist Literary History*, Basingstoke: Palgrave Macmillan, 2011.

Spiller, Elizabeth, *Seventeenth-century English Recipe Books: Cooking, Physic and Chirurgery in the Works of Elizabeth Talbot Grey and Aletheia Talbot Howard*, Aldershot: Ashgate, 2008.

Taavitsainen, Irma, and Jukka Tyrkkö, "The Field of Medical Writing with Fuzzy Edges", in *Early Modern English Medical Texts*, ed. by Irma Taavitsainen and Päivi Pahta, 2010, pp. 57–72.

Taavitsainen, Irma, and Päivi Pahta, eds, *Early Modern English Medical Texts*, Amsterdam: John Benjamins, 2010, CD ROM included.

–, eds, *Medical and Scientific Writing in Late Medieval English*, Cambridge: Cambridge University Press, 2004.

–, eds, *Medical Writing in Early Modern English*, Cambridge: Cambridge University Press, 2011.

Taavitsainen, Irma, Päivi Pahta, and Martti Mäkinen, eds, *Middle English Medical Texts*, a CD-ROM, Amsterdam: John Benjamins, 2005.

Teubert, Wolfgang, and Anna Čermáková, *Corpus Linguistics: A Short Introduction*, London: Continuum, 2007.

Thomas, Keith, *Religion and the Decline of Magic*, London: Penguin, 1991 (1971).

Thompson, C. J. S., *Quacks of Old London*, London: Brentano's, 1928.

Turner, E. S., *The Shocking History of Advertising*, London: Michael Joseph, 1952.

Vestergaard, T., and K. Schrøder, *The Language of Advertising*, Oxford: Blackwell, 1994.

Wales, Diane, "Equally Safe for Both Sexes: A Gender Analysis of Medical Advertisements in English Newspapers, 1690–1750", *Vesalius*, 11.1 (2005), pp. 26–32.

Walker, R. B., "Advertising in London Newspapers, 1650–1750", *Business History*, 15 (1973), pp. 112–30.

Wear, Andrew, *Health and Healing in Early Modern England*, Aldershot: Ashgate, 1998.

–, *Knowledge and Practice in English Medicine, 1550–1680*, Cambridge: Cambridge University Press, 2000.

–, "Medical Practice in Late Seventeenth- and Early Eighteenth-Century England: Continuity and Union", in *The Medical Revolution of the Seventeenth Century*, ed. by R. French and Andrew Wear, Cambridge: Cambridge University Press, 1989, pp. 294–320.

–, "The Popularization of Medicine in Early Modern England", in *The Popularization of Medicine 1650–1850,* ed. by Roy Porter, London: Routledge, 1992, pp. 17–41.

Weber, A. S., "Women's Early Modern Medical Almanacs in Historical Context", *English Literary Renaissance*, 33 (2003), pp. 358–402.

Woolley, Benjamin, *Heal Thyself: Nicholas Culpeper and the Seventeenth-Century Struggle to Bring Medicine to the People*, New York: HarperCollins, 2004.

Wright, Laura, "Street Addresses and Directions in Mid-Eighteenth Century London Newspaper Advertisements", in *News Discourse in Early Modern Britain*, ed. by Nicholas Brownlees, Bern: Peter Lang, 2006, pp. 199–215.

Zinato, Susanna, "Burnet's Heterobiography of John Wilton, Earl of Rochester", in *The Protean Forms of Life Writing: Auto/Biography in English, 1680–2000*, ed. by Angelo Righetti, Naples: Liguori, 2008, pp. 159–87.

Index

Interkulturelle Begegnungen.
Studien zum Literatur- und Kulturtransfer
Herausgegebenvon Rita Unfer Lukoschik und Michael Dallapiazza

Die Bände 1-12 sind im Martin Meidenbauer Verlag erschienen und können über den Verlag Peter Lang, Internationaler Verlag der Wissenschaften, bezogen werden: www.peterlang.de.

Ab Band 13 erscheint diese Reihe im Verlag Peter Lang, Internationaler Verlag der Wissenschaften, Frankfurt am Main.

Band 13 Corinna Ott: Zu Hause schmeckt's am besten. Essen als Ausdruck nationaler Identität in der deutsch-türkischen Migrationsliteratur. 2012.

Band 14 Maria Elisa Montironi: Riscritture tedesche del *Coriolanus* di Shakespeare (1609-1951). Ricezione politica e politica della ricezione. 2013.

Band 15 James Orao: Selbstverortungen. Migration und Identität in der zeitgenössischen deutsch- und englischsprachigen Gegenwartsliteratur. 2014.

Band 16 Arianna Di Bella: SAID – Ein Leben in der Fremde. 2014.

Band 17 Lilli Gebhard: Identitätskonstruktionen russlanddeutscher Mennoniten im Spiegel ihrer Literatur. 2014.

Band 18 Roberta Mullini: Healing Words. The Printed Handbills of Early Modern London Quacks. 2015.

www.peterlang.com

www.ingramcontent.com/pod-product-compliance
Ingram Content Group UK Ltd.
Pitfield, Milton Keynes, MK11 3LW, UK
UKHW041826100926
8556IPUK00002B/52

9 783631 664773